Rorschach Assessment of Senior Adults

This guide is a much-needed reference for clinicians on how to use the Rorschach Inkblot Test with senior adults, an essential tool for assessing personality functioning to better identify psychological interventions. The book integrates historical developments, current research, conceptual considerations, and therapeutic and diagnostic applications.

Chapters review basic guidelines for the understanding and interpretation of Rorschach variables, including protocol validity; interpretation of structural variables, thematic imagery, and cross-cultural normative data; sequence analysis; and more. The authors then provide 10 case illustrations of how the Rorschach indices of cognitive functioning, emotional experience, interpersonal relatedness, and self-perception can facilitate differential diagnosis and treatment planning in clinical work with older people. These case illustrations are rooted in previously non-existent Rorschach reference data based on an international sample of more than 250 senior adults and a second sample of more than 200 patients with Alzheimer's disease.

Clinicians will come away with a solid empirical basis for distinguishing between normal-range personality functioning and manifestations of psychological disorder in the elderly and for providing beneficial interventions to senior adult patients.

Irving B. Weiner, PhD, ABPP, is a retired professor of psychiatry and behavioral neurosciences at the University of South Florida. He is a past president of APA Division 12 (Clinical Psychology), APA Division 5 (Quantitative and Qualitative Methods), the Society for Personality Assessment, and the International Rorschach Society. His published books include *Psychodiagnosis in Schizophrenia* (1966), *Principles of Rorschach Assessment* (2nd ed., 2003), *Principles of Psychotherapy* (3rd ed., 2009), the *Handbook of Personality Assessment* (2nd ed., 2017), and, with Shira Tibon-Czopp, *Rorschach Assessment of Adolescents* (2016).

Liat Appel, PhD, is a clinical psychologist who is currently involved in an international research project on senior adults at Goldsmiths, University of London. Dr. Appel lectures in various clinical programs in Israel and practices clinical psychology in Tel-Aviv. She is a coauthor of the Rorschach Reality–Fantasy Scale Version 2.0 (RFS-2, 2016). Her recent publications include an article on adolescents with psychosomatic disorders in *Rorschachiana* (2011); a coauthored article on national trauma in *Psychology* (2011); and a coauthored article on Shedler–Westen assessment in *Psychoanalytic Psychology* (2012). She was the 2016 recipient of the Society for Personality Assessment Exner Scholar award.

Shira Tibon-Czopp, PhD, ABAP, is a clinical psychologist and visiting research fellow at Goldsmiths, University of London, where she co-conducts an international project on personality and attitudes in senior adults. She has been lecturing in various clinical programs in Israel and has worked in inpatient and outpatient public clinics. Some of her recent publications include an essay on the Rorschach Inkblot Method in the *Encyclopedia of Adolescence* (2012); a coauthored book with Irving B. Weiner entitled *Rorschach Assessment of Adolescents* (2016); and coauthored articles on the Rorschach Reality–Fantasy Scale Version 2.0 (RFS-2, 2016) and Rorschach psychometric validity in the *Journal of Personality Assessment* (2016).

Rorschach Assessment of Senior Adults

Irving B. Weiner, Liat Appel, and Shira Tibon-Czopp

Routledge
Taylor & Francis Group
NEW YORK AND LONDON

First published 2019
by Routledge
52 Vanderbilt Avenue, New York, NY 10017

and by Routledge
2 Park Square, Milton Park, Abingdon, Oxon, OX14 4RN

Routledge is an imprint of the Taylor & Francis Group, an informa business

Library of Congress Cataloging-in-Publication Data
Names: Weiner, Irving B., author. | Appel, Liat, author. | Tibon-Czopp, Shira, author.
Title: Rorschach assessment of senior adults / Irving B. Weiner, Liat Appel and Shira Tibon-Czopp.
Description: New York, NY : Routledge, 2019. | Includes bibliographical references and index.
Identifiers: LCCN 2019003216 (print) | LCCN 2019005094 (ebook) |
ISBN 9780429282171 (Ebook) | ISBN 9780367243814 (hardback : alk. paper) |
ISBN 9780367243838 (pbk. : alk. paper) Subjects: LCSH: Rorschach Test. |
Older people–Psychological testing. | Personality assessment. | Psychodiagnostics.
Classification: LCC BF698.8.R5 (ebook) | LCC BF698.8.R5 W45 2019 (print) | DDC 153.9/3–dc23
LC record available at https://lccn.loc.gov/2019003216

ISBN: 978-0-367-24381-4 (hbk)
ISBN: 978-0-367-24383-8 (pbk)
ISBN: 978-0-429-28217-1 (ebk)

Typeset in Minion
by Newgen Publishing UK

Contents

Preface

Recent years have seen an increasing percentage of senior adults in the population, together with a growing interest in gerontopsychology and increased attention being paid to the mental health care needs of older people. Addressing the mental health care needs of older people is facilitated by an adequate evaluation of their psychological functioning, personal concerns, and coping strengths and limitations. Such evaluations of the elderly assess their capacities to attend appropriately to their surroundings, perceive events accurately, think logically, experience and express their feelings comfortably, engage in rewarding relationships with other people, regard themselves in a positive light, and tolerate stress reasonably well. The Rorschach Inkblot Method provides validated indices of each of these dimensions of personality functioning, and it can accordingly provide valuable information in the psychological evaluation of senior adults.

With these considerations in mind, this book on the *Rorschach Assessment of Senior Adults* is addressed to Rorschach scholars and clinicians who are interested or engaged in assessing the personality functioning of senior adults as a means of understanding their concerns and identifying psychological interventions that are likely to benefit them.

The book begins in Part I with two introductory chapters that address current research and perspectives on aging and historical developments in the Rorschach assessment of senior adults. Chapter 1 describes a newly emerging image of aging and older people that runs counter to many traditional beliefs and stereotypes in two respects. First, advances in neuropsychological research have demonstrated that normal aging is not inevitably characterized by widespread cognitive decline, but instead by mostly mild declines in some cognitive capacities and not in others. Second, modified psychodynamic perspectives have led to the recognition that the elderly do not inevitably become closed-minded and fixed in their ways, and thereby unresponsive to psychotherapy, but are instead likely to be actively engaged in dealing with psychological issues in their lives and able to participate effectively in psychotherapy.

Chapter 2 reviews historical developments in the Rorschach assessment of senior adults, which since the inception of the inkblot method in 1921 has included attention not only to personality characteristics, but also to brain dysfunctions associated with the aging process. Over time, personality tests proved increasingly useful in distinguishing between so-called "organic" disorders and "psychological" disorders, and the Rorschach became recognized as helpful in making this distinction. First to examine the inkblot responses of elderly and "organically impaired" patients was Hermann Rorschach himself. Subsequent Rorschach clinicians and scholars have enriched our understanding of the Rorschach task and its applications in the assessment of senior adults.

Part II of the text comprises two chapters on conceptual considerations in using the Rorschach as a clinical gerontopsychology tool. Chapter 3 elaborates the nature of the Rorschach as a threefold measure of perception, association, and behavior. The discussion distinguishes between interpretations, which are transcendent, and their implications, which typically vary with a person's age, situational circumstances, and sociocultural environment. The chapter reviews behavioral variables that reflect how people experience and respond to the Rorschach situation and perhaps more generally to events in their lives, and it concludes with age-related considerations in examining senior adults.

Chapter 4 addresses the interpretive significance of the structural variables and thematic imagery in a Rorschach protocol, both in general and with particular respect to senior adults. Rorschach structural variables provide a quantitative basis for identifying probable characteristics of a person's cognitive functioning, affective experience, interpersonal relatedness, and self-perception, as well as for determining whether these characteristics fall within the normal range or instead signal some adaptive difficulties. Rorschach thematic imagery provides a qualitative basis for drawing inferences about a person's underlying needs, attitudes, and concerns and for judging the plausibility of these inferences.

Part III of the book continues with three chapters on normative Rorschach reference values related to nationality, age, and patient/nonpatient status. Chapter 5 analyzes Rorschach cross-cultural reference values found among cognitively healthy senior adults in several countries. Although elderly people constitute a heterogeneous group with respect to their background and personality styles, the cross-cultural uniformity of these reference data can assist clinicians in distinguishing between healthy and psychopathological personality functioning, irrespective of the social and cultural background of the person being tested.

Chapter 6 compares the cross-cultural Rorschach reference values of older senior adults with those of younger senior adults in several countries around the world. These data represent cognitively healthy senior adults at various ages and enable researchers and clinicians to observe developmental trends as reflected in normative changes in Rorschach scores.

Chapter 7 compares Rorschach reference data collected from senior adults who have Alzheimer's disease with those of elderly nonpatients. This chapter addresses in particular Rorschach markers of neuropsychological dysfunction and distinguishing them from manifestations of psychological disorder shown by deviant Rorschach structural scores and thematic imagery.

Part IV addresses the diagnostic and therapeutic applications of Rorschach assessment in senior adults with 10 case illustrations of both older adults with impaired personality functioning and seniors who show normal-range functioning. The case illustrations are drawn from five countries: Brazil, Iran, Israel, the UK, and the USA, and they are representative of the younger group of senior adults (aged 65–75). Four of the cases concern elderly individuals with impaired functioning: a 72-year-old American man diagnosed with dementia (Chapter 8); a 65-year-old American man with bipolar disorder (Chapter 9); a 65-year-old American man with Korsakoff's syndrome (Chapter 10); and a 65-year-old Israeli woman with an acute depressive reaction (Chapter 11).

Six of the cases concern elderly people who are normally adapted to reality: a 65-year-old Iranian woman with a chronic depressive syndrome (Chapter 12); a 75-year-old British man with manic defenses (Chapter 13); a 65-year-old British man with a medical condition and somatization (Chapter 14); a 67-year-old British man traumatized in childhood (Chapter 15); a 65-year-old Brazilian woman with fibromyalgia and alexithymia (Chapter 16); and a 67-year-old British man with obsessive–compulsive personality (Chapter 17).

Part V concludes the text with the presentation in Chapter 18 of final remarks on the utility of the Rorschach as a diagnostic and therapeutic tool and on its equal applicability across countries, cultures, and the adult lifespan.

Acknowledgments

We would like to thank our publisher for inviting us to work on this project. We are particularly grateful to the many productive Rorschach theorists, researchers, and practitioners who facilitated our work by providing us with their conceptual formulations, research data, and clinical experience on which we were able to draw in developing our conclusions and recommendations. In this respect, Bruce Smith at the University of California, Berkeley, was particularly helpful by inspiring the development of the Rorschach Reality–Fantasy Scale, which we use for interpreting the Rorschach data, and for providing us with two of the case illustrations. Our case illustrations also include protocols provided us by Norma Semer Lottenberg and Roberta Kats, Sao Paulo, Brazil; Kari Carstairs, London, UK; Efrat Lurie, Tel-Aviv, Israel; and Abufazel Hosseininasab, Tehran, Iran. We want to thank our colleagues Norma Semer Lottenberg and Roberta Kats, Sao Paulo, Brazil; Antonio Abel Pires, Porto, Portugal; Abufazel Hosseininasab, Tehran, Iran; and Piero Porcelli, Emanuela Brusadelli, and Alessandra Tomasich, Milan, Italy, who contributed data and enabled us to build a normative international reference sample, and Emiliano Muzio, Helsinki, Finland, who contributed Rorschach data concerning Alzheimer's disease. We have consulted with Roni Tibon from the MRC Cognition and Brain Sciences Unit, University of Cambridge, UK, about neuroscience issues and integrated her original and fruitful comments in the text. We are also most grateful to Herb Blumberg at Goldsmiths, University of London and to Ruth Zeligman at Tel-Aviv University for their contributions in allowing us to use empirical data and case illustrations from our coauthored projects on personality and attitudes in British and Israeli senior adults. Most importantly, we want to thank our beloved families for their keen interest in and support of our work.

Irving B. Weiner
Liat Appel
Shira Tibon-Czopp

About the Authors

Irving B. Weiner, PhD, ABPP, is a retired professor of psychiatry and behavioral neurosciences at the University of South Florida. He is a past president of APA Division 12 (Clinical Psychology), APA Division 5 (Quantitative and Qualitative Methods), the Society for Personality Assessment, and the International Rorschach Society. His published books include *Psychodiagnosis in Schizophrenia* (1966), *Principles of Rorschach Assessment* (2nd ed., 2003), *Principles of Psychotherapy* (3rd ed., 2009), the *Handbook of Personality Assessment* (2nd ed., 2017), and, with Shira Tibon-Czopp, *Rorschach Assessment of Adolescents* (2016).

Liat Appel, PhD, is a clinical psychologist who is currently involved in an international research project on senior adults at Goldsmiths, University of London. Dr. Appel lectures in various clinical programs in Israel and instructs students and interns. She has worked in inpatient and outpatient public clinics with children, adolescents, and adults at all ages and practices clinical psychology in Tel-Aviv, Israel. She is a coauthor of the Rorschach Reality–Fantasy Scale Version 2.0 (RFS-2, 2016). In addition to her coauthored articles on the RFS-2 in *Group Decision and Negotiation* (2014, 2016), her recent publications include an article on adolescents with psychosomatic disorders in *Rorschachiana* (2011); a coauthored article on national trauma in *Psychology* (2011); a coauthored article on Shedler–Westen assessment in *Psychoanalytic Psychology* (2012); a coauthored article on reference data for Israeli adolescents in the *Journal of Personality Assessment* (2012); and a coauthored article on personality dimensions and attitudes in the *Journal of Aggression, Conflict and Peace Research* (2017). She was the 2016 recipient of the Society for Personality Assessment Exner Scholar award.

Shira Tibon-Czopp, PhD, ABAP, is a clinical psychologist and a visiting research fellow at Goldsmiths, University of London, where she conducts with Herbert H. Blumberg and other colleagues an international project on personality and attitudes in senior adults. Professor Tibon-Czopp is a diplomate of the American Board of Assessment Psychology and a fellow of the American Academy of Assessment Psychology. She has lectured in various clinical programs, including those of Tel-Aviv University and Bar-Ilan University, and has worked in inpatient and outpatient public clinics. She practices clinical psychology in Tel-Aviv, Israel, and instructs students and interns who work with children, adolescents, and adults at all ages. Some of her recent publications include an essay on psychology in Israel in the *Corsini Encyclopedia of Psychology* (4th ed., 2010); an essay on the Rorschach Inkblot Method in the *Encyclopedia of Adolescence* (2012); a coauthored book with Irving B. Weiner entitled *Rorschach Assessment of Adolescents* (2016); and coauthored articles on the Rorschach Reality–Fantasy Scale, on Rorschach psychometric validity in the *Journal of Personality Assessment* (2016), and on personality dimensions and attitudes in the *Journal of Aggression, Conflict and Peace Research* (2017).

PART I

Introduction

CHAPTER 1

Current Research and Perspectives on Aging

Recent neuropsychological research and psychodynamic perspectives on aging, together with the growing percentage of high-functioning senior adults in populations throughout the Western world, have given rise to a new image of older people and challenged clinical psychologists to be adequately informed and skillful in assessing and treating them (Greenberg, 2016; Lockhart, DeCarli, & Fama, 2014). For clinical purposes, an accepted age for regarding a person as a senior adult has been 55 and above (Lingiardi & McWilliams, 2017, p. 752), although empirical studies have commonly used an age of 60 or 65 as the cutoff for including senior adults in age-based samples. Whichever age is used, contemporary senior adults increasingly include individuals who were exposed to unprecedented educational and economic opportunities in their childhood and adolescence (Barnett & Quenzel, 2017). As adults, they have additionally been faced with new developmental tasks of adapting themselves to a rapidly changing postmodern culture. Most importantly, what was once viewed as "normal" age-related mental decline has increasingly changed to much more complex and sometimes contradictory representations of what older people are like.

As background to discussing the Rorschach assessment of senior adults, this introductory chapter addresses how the new image of older people has emerged from contemporary neuropsychological research on the relation of brain functions to observable behavior and from current psychodynamic perspectives on the inner needs, attitudes, and concerns that influence a person's behavior.

Neuropsychological Research on Aging

With the increasing percentage of older adults in the population, the study of aging has become a major focus of attention in neuropsychological research. Older adults may undergo substantial changes in their cognitive functioning, as in people with dementia or mild cognitive impairment. Research has shown that healthy adults may also experience subtle cognitive changes associated with advancing age. It therefore becomes important to distinguish between mental abilities that are likely to be preserved or even improved over the years and those that are relatively likely to decline with normal aging, and also to distinguish normal mental decline from manifestations of psychological disorder.

As a general distinction in regard to mental decline, crystallized intellectual abilities (e.g., vocabulary and learned knowledge) show stability or even improve through the sixth and seventh decades of life, whereas fluid intelligence (e.g., abilities involving attention, reasoning, and spatial orientation) normally tends to decline. However, these terms are somewhat misleading for summarizing age trends because other capacities, such as processing speed and memory, are distinguished from fluid ability, and yet are highly sensitive to age.

Much of the cognitive decline in healthy older adults appears to result from slowed processing speed (Salthouse, 2010). Age-related slowing includes performance on many neuropsychological tests, as well as memory capabilities (Harada, Love, & Triebel, 2013). Indeed, decline in memory is one of the most common cognitive complaints among older adults. In addition to diminished processing speed, age-related memory decline may be due to reduced ability to register and retrieve new information, reduced ability to ignore irrelevant information, and decreased use of strategies for improving learning and memory. For such reasons, older adults as a group generally perform less well than younger adults on numerous tests of learning and memory (Harada et al., 2013).

To be more precise, however, it is important to distinguish between declarative and nondeclarative memory. Declarative memory is an explicit process that consists of conscious retrieval of information and includes semantic memory and episodic memory. Semantic memory involves the recollection of language usage and the meaning of concepts and is relatively preserved as people age. Episodic memory is the recall of personally experienced events that occurred at a specific time and place and can also be measured by how well people can remember stories and lists of numbers or words. Unlike semantic memory, episodic memory tends to decline with aging.

Nondeclarative memory, in contrast, is an implicit process that occurs automatically, outside of a person's awareness and without conscious intent to recall anything. A familiar type of nondeclarative memory is procedural memory, which is immediate recall for such motor and cognitive skills as driving a car, using a knife and fork, and adding and subtracting numbers. Like semantic memory, procedural memory does not normally diminish as people grow older.

Research has shown further that executive functions may decline with age, including reduction in the ability to select relevant information and to inhibit irrelevant stimuli, decreased ability to perform task switching, and deficits in attentional processing. The reduction in processing speed, working memory, and other executive functions may result in subtracted cognitive resources that increasingly limit older adults' processing capacity. Thus, aging affects the ability to modulate neural activity when a task becomes more demanding (Kennedy et al., 2015).

In addition to assessing the change in mental abilities with aging, neuroscientists have sought to identify the underlying brain mechanisms that are associated with variations in cognitive performance of senior adults. Many brain structures show reduction of brain volume, cortical thickness, and white-matter integrity, as well as depletion in dopamine receptors. In contrast to the age-related decline in cognitive functions and brain structures, functional brain activity increases with age, particularly in the frontal cortex. The Scaffolding Theory of Aging and Cognition Revised (STAC-R; Reuter-Lorenz & Park, 2014) suggests that the increase in functional activity is due to compensatory scaffolding. A key element of the model is that the aging brain has the capacity to adapt to brain degradation by developing neural scaffolds (i.e., supportive neural structures and neural activity) that minimize or compensate for some aspects of neural degradation and in turn minimize the impact of this degradation on cognition.

Furthermore, life events and developmental processes can also be important factors that either deplete or enrich neural resources. Neural enrichment may result from various factors such as intellectual engagement, higher education, and cognitive ability, as well as physical fitness. Depletion of neural resources may result from many risk factors such as lower socioeconomic status, depression, and anxiety symptoms.

The neurocognitive structural changes as well as the developmental factors are responsible for what is called the *neuroplasticity* of the brain in older adults (Lingiardi & McWilliams, 2017, p. 753) and might explain their capacity to function quite well in demanding personal, familial, social, and other surrounding environments. The interplay between neurological and contextual changes thus acts as a protective agent against the age-related decline in neural structures and cognitive processing efficiency.

For the reader's further information, the measures most commonly used for rapid screening of general cognitive and other areas of neuropsychological functioning in senior adults include the following: Mini-Mental State Examination (MMSE; Folstein, Folstein, & McHugh, 1975); the short form of the Cambridge Mental Disorders of the Elderly Examination Revised (CAMDEX-R; Roth, Hupert, Mountjoy, & Tym, 1998); the Dementia Rating Scale (DRS; Mattis, 1988); and the Alzheimer Disease Assessment Scale (ADAS; Rosen, Mohs, & Davis, 1984), which consists of 11 cognitive performance items (ADAS Cog) and 10 noncognitive observation items (ADAS Non-Cog). In addition, some tests are used for assessing specific cognitive capacities. These include the Visual Pattern Test (VPT; Della Sala, Gray, Baddely, & Wilson, 1999), which is useful for evaluating attention and mental imagery, and the Rey–Osterrieth Complex Figure Test (CFT; Corwin & Bylsma, 1993), which was developed to assess visual–spatial constructional ability and visual memory.

Among more general measures, the Bender Gestalt Test and some Wechsler Adult Inelligence Scale-5 (WAIS-5) subtests can also be helpful for assessing neuropsychological functioning in senior adults. In addition, recent developments in brain imaging techniques indicate that the Rorschach Inkblot Method (Rorschach, 1921/1942) can prove useful in evaluating neurocognitive functioning in senior adults (Porcelli, Giromini, Parolin, Pineda, & Viglione, 2013). Moreover, as elaborated in the present text, the Rorschach brings to the clinical assessment process an evidence-based and psychodynamically oriented measure of personality functioning that provides information about a person's cognitive functioning, affective experience, interpersonal relatedness, self-perception, and inner subjective experience.

Psychodynamic Perspectives on Aging

In conjunction with innovations in neuropsychology, contemporary psychodynamic perspectives on aging have helped to modernize the image of older people by challenging entrenched stereotypes and false assumptions about the elderly. Among these stereotypes and false assumptions is the expectation that growing older causes people to become increasingly rigid and fixed in their ways, incapable of solving problems and exercising good judgment, and likely to show psychopathological manifestations. Youth-oriented societies are particularly likely to harbor such negative and unwarranted attitudes toward aging, and most people, including mental health professionals, are susceptible to adopting such attitudes. Changes in these and other traditional images of older people have been emerging, but only gradually, and there is a continuing need to counter biased attitudes toward aging with new facts and revised conceptions.

As a case in point, common attitudes in most societies consider the elderly to lack an active mind and a complex set of motivations, and the presumed rigidity and inability to change of older people has often been regarded as precluding their being responsive to psychodynamic psychotherapy or able to benefit from it. To the contrary, however, the neuroscience research mentioned earlier in this chapter has introduced the concept of *neuroplasticity*, according to which changes in the brain and improved cognitive capacities are possible even in old age. As reported by Lingiardi and McWilliams (2017, p. 751), moreover, accumulating clinical experience has shown that senior adults can in fact participate beneficially in psychodynamic psychotherapy.

To put these considerations in their historical context, the traditional psychodynamic image of rigidity and incapacity for change in older people traces back to the views of Freud (1904/1953), who wrote:

> Near or above the age of fifty the elasticity of the mental processes, on which the treatment depends, is as a rule lacking—old people are no longer educable—and, on the other hand, the mass of material to be dealt with would prolong the duration of the treatment indefinitely.
>
> (p. 161)

Over the years, this classical image of older people has given way to more positive psychoanalytic views of aging, with increasing appreciation of the poor fit that has existed between the needs and abilities of older people and the limited expectations and opportunities in their society. There has also been increasing recognition that, far from lacking an active mind and a complex set of motivations, elderly individuals are likely to be grappling with a variety of unresolved conflicts, contradictions, and tensions. As elaborated by Lomranz (1998), such conflicts, contradictions, and tensions are part of the reason why older people have proved able to engage effectively in psychodynamic psychotherapy.

With further respect to contemporary views on aging, the phrase *growing old* as commonly used today reflects a developmental perspective on late as well as early life. From this perspective, aging is currently viewed as a developmental process that occurs in reciprocal relationships between individuals and their contexts (Baltes, 1979, 1987; Baltes, Lindenberger, & Staudinger, 1998; Boyer, 2006; Lerner, 2015; Overton, 2015). Important developments in psychodynamic theories jointly with advances in contemporary neuroscience findings and accumulating empirical evidence support the view that personality changes with age occur within a context of surrounding environments.

Erikson (1956, 1959) was one of the first developmental psychologists to assert that some type of psychosocial development continues throughout the life cycle. He identified eight stages, each with its particular age-related concerns and challenges to be met. For older people, Erikson differentiated between a healthy outcome of *contentment* with one's life and accomplishments and an unhealthy sense of *despair* over not having lived life to the full or done much to feel good about. In addition, concerns related to *separation–individuation*, once regarded solely as childhood and adolescent phenomena, are now known to play a role in the life satisfaction of adults as well. Elaborating Erikson's theory, Cohen (1999) formulated a new and empowering view of older adults in which he divided Erikson's late adulthood stage into four phases of growth and development. These phases reflect evolving mental maturity, ongoing human development, and continuing psychological growth, and commonly occur in separate periods of time, although they may also coexist, intersect, and interact.

Influenced by developmental theories, modern psychoanalytic conceptualizations of what constitutes healthy functioning have changed substantially from the *ego psychology* definition, and adaptation is now more commonly defined in terms of internal as well as external reality. Rapaport (1967) amplified the definitions of internal and external reality by contrasting two notions: the *relative autonomy of the ego from the id*, which consists of one's solid relationship with the outside world, and the *relative autonomy of the ego from external reality*, which consists of being free from the constraints of the outer world to experience one's subjective inner world. He then used these notions to demonstrate how reality can serve as a defense against fantasy and, conversely, how fantasy can serve as a defense against reality. Rapaport attributed the literal and concrete thinking of individuals with schizophrenia to impairment in the ego's autonomy from the id and the fanciful thinking and intrapsychic blocking of instinctual drives in people with neurotic conditions (e.g., obsessive–compulsive disorder) to an impairment in the ego's autonomy from external reality.

Taken together, modern revisions of the negative image of aging and of the conception of normality as measured only by adaptation have fostered a marked shift in the focus of personality assessment. This newer focus involves exploring developmental issues that have shaped an individual's personality and assessing not only the individual's symptoms, but also the experiences that have given rise to these symptoms.

In this regard, psychodynamically oriented clinicians are generally agreed that the descriptive diagnostic categories of the *Diagnostic and Statistical Manual of Mental Disorders, Fifth Edition* (*DSM-5*; American Psychiatric Association, 2013) are not particularly helpful in understanding personality functioning in senior adults. Among other shortcomings, the *DSM-5* descriptive approach to diagnosis results in heterogeneous and overlapping categories, and the *DSM-5* does not refer specifically to the nature or manifestations of psychopathology in older people.

As an alternative to the *DSM-5* symptom-based classification system, the US National Institute of Mental Health initiated the research-based *Research Domain Criteria* (*RDoC*) project. By incorporating information from neuroscience research, the *RDoC* project is intended to achieve a biologically valid framework for understanding mental disorders. The *RDoC* delineates five domains of impaired brain functioning related to regulatory, cognitive, social process, and positive (e.g., habits) and negative (e.g., anxiety) valence systems. Along with focusing on the neural circuits associated with these domains, the *RDoC* employs a dimensional approach to the classification of disorders, rather than the categorical *DSM-5* approach (Casey et al., 2013; Widiger & Gore, 2014). In common with the *DSM-5*, however, the *RDoC* does not address patterns of psychopathology likely to be seen in older people.

Advances in theory and research have gradually been establishing the personality assessment of senior adults as a specialty in clinical psychogerontology and a feature of evidence-based psychodynamic practice. As just noted, however, the psychological assessment of older people has lacked a classification system and an empirical database that would help clinicians distinguish between normal and psychopathological aging in the elderly, who more than any other age group deal with such profound issues as their health, mobility, and mortality. To meet this need, a classification scheme for sharpening the assessment of senior adults has recently appeared in the second edition of the *Psychodynamic Diagnostic Manual* (*PDM-2*; Lingiardi & McWilliams, 2017), which includes for the first time in a major diagnostic manual a separate section on the elderly. The previously noted aging of modern societies and increasing attention to the psychological needs of older people lend considerable importance to this psychodynamic innovation in classifying psychological disorders in senior adults.

The *PDM-2* conceptualization of aging, shaped by the established clinical utility of psychodynamic formulations, provides a diagnostic framework for assessing the elderly along three axes: a Profile of Mental Functioning for the Elderly (ME Axis), a Personality Patterns and Syndromes in the Elderly (PE Axis), and a Symptom Patterns and Subjective Experiences in the Elderly (SE axis). Taken together, these three axes facilitate a systematic description of healthy and disordered personality functioning in senior adults. To provide an empirical database as well as the

PDM-2 conceptual framework for use in assessing older people, Part III of the present volume reports newly compiled Rorschach reference values for large samples of patient and nonpatient senior adults.

Conclusion

Empirical research and clinical experience have given rise to changes in the traditional image of senior adults. Contrary to long-held views of normal aging as a process of decline and decay, neuropsychological findings have shown that, although decline in some cognitive capacities does occur over time, this decline is for the most part minimal and does not ordinarily lead to functional impairments. To the contrary, there is ample evidence that normal aging often includes elements of enrichment, integration, and personal growth of an individual. Although aging may be associated with chronicity and multiple problems, it is often associated as well with such positive emotional and mental health developments as increased life satisfaction (Lingiardi & McWilliams, 2017, p. 753).

Clinicians evaluating older people should accordingly formulate not only a descriptive diagnosis of their condition, but also a psychodynamic diagnosis that addresses the underlying needs, attitudes, and concerns that motivate them to behave in certain ways. The case studies presented in Part IV of the present volume illustrate the considerable utility of the Rorschach in assessing both the descriptive and psychodynamic features of personality. In arriving at these diagnostic formulations, clinicians must also keep in mind that senior adults are an extremely heterogeneous group with respect to their age subgroup, their physical and mental health, their personality style, and their current family and sociocultural circumstances. In this latter regard, psychological assessment of older people should take special account of cross-cultural variability in attitudes toward aging that may have a substantial bearing in the detection of mental health problems in senior adults.

Assessing the mental functioning and subjective experience of older people requires distinguishing among the following abilities: mental abilities impaired by aging; mental abilities preserved despite aging; mental abilities impaired by transitional developmental crises; mental abilities impaired by the individual's faltering developmental history; and mental abilities on which aging has not exercised any special influence. To address these issues, practitioners who work with senior adults in the twenty-first century should be familiar with both the special needs of older people, their resilience and even potential for further development.

References

American Psychiatric Association (2013). *Diagnostic and statistical manual of mental disorders* (5th ed.). Arlington, VA: Author.

Baltes, E. B. (1979). Life-span developmental psychology: Some converging observations on history and theory. In *Life-span development and behavior* (Vol. 2, pp. 255–279). New York, NY: Academic Press.

Baltes, P. B. (1987). Theoretical propositions of life-span developmental psychology: On the dynamics between growth and decline. *Developmental Psychology, 23*(5), 611–626.

Baltes, P. B., Lindenberger, U., & Staudinger, U. M. (1998). Life-span theory in developmental psychology. In *Handbook of child psychology* (pp. 1029–1143). New York, NY: Wiley.

Barnett, J. E., & Quenzel, A. P. (2017). Innovating to meet the needs of our aging population. *Practice Innovations, 2*, 136–149.

Boyer, T. W. (2006). The development of risk taking: A multi-perspective review. *Developmental Review, 26*, 291–345.

Casey, B. J., Craddock, N. Cuthbert, B. N., Hyman, S. E., Lee, F.S., & Ressler, K. J. (2013). *DSM-5* and *RDoC*: Progress in psychiatry research? *Nature, 14*, 810–814.

Cohen, G. D. (1999). Human potential phases in the second half of life: Mental health theory development. *The American Journal of Geriatric Psychiatry, 7*(1), 1–7.

Corwin, J., & Bylsma, W. F. (1993). Psychological examination of traumatic encephalopathy. *Clinical Neuropsychologist, 7*, 3–21.

Della Sala, S., Gray, C., Baddeley, A., Allamano, N., & Wilson, L. (1999). Pattern span: A tool for unwelding visuo-spatial memory. *Neuropsychologia, 37*(10), 1189–1199.

Erikson, E. H. (1956). The problem of ego identity. *Journal of the American Psychoanalytic Association, 4*, 56–121.

Erikson, E. H. (1959). Identity and the life cycle. *Psychological Issues, 1*, 1–171.

Folstein, M. F., Folstein, S. E., & McHugh, P. R. (1975). Mini-Mental State: A practical method for grading the cognitive state of patients for the clinicians. *Journal of Psychiatric Research, 12*, 189–198.

Freud, S. (1953). On psychotherapy. In *Standard edition* (Vol. 7, pp. 157–268). London, UK: Hogarth Press (original work published in 1904).

Greenberg, T. M. (2016). When the body intrudes: Psychotherapy with older and medically ill adults. In *Psychodynamic perspectives on aging and illness* (pp. 1–22). New York, NY: Springer.

Harada, C. N., Love, M. C. N., & Triebel, K. L. (2013). Normal cognitive aging. *Clinics in Geriatric Medicine, 29*(4), 737–752.

Kennedy, K. M., Rodrigue, K. M., Bischof, G. N., Hebrank, A. C., Reuter-Lorenz, P. A., & Park, D. C. (2015). Age trajectories of functional activation under conditions of low and high processing demands: An adult lifespan fMRI study of the aging brain. *Neuroimage, 104*, 21–34.

Lerner, R. M. (2015). Promoting positive human development and social justice: Integrating theory, research and application in contemporary developmental science. *International Journal of Psychology, 50*(3), 165–173.

Lingiardi, V., & McWilliams, N. (2017). *Psychodynamic diagnostic manual* (2nd ed.). New York, NY: Guilford Press.

Lockhart, S., DeCarli, C., & Fama, R (2014). Neuroimaging of the aging brain: Introduction to the special issue of neuropsychology review. *Neuropsychology Review, 24*, 267–270.

Lomranz, J. (1998). An image of aging and the concept of aintegration. In J. Lomranz (Ed.), *Handbook of aging and mental health: An integrative approach* (pp. 217–250). New York, NY: Plenum Press.

Mattis, S. (1988). *Dementia Rating Scale. Professional manual.* Odessa, FL: Psychological Assessment Resources.

Overton, W. F. (2015). Process and relational developmental systems. In *Handbook of child psychology and developmental science*, Vol. 1: Theory and method (7th ed., pp. 9–62). Hoboken, NJ: Wiley.

Porcelli, P., Giromini, L., Parolin, L., Pineda, J. A., & Viglione, D. J., (2013). Mirroring activity in the brain and movement determinant in the Rorschach test. *Journal of Personality Assessment, 95*(5), 444–456.

Rapaport, D. (1967). The theory of ego autonomy. In M. Gill (Ed.), *Collected papers of David Rapaport* (pp. 722–744). New York, NY: Basic Books (original work published 1957).

Reuter-Lorenz, P. A., & Park, D. C. (2014). How does it STAC up? Revisiting the scaffolding theory of aging and cognition. *Neuropsychology Review, 24*(3), 355–370.

Rosen, W. Mohs, R., & Davis, K. (1984). A new rating scale for Alzheimer's disease. *American Journal of Psychiatry, 141*, 1356–1364.

Roth, M., Huppert, F. A., Mountjoy, C. Q., & Tym E. (1998). *The Cambridge Examination for Mental Disorders of the Elderly – Revised*. Cambridge, UK: Cambridge University Press.

Rorschach, H. (1921/1942). *Psychodiagnostics: A diagnostic test based on perception*. Bern, Switzerland: Hans Huber.

Salthouse, T. A. (2010) Selective review of cognitive aging. *Journal of the International Neuropsychological Society, 16*, 754–760.

Widiger, T. A., & Gore, W. L. (2014). Mental disorders as discrete clinical conditions: Dimensional versus categorical classification. In *Adult psychopathology and diagnosis* (pp. 3–33). Hoboken, NJ: Wiley.

CHAPTER 2

Historical Developments in the Rorschach Assessment of Senior Adults

The Rorschach assessment of senior adults has a long but modest history. It begins with Hermann Rorschach himself and extends through the gradual accumulation of standardized Rorschach data for senior adults and companion developments in applying the Rorschach as a neuropsychological tool.

Early History

Rorschach presented 24 case examples in his 1921 *Psychodiagnostics*, three of which were the records of senior adults: an 80-year-old normally functioning woman; a 69-year-old woman with depression and dementia; and a 78-year-old man with senile dementia (Rorschach, 1921/1942). Rorschach commented on probable age changes in the frequencies of certain variables, but he did not elaborate on the kinds of protocols likely to be given by older people or on the use of their protocols in clinical evaluations.

Basic texts on the administration, scoring, and interpretation of the Rorschach Inkblot Method have similarly made little mention of assessing the elderly. Beck (1950) did comment as follows on the propriety of administering the Rorschach to older people: "If a person can see and talk, he can take the Rorschach" (p. 11). Nevertheless, neither Beck (1950), Klopfer, Ainsworth, Klopfer, and Holt (1954), Exner (2003), Lerner (1998) nor Weiner (2003) discuss the typical nature, customary interpretation, and clinical utility of senior adult protocols.

With respect to age-related considerations, numerous books have discussed the Rorschach assessment of children and adolescents (e.g., Ames, Metraux, & Walker, 1959; Ames, Metraux, Rodell, & Walker, 1974a; Exner & Weiner, 1995; Leichtman, 1996; Tibon-Czopp & Weiner, 2016). However, the only book prior to the present volume that has addressed Rorschach assessment of older people is the 1974 second edition of *Rorschach Responses in Old Age*, authored by Ames, Metraux, Rodell, and Walker (1974b). The Ames et al. book is a research monograph that presents normative Rorschach reference data on 140 women and 60 men between the ages of 70 and 100. There were 102 70-year-olds, 85 80-year-olds, and 13 90-year-olds in the sample. Sixty-seven of these participants were living in their own homes and 133 in institutions for the aged, but all were considered to be "reasonably healthy, active, and alert" (p. 14).

The three age groups in the Ames et al. study did not show any consistent differences in their Rorschach responses. Some of the participants in each of the age groups responded similarly to normally functioning younger adults, and some in the oldest group responded more adequately than some in the youngest group. Ames et al. concluded from these findings that a person's psychological age is not necessarily the same as his or her chronological age. However, on the basis of certain characteristics of their participants' Rorschach responses, Ames et al. differentiated 41 of them as *normal* (responses resembling any normally functioning adult), 140 as *presenile* (showing some signs of diminished cognitive capacity), and 19 as *senile* (indications of substantial cognitive decline, but not to the extent of dementia). The presenile and senile groups differed on the average from the normal group in the following respects: fewer responses; less varied content, with higher *A%*; presence of perseveration; increased *F%* and decreased *F+%*; increased *W%* and decreased *D%* and *Dd%*; fewer *M* and *FM* responses, with more *FM* than *M*; fewer shading responses; and fewer color responses, with more *CF* than *FC*.

Turning from the Ames et al. book to the periodical literature, the first English-language article on the Rorschach assessment of senior adults was a 1946 report by Walter Klopfer on the performance of 50 respondents aged 62–93, 30 of whom were living in a home for the aged and 20 of whom were not institutionalized (Klopfer, 1946). There were few differences between the institutionalized and noninstitutionalized groups in their test responses, and both groups displayed a variety of personality styles. Walter Klopfer's specific findings concerning the Rorschach responses of older people closely resembled those subsequently obtained by Ames et al. with their much larger sample. Also similar to the Ames et al. data were the findings in two small-sample Rorschach studies that were published shortly after Walter Klopfer's report: one by Prados and Fried (1947) on 35 older people aged 50–70; and the other by Chesrow, Wosika, and Reinitz (1949) on 20 senior adults aged 64–83.

This early work was summarized and elaborated by Walter Klopfer in a 1956 book chapter on "The Application of the Rorschach Technique to Geriatrics" (Klopfer, 1956). This chapter was notable not only for its discussion of the standardization of Rorschach response patterns in the elderly, but also for providing the first published elaboration of guidelines for using the Rorschach in clinical work with older people. Walter Klopfer described how the Rorschach can illuminate personality patterns in older people, illustrated how the Rorschach can facilitate differential diagnosis in the elderly, and commented on how Rorschach findings can be useful in planning treatment and rehabilitation programs for the aged. Hayslip and Lowman (1986), in a later commentary on the utility of the Rorschach in facilitating clinical decisions, extended its applications with the aged to include assessment of competency, need for institutionalization, suicidal risk, and aggressive proclivities.

Standardized Data for Senior Adults

With respect to the available standardized data for senior adults, nine studies can be noted, five in the US and four from abroad. In the US studies, Light and Amick (1956) presented Rorschach data for 50 noninstitutionalized men and women aged 65–85; Eisdorfer (1963) reported Rorschach data on 242 men and women aged 60–94; Insua and Loza (1986) evaluated the Rorschach response patterns of 30 adults aged 52–71, 15 of whom were functioning normally and 15 of whom were showing early signs of dementia; Gross, Newton, and Brooks (1990) examined age, intellectual level, and Rorschach variables in 47 healthy, community-dwelling men and women aged 65–87; and Pertchik, Shaffer, Erdberg, and Margolin (2007) provided Rorschach data on 52 well-functioning older adults aged 60–80.

From Finland, Mattlar, Knuts, and Virtanen (1985) compared the Rorschach responses of 48 female and 33 male 71-year-old noninstitutionalized elderly people to the responses of middle-aged and young adult samples, and Mattlar, Carlsson, Forsander, and Karppi (1992) used the Rorschach to study the personality structures of 18 physically fit 80-year-old men. From India, Chaudhury et al. (2007) reported on the Rorschach protocols of 442 men and women aged 65 or older, 282 of whom were functioning normally and 160 of whom were psychiatric patients with a variety of formal diagnoses. From Japan, Shimonaka and Nakazato (1991) reported on the Rorschach responses of 236 persons aged 60–96 living in nursing homes.

Notable in this literature review is the fact that all of the cited Rorschach studies of psychological functioning in senior adults, except for the Chaudhury et al. (2007) and Pertchik et al. (2007) reports, were published in the twentieth century. The limited twenty-first-century data are part of the motivation for preparing the present book. However, there has been another thread of research that has substantial implications for the Rorschach assessment of older people—a thread that addresses neuropsychological as well as psychological functioning. As noted in Chapter 1, neurocognitive impairment and decline are often perceived as being associated with the aging process, which makes the neuroscience of Rorschach assessment quite relevant to the clinical evaluation of senior adults.

Historical Developments in Applying the Rorschach as a Neuropsychological Tool

The neuroscience of Rorschach assessment has as long a history as its psychological science, and it has been the subject of extensive research and the focus of considerable contemporary attention. Once again, the story begins with Rorschach himself, who included in his *Psychodiagnostics* a section of case examples on "Organic Psychoses." The utility of the Rorschach in assessing brain damage was a central topic of the first volume of the *Journal of Personality Assessment* (then the *Rorschach Research Exchange*). Piotrowski (1936) led off with a seminal article titled "On the Rorschach Method and its Application in Organic Disturbances of the Central Nervous System." Piotrowski's article was followed by articles on "Personality Studies of Cases with Lesions of the Frontal Lobes" by Kurt Goldstein (1936), "Rorschach Study of a Bilateral Lobectomy Case" by Gladys Tallman (1937), and "Rorschach Interpretation of the Bilateral Lobectomy Case" by Bruno Klopfer (1937).

In this and a later publication, Piotrowski (1937) listed 10 Rorschach signs and proposed that any five or more in a record should be considered indicative of *organicity*, which would currently be referred to as *neuropsychological disorder* or *neurocognitive impairment*. These 10 signs of Piotrowski are the following:

Low number of responses
Slow reaction time
Fewer than two *M* responses
One or more color naming responses
Fewer good-form responses—$F+\% < 70$
Fewer popular responses—$P\% < 25$
Repetition—perseveration of the same response in several blots
Impotence—difficulty correcting or improving responses despite perceiving them as inadequate or of poor quality
Perplexity—expressions of uncertainty about how to respond, self-doubts about being able to perform the task, and frequent requests for clarification and reassurance from the examiner
Automatic phrases—recurring use of particular expressions, as in beginning every card with "This is a nice piece of artwork that …" or of a single word for many different objects, as in "This is one of those units" or "He's got some kind of unit in his hand"

Numerous subsequent studies comparing brain-injured patients with normal controls attested to the validity of five or more of the Piotrowski signs as suggestive of brain damage (Aita, Reitan, & Ruth, 1947; Birch & Diller, 1959; Chaudhury, John, Bhatoe, & Rohatgi, 1999; Eckhardt, 1961; Hertz & Loehrke, 1954). In qualifying statements, however, Hertz and Loehrke cautioned that the absence of these signs is not contraindicative of organic disturbances (i.e., the occurrence of false-negative findings), and Aita et al. noted that five signs accounted for much of the variance in their findings: color naming, repetition, impotence, perplexity, and automatic phrases. Notably, these five critical signs, except for color naming, provide behavioral rather than structural data in Rorschach assessment. This distinction, together with the conceptual formulation of how the Rorschach facilitates neurocognitive as well psychological assessment, is elaborated in Chapter 4 of the present book.

Returning to historical developments, interest in the Rorschach assessment of neuropsychological dysfunction was greatly stimulated when John Exner published his 1974 book introducing the Rorschach Comprehensive System (CS).

Exner defined the Rorschach as a perceptual–cognitive and problem-solving task, and his system included numerous empirically quantified and reliably scored variables that measure how people use language, attend to their surroundings, perceive people and events, think about their experience, and make decisions. The resemblance of Exner's perceptual–cognitive and problem-solving emphasis in Rorschach assessment to the typical focus of neuropsychological assessment led to a resurgence of the interest in combining the two types of assessment that also characterized the previously mentioned 1936–1937 first volume of the *Rorschach Research Exchange*.

Three examples of this revised interest are articles by Acklin and Wu-Holt (1996) on "Contributions of Cognitive Science to the Rorschach Technique: Cognitive and Neuropsychological Correlates of the Response Process," by Zillmer and Perry (1996) on "Cognitive–Neuropsychological Abilities and Related Psychological Disturbances: A Factor Model of Neuropsychological, Rorschach, and MMPI Indices," and by Exner, Colligan, Boll, Stischer, and Hillman (1996) on "Rorschach Findings Concerning Closed Head Injury Patients."

The CS interpretive focus on perceptual–cognitive aspects of the response process is also prominent in the recent development of an alternative Rorschach method, the Rorschach Personality Assessment System (R-PAS; Meyer, Viglione, Mihura, Erard, & Edberg, 2011). The R-PAS differs from the CS in certain features of how the test is administered and coded, but there are few differences between them in the nature and interpretation of the variables that are coded. With respect to assessing neurocognitive functioning, the R-PAS pays particular attention to the complexity and synthesis of the responses that are given.

Also of note with respect to Rorschach assessment of neurocognitive functioning are ways in which it can complement assessment with such traditional neuropsychological measures as the WAIS, the Wechsler Memory Scale, and the Trail-Making Test. In taking such neuropsychological tests, people are encouraged to do their best and ordinarily do so. The test results are thus a *maximal* indicator of what people are capable of doing in a relatively structured situation in which there are obvious indications of whether they are doing well or poorly, such as being able to answer test questions. By contrast, a Rorschach examination is a relatively unstructured situation in which examinees have little conception of what is expected of them or of what constitutes doing well. For this reason, Rorschach findings are not a *maximal* indicator of what people are able to do when being urged to do it, but are instead a *typical* indicator of what they are likely to do when left to their own preferences. Information about both maximal and typical patterns of perceptual–cognitive functioning enriches the results of a neuropsychological evaluation, and the Rorschach can accordingly serve as a neuropsychological as well as a personality assessment instrument.

The designation of the Rorschach as a neuropsychological tool has been proposed as well by Perry and Potterat (1997) and numerous other authors, but only recently have advances in the neuroscience of Rorschach assessment identified discrete relationships between certain Rorschach variables and structural and functional features of the brain. As reviewed by Muzio (2016) and Schott (2014), this contemporary line of research has involved taking brain wave (electroencephalogram) and brain imaging (functional magnetic resonance imaging) measurements while people were observing or giving responses to the inkblots. Among other findings, these studies have shown that viewing the chromatic and achromatic cards simulates activity in different regions of the brain (Ishibashi et al., 2016); that activation of the mirror nervous system (MNS) leads to increased production of human movement (*M*) responses (Giromini et al., 2016); and that interfering with MNS activity decreases the propensity to see *M* in the inkblots (Ando et al., 2015).

Conclusion

As this brief introductory review indicates, the Rorschach has a long history of application in clinical evaluations of senior adults, as both a personality and a neuropsychological assessment instrument. However, there has been little elaboration in the literature of how Rorschach assessment can measure psychological concerns and neurocognitive dysfunctions in older people, and there has been no extensive presentation of normative Rorschach reference data in the last 40 years. The chapters in Part III of this volume present recently obtained reference values for a large international sample of senior adult nonpatients, for age-related differences within this nonpatient sample, and for a patient sample of senior adults with Alzheimer's disease. The chapters in Part IV address the diagnostic and therapeutic applications of Rorschach assessment with case illustrations of senior adults with both impaired and normal-range personality functioning. Part II that follows comprises two chapters: Chapter 3 on the Rorschach as a clinical gerontopsychological tool, with attention to how older people experience and respond to the Rorschach; and Chapter 4 on the parameters of Rorschach interpretation, with attention to response patterns that are suggestive of certain psychological disorders and adjustment difficulties.

References

Aita, J. A., Reitan, R. M., & Ruth, J. M. (1947). Rorschach's test as a diagnostic aid in brain injury. *American Journal of Psychiatry, 103*, 770–779.

Ames, L. B., Metraux, R. W., & Walker, R. N. (1959) *Adolescent Rorschach responses.* Oxford, UK: Hoeber.

Ames, L. B., Metraux, R. W., Rodell, J. L., & Walker, R. N. (1974a). *Child Rorschach responses: Developmental trends from two to ten years.* Oxford, UK: Brunner/Mazel.

Ames, L. B., Metraux, R. W., Rodell, J. L., & Walker, R. N. (1974b). *Rorschach responses in old age.* New York, NY: Brunner/Mazel.

Ando, A., Salatino, A., Giromini, L., Ricci, R., Ignollo, C., Cristofanelli, S., ... Zennaro, A. (2015). Embodied simulation and ambiguous stimuli: The role of the mirror neuron system. *Brain Research, 1629*, 135–142.

Beck, S. J. (1950). *Rorschach's test: I. Basic processes.* New York, NY: Grune & Stratton.

Birch, H. G., & Diller, L. (1959). Rorschach signs of "organicity": A physiological basis for perceptual disturbances. *Journal of Projective Techniques, 23*, 184–197.

Chaudhury, S., John, T. R., Bhatoe, H. S., & Rohatgi, S. (1999). Evaluation of Piotrowksi's organic signs of head injury. *Journal of Projective Psychology & Mental Health*, 6, 53–67.

Chaudhury, S., Sudersanan, S., Seby, K., Salujha, S. K., Srivastava, K., Kundeyawala, S. M., & Rathee, P. (2007). Rorschach responses of older Indians. *Journal of Projective Psychology and Mental Health, 14*, 30–43.

Chesrow, E. J., Wosika, P. H., & Reinitz, A. H. (1949). A psychometric evaluation of aged white makes. *Geriatrics, 4*, 169–177.

Eckhardt, W. (1961). Piotrowski's signs: Organic or functional? *Journal of Clinical Psychology*, 17, 36–38.

Eisdorfer, C. (1963). Rorschach performance and intellectual functioning in the aged. *Journal of Gerontology, 18*, 358–363.

Exner, J. E., Jr. (2003). *The Rorschach: A comprehensive system. Vol. 1, Basic foundations and principles of interpretation* (4th ed.). New York, NY: Wiley.

Exner, J. E, Jr., & Weiner, I. B. (1995). *The Rorschach: A comprehensive system: Vol. 3, Assessment of children and adolescents* (2nd ed.). Hoboken, NJ: Wiley.

Giromini, L., Viglione, D. J., Brusadelli, E., Zennaro, A., DiGirolamo, M., & Porcelli, P. (2016). The effects of neurological priming on the Rorschach. *Rorschachiana, 37*, 58–73.

Goldstein, K. (1936). Pesonality studies of cases with lesions of the frontal lobes: 1. The psychopathology of Pick's disease. *Rorschach Research Exchange*, 1, 57–65.

Gross, A., Newton, R. R., & Brooks, R. B. (1990). Rorschach responses in healthy, community, dwelling older adults. *Journal of Personality Assessment, 55*, 335–343.

Hayslip B., & Lowman, R. L. (1986). The clinical use of projective techniques with the aged: A critical review and synthesis. *The Journal of Aging and Mental Health, 5*, 63–94.

Hertz, M. R., & Loehrke, L. M. (1954). The application of the Piotrowski and the Hughes signs of organic defect to a group of patients suffering from post-traumatic encephalopathy. *Journal of Projective Techniques*, 18, 183–196.

Insua, A. M., & Loza, S. M. (1986). Psychometric patters on the Rorschach of healthy elderly persons and patients with suspected dementia. *Perceptual and Motor Skills, 63*, 931–936.

Ishibashi, M., Uchiumi, C., Jung, M., Azawa, N., Makita, K., Nakamura, Y., & Saito, D. N. (2016), Differences in brain hemodynamics in response to achromatic and chromatic cards of the Rorschach: A fMRI study. *Rorschachiana, 37*, 41–57.

Klopfer, B. (1937). Rorschach interpretation of the bilateral lobectomy case. *Rorschach Research Exchange, 1*, 83–88.

Klopfer, B., Ainsworth, M. D., Klopfer, W. G., & Holt, R. R. (1954). *Developments in the Rorschach technique: Vol. 1. Technique and theory.* Yonkers-on-Hudson, NY: World Book.

Klopfer, W. G. (1946). Personality patterns of old age. *Rorschach Research Exchange, 10*, 145–166.

Klopfer, W. G. (1956). The application of the Rorschach technique in geriatrics. In B. Klopfer (Ed.), *Developments in the Rorschach technique. Vol. 2. Fields of application* (pp. 195–214). Burlingame, NY: Harcourt, Brace, & World.

Leichtman, M. (1996). *The Rorschach: A developmental perspective.* Hillsdale, NJ: Analytic Press.

Lerner, P. M. (998). *Psychoanalytic perspectives on the Rorschach.* Hillsdale, NJ: Analytic Press.

Light, B. H., & Amick, J. H. (1956). Rorschach responses of normal aged. *Journal of Projective Techniques, 20*, 185–195.

Mattlar, C.-K., Carlsson, A., Forsander, C. & Karppi, S.-L. (1992).Personality characteristics for a group of physically fit 80 year old men. *British Journal of Projective Psychology, 37*, 41–51.

Mattlar, C.-K., Knuts, L.-R, & Virtanen, E. (1985). Personality structure on the Rorschach for a group of healthy 71-year-old females and males. *British Journal of Projective Psychology & Personality Study, 30*, 3–8.

Muzio, W. (2016). Inkblots and neurons: Correlating typical cognitive performance with brain structure and function. *Rorschachiana, 37*, 1–6.

Piotrowski, Z. A. (1936). On the Rorschach method and its application in organic disturbances of the brain. *Rorschach Research Exchange, 1*, 23–39.

Perry, W., & Potterat, E. G. (1997). Beyond personality assessment: The use of the Rorschach as a neuropsychological instrument in patients with amnestic disorders. In J. R. Meloy, M. W. Acklin, C. B. Gacono, & J. F. Murray (Eds.), *Contemporary Rorschach interpretation* (pp. 557–575). Mahwah, NJ: Lawrence Erlbaum Associates.

Pertchik, K., Shaffer, T. W., Erdberg, P., & Margolin, D. I. (2007). Rorschach Comprehensive System data from a sample of 52 older adult nonpatients from the United States. *Journal of Personality Assessment, 89*(Suppl. 1), 166–173.

Piotrowski, Z. A. (1937). The Rorschach Ink Blot Method in organic disturbances of the central nervous system. *Journal of Nervous and Mental Disease, 86*, 525–537.

Prados, M., & Fried, E. (1947). Personality structure of the older age groups. *Journal of Clinical Psychology*, 3, 113–120.

Rorschach, H. (1921/1942). *Psychodiagnostics: A diagnostic test based on perception.* Bern, Switzerland: Hans Huber.

Schott, G. D. (2014). Revisiting the Rorschach ink-blots: From iconography and psychology to neuroscience. *Journal of Neurology, Neurosurgery, and Psychiatry, 85*, 699–706.

Shimonaka, Y., & Nakazato, K. (1991). Aging and terminal changes in Rorschach responses among the Japanese elderly. *Journal of Personality Assessment, 57*, 10–18.

Tallman, G. (1937). Rorschach study of a bilateral lobectomy case. *Rorschach Research Exchange, 1*, 77–83.

Tibon-Czopp, S., & Weiner, I. B. (2016). *Rorschach assessment of adolescents.* New York, NY: Springer.

Weiner, I. B. (2003). *Principles of Rorschach interpretation* (2nd ed.). Hillsdale, NJ: Lawrence Erlbaum Associates.

Zillmer, E. A., & Perry, W. (1996). Cognitive–neuropsychological abilities and related psychological disturbance: A factor model of neuropsychological, Rorschach, and MMPI indices. *Assessment*, 3, 209–224.

PART II

Conceptual Considerations

CHAPTER 3

Effective Utilization of the Rorschach Task in Clinical Gerontopsychology

Effective utilization of the Rorschach Inkblot Method in the clinical evaluation of senior adults requires awareness of its nature as an assessment instrument, of the ways in which people typically experience and respond to it, and of age-related considerations in examining older people and obtaining test data from them.

The Nature of the Rorschach Task

What is the Rorschach test? As is often the case in describing psychological phenomena, the answer to this question is that "it depends." Specifically, the nature of the Rorschach as an assessment instrument depends on how a person is responding to it at a particular moment in time. Suppose a person when handed Card I neither perceives nor associates to it, but instead hands it back and says, "I don't think I can do this, because tests make me nervous, I never do well on them, and anyway I was made to come here." Now the Rorschach is clearly acting as a test of behavior, eliciting in this instance some possible indications of oppositional or passive–aggressive tendencies, low self-esteem, and resentment at being ordered about by people in authority. Consider, however, a respondent who looks at Card I and says, "I see a bat here, with the wings on the side." In this response, the Rorschach is clearly serving as a test of perception. Suppose instead the person looks at Card I and says, "It reminds me of a vicious bat, something flying around that could hurt me." In this response, the Rorschach is clearly functioning as a test of association.

To answer the opening question, then, the Rorschach test is a threefold measure of behavior, perception, and association. In the course of an examination, respondents always display some test-taking behavior, which can be observed by the examiner; they engage in some perception, which is coded with the structural variables; and they always express some associations, which are reflected in the thematic imagery.

Taken together, these behavioral, structural, and thematic elements of respondents' Rorschach performance provide information about their cognitive functioning, affective experience, interpersonal relatedness, self-perception, and underlying attitudes and concerns. Notably, the basic principles of interpreting these behavioral, structural, and thematic Rorschach variables are not age-related, and examiners need to be familiar with just one set of interpretive guidelines, whatever the age of the person they are examining. However, the same interpretation can have different implications for different people, depending on their age and also on their current circumstances and sociocultural environment.

To illustrate the distinction between interpretations and their implications, consider the *FC:CF* relationship. *FC* responses represent relatively well-modulated and reserved processing of affect in which feelings emerge and dissipate slowly and are deeply felt but mild to moderate in their intensity. In contrast, *CF* responses reflect relatively unmodulated and spontaneous processing of affect in which feelings arise and dissipate quickly but are often quite intense while they last. Reserved and well-modulated affect is by and large an adult characteristic, whereas spontaneous and unmodulated expression of feelings is more typical of children than adults. With respect to interpretation, then, *FC* and *CF* responses mean what they mean, whoever gives them. With respect to implications, however, a predominance of *FC* responses is likely to be associated with good psychological adjustment in adults, but in children it is likely to identify pseudo-mature emotional restraint and limited ability to engage in the free-flowing affective interchange of youthful peer relationships. Conversely, a predominance of *CF* responses indicates the emotional intensity, spontaneity, and lability that commonly characterize children, but in adults can lead to a person's being seen as childishly immature, intense, and excitable.

As for a respondent's current circumstances, psychology has a long history of attention to situational determinants of behavior. In a seminal volume titled *Personality and Assessment*, Walter Mischel (1968) observed that people may be generally disposed to act in certain ways, but are likely to behave differently in certain circumstances. A common example of situation-specific behavior is the aggressive bully who delights in dominating and belittling other people but, in the presence of a more powerful or authoritarian person, becomes passively subservient and ingratiating. Another easily recognizable example of situation-specific behavior is a person who is generally fearless, but trembles at the prospect of having to speak in public.

Recognition of environmental influences on the adaptability of personality characteristics traces back to the classical anthropological studies of Margaret Mead (1928), as reported in her book, *Coming of Age in Samoa*. Mead's findings demonstrated that a passive–dependent individual is likely to adapt well in an easygoing, collaborative, and group-oriented society in which people are devoted to taking care of each other, but would find it difficult to adapt to being in an energetic, competitive, and individual-oriented society that values striving, assertiveness, and taking care of one's own needs. Conversely, a person who is by nature self-centered, assertive, and competitive is likely to thrive in an individual-oriented society, but be uncomfortable, out of step, and unpopular in a group-oriented society. These indications that personality characteristics can be adaptive in one society and maladaptive in another apply as well to such smaller sociocultural environments as a person's family, neighborhood, school, and workplace.

Returning to the threefold nature of the Rorschach as a perceptual, associational, and behavioral measure, this chapter focuses on the interpretive significance of test behaviors that reflect how people are experiencing and responding to the Rorschach task and perhaps more generally to events in their lives.

Interpretive Significance of Test Behaviors

Rorschach test behaviors are representative samples of a person's customary ways of dealing with problem-solving and decision-making situations. How people conduct themselves when taking the Rorschach often reflects the kind of person they are, their attitudes toward themselves, and their manner of relating to other people. Three types of test behaviors that are especially likely to have such interpretive significance are comments, expressive style, and interpersonal manner. Conceptually, each type of test behavior can be interpreted from one or more theoretical perspectives. For example, rejecting a card can be viewed as indicating problems of adaptation to the task from an *ego psychology* perspective, difficulties in interpersonal relatedness in terms of *object relations* theory, difficulties in preserving self-confidence in terms of *self psychology*, and problems in playfully coping with the task by providing responses located within the transitional space between reality and fantasy from a *relational psychology* perspective (Blatt, Tuber, & Auerbach, 1990; Handler, 1999; Lerner, 1998; Silverstein, 1999; Smith, 1990; Tibon-Czopp, Appel & Zeligman, 2016; Weiner, 2003).

Comments

Comments during a Rorschach examination consist of what people say in addition to giving direct responses to the customary questions "What might this be?" "Where did you see it?" and "What made it look like that?" Some such comments are intended to explain or justify a response on the basis of personal experience and are coded as *Personal* (*PER*), as are comments that merely share personal information with the examiner. In this respect, *PER* responses frequently mention the resemblance of an object to something the respondent has seen elsewhere, as in "It's a cartoon figure, like ones I've seen in comic strips." In other instances, respondents may justify a response by referring to how much they know about an object, as in "It looks like the stabilizer on an airplane, which I know about from my experience as a pilot." Both types of personalized justification of a response are likely to reflect some underlying insecurity or self-doubt that inclines respondents to verbalize a resemblance as a basis for what they have reported, as if to prove themselves capable, or to tout their talents and accomplishments, as if to prove themselves admirable. The detection of underlying concerns about adequacy that most often arise in senior adults, even when they are not otherwise apparent or within the person's conscious awareness, can point to potential therapeutic interventions that will help the person recognize and deal realistically with them.

Some comments that share personal information with the examiner refer to objects and events in the respondent's life, but these self-revelations are neither explanatory nor self-glorifying. Instead, they often indicate a respondent's interest in reaching out to the examiner, as if to say, "I want you to know more about me as a person." Self-revealing comments about objects might take the form of "I'm fond of dogs, and this part looks like the cute little puppy I have at home." A self-revealing *PER* response about events might take the form of "A lake here that reminds me of when I was young and would visit my grandparents at their summer cottage." Such positively toned sharing of personal information with the examiner is likely to have implications for a respondent being generally able to enjoy life and relate comfortably to other people. In addition, the content of self-revealing *PER* responses is often a rich source of information about the thoughts, feelings, and experiences that have shaped a respondent's personality development and characteristics.

With further regard to self-revealing *PER* responses, older adults may be more likely than younger adults to relate reminiscences, for three reasons. First, they will on the average have had more experiences and more memories of the past than younger adults. Second, older adults are more inclined than younger adults to look back at what has happened in the past. Third, and especially when they are experiencing loneliness, older adults may be more inclined than younger adults to reach out for relationships by sharing personal information. The potentially positive influence of reminiscence on the enhancement of life satisfaction and emotional well-being in older adults is discussed further in Chapter 6.

Along with *PER* responses, people may make interpretively significant comments that reflect attitudes toward their being tested, toward themselves, toward the examiner, or toward the examiner's test. Attitudes toward being examined can have a positive flavor, as in "It's interesting to see how many different things I can find in these cards," but more often they reflect concern about what the test results might show, as in "I hope I'm doing okay on these." Particularly in testing older people, who with aging may be finding it increasingly difficult and therefore stressful to deal with problem-solving and decision-making situations, examiners should stand ready to assuage such concerns with support and encouragement, as in saying, "You're doing just fine." Of further note, expressed concerns about being examined illustrate the concept of perplexity that was identified in Chapter 2 as one of the Piotrowski signs of neurocognitive impairment. Perplexity consists of frequent statements of uncertainty about how to respond, repeated self-doubts about being able to perform the Rorschach task, and numerous requests for clarification and reassurance from the examiner.

Respondents' attitudes toward themselves usually emerge in the form of evaluative comments on their responses, as in "I like that one, and I guess I'm pretty good at doing this," or "That's probably another poor response that I've just given." Negative opinions of their responses can indicate low self-esteem, sometimes of recent origin and related to aging. Positive response evaluations can also reflect diminished self-esteem, however, should these evaluations be serving as a way of denying or counteracting self-depreciation. Such defensiveness is especially apparent when respondents seek examiner confirmation of having done well, as in "I've got a really good imagination, haven't I?"

Evaluative comments addressed to the examiner can also have a positive or a negative flavor. Positive comments are directly or indirectly intended to please and curry favor with the examiner. Examples of expressing positive attitudes directly would be thanking examiners for their effort ("I appreciate your spending so much time with me") or complimenting them on their manner ("You have a pleasant way about you"), their abilities ("I've heard that you have an excellent reputation"), or their appearance ("I like that tie you're wearing"). Indirectly, respondents may express positive attitudes with comments about the examiner's profession ("I have a lot of respect for psychologists") or possessions ("You have a nicely furnished office").

Expressed negative attitudes toward examiners, by contrast, often involve challenging or demeaning them. Direct examples of such negative comments might be "I don't think you're going about this in a good way," or "You seem too young to have had much experience." Indirectly, a respondent may find fault with the examiner's location, facilities, or occupation, as in "Your office was really hard to find," "This is a very uncomfortable chair," or "It must be pretty dull doing what you do all day long." Like self-revealing *PER* responses, expressions of positive attitudes toward the examiner can indicate respondents' needs to reach out for close relationships and have other people like and approach them. As for expressions of negative attitudes that demean and devaluate the examiner, such unwarranted comments may reflect underlying concerns about adequacy and a need to denigrate others as a way of bolstering their own self-esteem.

With respect to attitudes toward the Rorschach task, respondents receiving their initial instructions may interject with enthusiasm ("I've heard a lot about these inkblots, and I'm looking forward to seeing them") or disavowal ("As far as I know, these inkblots aren't a valid measure of anything and won't tell you much about me"). Similar to the other types of comments, positive pronouncements about the Rorschach are likely to indicate a generally upbeat outlook on life and a wish to please the examiner, whereas casting aspersions on the inkblot method suggests a generally negative outlook and a self-protective way of denying the accuracy or implications of whatever the test results may suggest.

Expressive Style

Much can be learned about people from their expressive style in giving Rorschach responses and using language. The delivery of Rorschach responses can be categorized by its rate, certainty, and flexibility. With respect to rate of responding, some people may go about the task deliberately, taking time to study the blots and considering carefully what they want to say about them, whereas other people may deal with the blots hastily, giving them a cursory glance and voicing the first thought that comes to mind. These long and short reaction times are likely to identify a general propensity for either a contemplative or an unreflective approach to making decisions. Additionally, prolonged reaction times can be a manifestation of depleted energy associated with depression. However, diminished processing speed, which is known to characterize older people, may sometimes be the main reason for extended reaction times in focusing their attention on the blots and formulating impressions of them.

In similar fashion, rate of speech in delivering responses can be an indication of how rapidly or slowly people are generally inclined to express themselves. At the extremes, very rapid speech may reflect the excitement of a hypomanic condition, and very slow speech may be a manifestation of the depleted energy associated with a depressive condition. The possibility of depleted energy is especially relevant in the assessment of older people, in whom slowed speech, like long reaction times, can suggest not only depression, but also neurocognitive impairment of the ability to find words and sustain attention.

The certainty with which responses are delivered refers to whether they are expressed in definite or qualified terms. An example of a definite response would be "That's a bat," or, even more definitely, "That must be a bat," or "It's definitely a bat." A less certain response would be "It might be a bat," or "Possibly a bat." Even further from being definite, a respondent might qualify responses in ways that disavow responsibility for them, as in "If I have to say something, I'd say a bat, but it doesn't really look like that," or "If this part were bigger and this part were smaller, it might resemble a bat, but I'm not sure of that."

Consistently delivering responses with certainty is likely to reflect a general style of being assertive and self-assured in expressing opinions, whereas repetitive qualification of responses points to characterological passivity and reluctance to commit to a point of view. In older people, both repetitive certainty and pervasive qualification in delivering Rorschach responses can be a defensive reaction to concerns about diminished capacities. Being quite definite serves defensive purposes by preempting further inquiry into how and why something has been seen, and being quite uncertain similarly spares respondents from having to justify a percept they have reported.

The flexibility of Rorschach responses refers to the variety of the language that is used in giving them. Responses are ordinarily phrased differently from each other, as in "This looks like …" for one response, "What I see in this one is …" for another response, and "The top part here resembles a …" for a third response. The location, determinants, and content categories also vary across the responses in most records. As described in Chapter 2, deviations from this expected flexibility in language are captured by two other Piotrowski signs of neurocognitive impairment: repetition and automatic phrases.

Repetition refers to perseveration, coded in the CS as *PSV*, and captures repetitive responses either within or between cards. Within-card perseveration consists of two successive responses to a card that are identical in location, determinants, content category, and form quality. Between-card perseveration consists of identifying an object seen on a card as being the same object that was seen on a previous card, as in saying for Card III, "It looks like two people cooking over a pot," and for Card VII, "Here's the same two people I saw before, but now they're just sitting there." As for automatic phrases, they sometimes take the form of introducing responses with the same set of words, as in saying for Card I, "This is a nice piece of artwork that shows a bat"; for Card II, "This is a nice piece of artwork that shows two bears"; for Card III, "This is a nice piece of artwork that shows two people with a pot between them"; and so forth. In other instances, automatic phrases consist of substituting some general noun for specific object names, as illustrated by the following responses: "This is a unit for writing with" (instead of pen or pencil); "This is a unit for digging up things" (instead of spade or shovel); and "On this one he's got some kind of unit in his hand."

Such perseveration and automatic phrasing in delivering Rorschach responses usually indicate a need to cling to ways of thinking and acting that have previously seemed to work well for the person, even when changing circumstances make them no longer appropriate and adaptive. Like being quite definite in expressing responses, perseveration and automatic phrasing can be understood as self-protective efforts by respondents to keep themselves feeling safe and secure and thereby ward off underlying concerns about inadequacy or diminished capacities. Unusual word substitutions may also reflect short-term memory loss, with difficulty remembering the names of people or objects. Minor and occasional instances of such diminished flexibility and short-term memory loss are common features of the normal aging process. The more frequent and maladaptive they become, however, the more likely they are to identify clinically significant neurocognitive impairment.

Interpersonal Style

How respondents experience and interact with the Rorschach examiner is likely to reflect how they typically relate to other people, especially in such uncertain circumstances as having to say what inkblots might be. This uncertainty in a standard Rorschach administration typically elicits four alternative ways in which respondents tend to perceive their examiners. They may see them as an over-controlling authority who is dictating what must be done (as in saying, "I'm going to show you some inkblots, and I want you to tell me what they look like to you") or as an under-controlling observer who is giving insufficient guidance in how it should be done (as in saying, "It's up to you"). They may regard them as properly investigating their psychological problems or as improperly invading their personal privacy. They may experience them as being supportively focused on bringing to light their psychological assets and capacities or as being critically focused on uncovering their faults and limitations. They may consider them sincerely interested in being helpful or as indifferently going through the motions of conducting the evaluation. These alternative perceptions of the examiner are likely to reflect tendencies of a respondent to regard other people as being under- or over-controlling, interested or intrusive, supportive or critical, and helpful or uncaring.

As for revealing styles of relating to the Rorschach examiner, imagine soft-spoken respondents who comply quietly with the examination process and collaborate without complaint. They are friendly, pleasant, and polite. During the examination, they handle the examiner's cards gently and reach out to take and hand them back. Such test behavior might suggest a passive–dependent style of interpersonal relatedness.

In contrast, imagine abrasive respondents who distance themselves from the examination process by questioning its necessity ("I don't think there is any reason for my being examined"), expressing disdain for it ("I don't see how this will do any good"), and participating in it grudgingly ("If I have to say something, I will"). Such hypothetical respondents are hostile, surly, and scornful. During the examination, they lean back, forcing the examiner to reach out to give them the cards, which they then handle roughly and, after responding, toss on the desk instead of handing them back. Test behavior of this kind is likely to identify a passive–aggressive or just plain aggressive style of conducting interpersonal relationships. Although Rorschach test behavior cannot by itself document passive–dependent and passive–aggressive personality characteristics, these two hypothetical examples illustrate how expressive style during an examination can raise these possibilities for further consideration.

Conclusion

With respect to the utility of the Rorschach as an assessment tool in the clinical gerontopsychology field, it is reasonable to ask why the test should be administered to senior adults. The answer to this question is that the Rorschach should be administered to seniors for the same reason that it is administered to younger people, which is to assess their personality characteristics and the extent of their psychological capacities and limitations, with particular attention to any conditions or concerns that call for therapeutic intervention. To serve these purposes, a properly administered and scored Rorschach protocol provides the following four types of information about respondents: (1) their cognitive ability to attend adequately to their surroundings, perceive their world accurately, and think clearly and logically about relationships between events; (2) their manner of experiencing and expressing affect without becoming unduly upset by events; (3) their attitudes toward themselves, toward other people, and toward interpersonal relationships; and (4) underlying concerns and sources of distress of which they may not be fully aware. In each of these respects, deviations from normative expectations help to identify adjustment difficulties and psychological disorders and to suggest therapeutic interventions for alleviating them. These Rorschach contributions to differential diagnosis and treatment planning typify clinical work with older as well as younger people, as described in the case illustrations presented in Part IV of the current volume.

However, given the previously noted likelihood of at least some older people becoming uneasy when required to solve problems and make decisions, supportive and encouraging comments by the examiner may be called for more frequently than in the testing of younger people. Nonetheless, examiners should guard against being influenced by any preconceived notions of what older people are like and what can be expected of them, such as their being emotionally frail or limited in their ability to participate in a psychological evaluation. Stereotyped notions and expectations of this kind can affect how examiners administer the Rorschach. Consequently, treating older people as if they were emotionally frail can result in their responding with frailty. Such negative clinical consequences of mistaken perceptions of older people and biased attitudes toward them are elaborated in the American Psychological Association's *Guidelines for Practice with Older Adults* (American Psychological Association, 2014) and more recently by Barnett and Quenzel (2017), who review psychological issues associated with the aging process, considerations in the assessment and psychological treatment of older people, and the necessity of appropriate training and continuing professional education in the field of gerontopsychology for clinicians working with the elderly. Reyes, Krishnamurthy, and Puente (2018) similarly stress the importance of avoiding age-related stereotypy in psychological assessment and treating the elderly in a respectful and noncondescending manner, while being alert to indications of distress when testing senior adults and prepared to counter them with support and encouragement, then, examiners should administer the Rorschach exactly as they would when testing younger adults.

References

American Psychological Association (2014). Guidelines for practice with older adults. *American Psychologist, 69*, 34–65.

Barnett, J. E., & Quenzel, A. P. (2017). Innovating to meet the needs of our aging population. *Practice Innovations, 2*, 136–149.

Blatt, S. J., Tuber, S. B., & Auerbach, J. S. (1990). Representation of interpersonal interactions on the Rorschach and level of psychopathology. *Journal of Personality Assessment, 54*(3–4), 711–728.

Handler, L. (1999). Assessment of playfulness: Hermann Rorschach meets D. W. Winnicott. *Journal of Personality Assessment, 72*, 208–217.

Lerner, P. M. (1998). *Psychoanalytic perspectives on the Rorschach*. Hillsdale, NJ: Analytic Press.

Mead, M. (1928). *Coming of age in Samoa*. Oxford, UK: William Morrow.

Mischel, W. (1968). *Personality and assessment*. Hoboken, NJ: John Wiley & Sons

Reyes, V. P., Krishnamurthy, R., & Puente (2018). Age as diversity in psychological assessment. In S. R. Smith & R. Krishnamurthy (Eds.), *Diversity-sensitive personality assessment* (pp. 203–219). New York, NY: Routledge.

Silverstein, M. L. (1999). *Self psychology and diagnostic assessment*. Mahwah, NJ: Lawrence Erlbaum Associates.

Smith, B. L. (1990). Potential space and the Rorschach: Application of Object Relations theory. *Journal of Personality Assessment, 55*, 756–767.

Tibon-Czopp, S., Appel, L., & Zeligman, R. (2016). Assessing personality patterns of functioning in a decision-making ambiguous task: The Rorschach Reality–Fantasy Scale (RFS-2). *Group Decision and Negotiation*, *25*, 65–75.

Weiner, I. B. (2003). *Principles of Rorschach interpretation* (2nd ed.). Mahwah, NJ: Lawrence Erlbaum Associates.

CHAPTER 4

Parameters of Rorschach Interpretation

Interpretation, which is the most complex facet of Rorschach assessment, consists of a threefold analysis of the clinician's behavioral observations and the respondent's perceptions and associations. As described in Chapter 3, the behavioral observations describe how respondents conduct themselves during the examination, deliver their responses, and relate to the examiner. The present chapter addresses the interpretive significance of the structural variables and the thematic imagery in a Rorschach protocol. The perceptual features of responses are coded with structural variables based on their location choice, determinants, and content category, and the associational features of responses consist of the thematic imagery they contain.

Many clinicians rely on the Rorschach as an assessment tool for helping to distinguish between healthy and psychopathological functioning. As a standardized task that does not require respondents to engage in conscious self-reflection, it is well suited for this purpose, if properly used. The structural variables in a Rorschach protocol provide a quantitative basis for identifying probable characteristics of a person's cognitive functioning, affective experience, interpersonal relatedness, and self-perception and for determining whether these characteristics fall within the normal range or instead signal some adaptive difficulties. Thematic imagery is explored by using content and sequence analysis.

The following discussion elaborates the interpretive significance of the Rorschach Comprehensive System (CS; Exner, 2003; Exner & Weiner, 1995) structural variables and thematic imagery both in general and with respect to senior adults in particular. These two sources of information are integrated into a clinically relevant classification of mental functioning that is anchored in the assumption that mental health is more than simply the absence of symptoms. Delineating deficiencies in mental health must accordingly consider impairment in a variety of capacities, some of which are not overtly manifest, and the Rorschach is a particularly useful tool for assessing implicit as well as explicit personality characteristics.

As just noted, we use the CS structural variables to assess four domains of personality: cognitive functioning, affective experience, interpersonal relatedness, and self-perception. Rorschach clinicians working with elderly people have until now relied for normative reference data on the composite international sample of nonpatient adults reported by Meyer, Erdberg, and Shaffer (2007). The present volume reports Rorschach data newly collected from an international sample of nonpatient senior adults, aged 60 or older, and compares them with the reference values of Meyer et al. (see Chapter 5).

Prior to turning to these new Rorschach reference values for senior adults, the present chapter discusses protocol validity, describes CS-based variables that measure each of the four domains just mentioned, and reviews considerations in utilizing the thematic imagery and sequence analysis in Rorschach responses as a source of information about a person's underlying needs, attitudes, and concerns. The discussion includes interpretive guidelines for drawing inferences about an individual's personality strengths, mental functioning, and subjective experience. The case reports in Part IV of this volume illustrate application of these interpretive guidelines in the evaluation of both patient and nonpatient senior adults presenting with a broad range of personal issues and life circumstances.

Protocol Validity

It is generally recognized that the validity of a test protocol depends in part on its reliability, which is the extent to which its findings will remain stable over time, barring any major changes in a person's psychological condition or life situation. Hence, a measuring instrument is likely to demonstrate valid corollaries only if it is reliable. The shorter a test, as defined by the number of items it contains, the less likely it is to be reliable. This psychometric principle translates into Rorschach assessment as consideration of the number of responses (R) that are needed for a protocol to be reliable and thus likely to yield valid inferences. In research reviewed by Exner (1988), participants in Rorschach retest studies who gave fewer than 14 responses on either their first or second testing showed little temporal consistency in their scores. Accordingly, the criterion for Rorschach protocol validity has been set at $R > 13$, and a protocol with $R < 14$ is considered too brief to support dependable interpretation of its various scores, percentages, ratios, and indices.

As standard CS procedure, respondents who give fewer than 14 responses are shown the cards a second time and asked to give more responses to them. Even a brief record should not necessarily be discarded, however, should it contain some dramatic features. For example, a 12-response record in which there are six perceptual distortions and four occasions of illogical thinking provides fairly strong evidence of impaired reality testing and disordered thinking, and a brief record with multiple *Morbid* responses probably identifies concerns about bodily integrity and/or depressive thinking. Long records, on the other hand, do not pose any threat to protocol validity or call for modified interpretive guidelines. The more the number of responses exceeds 30, the more likely it is that the respondent is a creative person who enjoys the challenge of the Rorschach task, or is an interpersonally needy person who is attempting to please the examiner, or is an obsessive–compulsive person who needs to exercise control, or is an energetic and up-tempo person, perhaps to the extent of appearing hypomanic.

Interpretation of Structural Variables

The structural variables in a Rorschach protocol comprise scores and indices that are based on the location, determinants, content, and special features of a person's responses and are identified in a Structural Summary. As elaborated next, all of these scores and indices have interpretive implications for one or more of the four domains of personality.

Cognitive Functioning

Cognitive functioning consists of the manner in which people attend to their experience and circumstances, perceive objects and events in their lives, and think about the meaning and connections between these objects and events. Three general Rorschach indices and several individual variables help to identify limitations or impairments in these cognitive functions. The three general Rorschach indices for evaluating the adequacy of a person's cognitive functioning are the CS *Perceptual Thinking Index* (*PTI*), the *Ego Impairment Index* (*EII-2*; Viglione, Perry, & Meyer, 2003), and the *Reality–Fantasy Scale Version 2.0* (*RFS-2*; Tibon-Czopp, Appel, & Zeligman, 2016).

PTI. The *PTI* is a five-item set of criteria based on the percentage of poor form quality responses in a record (*X–%*) and the frequency of the cognitive special scores *DV*, *INC*, *DR*, *FAB*, *ALOG*, and *CONTAM*. A positive finding for more than three of the five *PTI* criteria identifies an extent of inaccurate perception and disordered thinking that is usually associated with a schizophrenia-spectrum or other psychotic disorder (Benedik, Coderl, Bon, & Smith, 2013; Dao & Prevatt, 2006; Hilsenroth, Eudell-Simmons, DeFife, & Charnas, 2007; Kumar & Khess, 2005; Smith, Baity, Knowles, & Hilsenroth, 2001).

EII-2. The *EII-2* is similarly based on the percentage of poor form quality and the frequency of cognitive special scores in a record, but it additionally takes into account problematic interpersonal relationships, as measured by the ratio of *Good Human Representation* to *Poor Human Representation* (*GHR:PHR*), and the frequency of content categories suggestive of troubling thoughts (e.g., Anatomy, Blood, Explosion, Morbid, Sex). Any score greater than 0 on the *EII-2* is indicative of maladaptive cognitive functioning (Auslander, 2002; Diener, Hilsenroth, Shaffer, & Sexton, 2011; Minassian, Cadenhead, Sprock, & Braff, 2003; Perry, Viglione, & Braff, 1992; Viglione, Perry, & Meyer, 2003).

RFS-2. Whereas the *PTI* and *EII-2* are primarily empirical approaches to assessing cognitive malfunction, the *RFS-2* emerged from a theoretical conceptualization of the space people maintain between their inner and outer experience; that is, between attending to reality and accessing their inner thoughts and feelings. The *RFS-2* rates responses on an 11-point scale, from –5 (extremely immersed in fantasy) to +5 (extremely bound to reality). An example of a –5 response would be a relatively severe cognitive special score; an example of a +5 score would be an *FQo* response with no movement, no abstraction, and just one bland content, such as "It's an animal."

The *RFS-2* response ratings yield two summary scores: the *RFS-P* and the *RFS-S*. The *RFS-P* is a mean of the response ratings, with 0 indicating an adaptive balance between reality and fantasy. An *RFS-P* of less than −0.51 in adults suggests excessive distance from realistic considerations and a preoccupation with inner thoughts and feelings, whereas an *RFS-P* of more than +0.65 reflects too little distance from reality and limited capacity for awareness of internal experiences. *RFS-S* is a measure of scatter among the *RFS-2* ratings of each of the responses in a protocol. It is based on their standard deviation and takes account of extreme variations of the collapse of reality into fantasy (the *RFS-2* negative scores) and the collapse of fantasy into reality (the *RFS-2* positive scores). An *RFS-S* score of more than 2.70 in adults is considered indicative of proneness to dissociation (Tibon- Czopp, Appel, & Zeligman, 2016). Of note, the conceptually based scale derivations have shown significant correlation with the empirically based *EII-2* (Diener et al., 2011; Tibon, Porcelli, & Weinberger, 2005). On both of the *RFS-2* measures, as on the *PTI*, markedly deviant scores are usually associated with psychotic personality organization although children and adolescents may differ from adults in this regard (Appel, 2011).

In addition to these general indices, as was noted, several individual CS variables can provide useful information about a person's cognitive functioning. These variables comprise three subdomains of cognitive functioning: Attention (Processing), Perception (Mediation), and Thinking (Ideation).

Attention. How people attend to their experience is measured on the Rorschach by indices of openness, focus, organization, and precision (*Lambda*, *W:D:Dd*, *Zd*, and *DQv*, respectively). As noted in Chapter 1, difficulties in attention appear to be normative in elderly people. These difficulties often result from a decline in fluid capabilities. Whereas younger people are able to receive and process new stimuli readily, the elderly may often process only stimuli that they have processed previously or that are at least recognizable. Accordingly, slightly deviant scores on *Lambda*, *W:D:Dd*, *Zd*, and *DQv* in Rorschach protocols of older people should not be regarded as manifestations of neuropsychopathology, but rather as normal age-related patterns of cognitive functioning. Moreover, research has shown that senior adults can be helped to maintain their attention and learning capacities by being exposed to training techniques that promote attention or even just by being involved in a stimulating environment (e.g., Chaffin & Harlow, 2005).

***Lambda* (*L*)**. Openness to experience is shown by *Lambda*, which consists of the number of pure form (*F*) responses in a record divided by the number of responses with determinants other than *F* (i.e., *R* minus *F*). A *Lambda of* between 0.30 and 0.99 usually identifies an adaptively balanced openness to experience. A *Lambda* > 0.99 is likely to indicate a limited openness to experience characterized by a narrow frame of reference, minimal tolerance for ambiguity or uncertainty, detachment from thoughts and feelings, and a preference for simple solutions even to complex problems. A *Lambda* < 0.30, in contrast, suggests considerable openness to experience and wide-ranging perspectives, but also a tendency to become overly involved in contemplating the meaning of events and to make matters more complicated than they need to be.

W:D:Dd. A person's focus of attention is indicated by the location choices in the *W:D:Dd* ratio. Adults ordinarily give about half of their responses to common details (*D*), from a third to half of their responses to the whole blot (*W*), and the remaining sixth or fewer to unusual details (*Dd*). A Rorschach protocol with $W > 0.50$, $D < 0.50$, or $Dd > 0.15$ reflects inordinate attention to either global or unusual aspects of experience at the expense of attention to what is ordinary and commonplace, and it may also be associated with unconventional attitudes or behavior.

Zd. The organization of a person's attention is measured by the *Zd* score. *Zd* is a difference score that is calculated by adding all of the *Z* scores that are assigned to the responses in a record to provide a *Zsum* and then subtracting from this *Zsum* an estimated total *Z* (*Zest*), as shown in a table of *Zest* values for the total number of responses with a *Z* score. A *Zd* score of between +3.0 and −3.0 identifies a relatively adequate capacity for keeping balance between the amount of information that people take in while attending to their experience and the amount of information they can organize efficiently. When their *Zd* exceeds +3.0, people are likely to be examining their experience more thoroughly than is necessary and taking in more information than they can organize efficiently. Being overly careful, they may have difficulty making decisions because of uncertainty about whether they have enough information in hand to warrant opinions and conclusions. When their *Zd* falls below −3.0, on the other hand, people are likely to be examining their experience less thoroughly than would be desirable and taking in less information than they should. As a consequence, they are more likely to be careless than careful and prone to coming to conclusions hastily, with insufficient attention to relevant considerations.

DQv. Precision in attending to experience is measured on the Rorschach by the frequency of responses with vague developmental quality, coded as *DQv*. Vague responses—that is, objects that have no definite shape or can take almost any form, such as grass, clouds, or rocks—rarely occur more than twice in a typical record. $DQv > 2$ usually indicates an impressionistic style of processing information that sometimes results from insufficient energy to determine precisely what external objects might be and at other times from a defensive avoidance of potentially self-revealing commitment to a specific form response.

Perception. How people perceive objects and events is measured on the Rorschach by indices of accuracy (*XA%*, *WDA%*, and *X−%*) and conventionality (*Xu%* and *P*). Perceptual accuracy consists of the extent to which the objects people report seeing in blot areas conform to their actual shape in the real world, and conventionality consists of the extent to which these objects are commonly seen in these blot areas.

XA%. *XA%* is the percentage of responses with appropriate form quality (*FQo*, *FQ+*, or *FQu*). Normally functioning adults tend to have an *XA%* in the range of 0.80–0.89, and an *XA%* of 0.70 or more ordinarily indicates at least fairly good ability to perceive objects and events realistically. As *XA%* decreases toward 0.70, people become increasingly prone to misperceiving events, to forming mistaken impressions of other people and their intentions, and to exercising poor judgment concerning the advisability and impact of their own actions. An *XA%* falling below 0.70 is likely to identify a clinically significant impairment of reality-testing capacities, in particular the possibility of perceptual impairment. However, the interpretive significance of a low *XA%* can be attenuated by an adequate *WDA%*.

WDA%. *WDA%* is the percentage of appropriate form responses given to the commonly used *W* and *D* locations. The *WDA%* accordingly provides an index of respondents' reality testing when they are attending to common and relatively obvious features of their experience and environment. When *XA%* falls below 0.70, but *WDA%* is at least 0.75, misperceptions of reality are occurring mainly when respondents are focusing on unusual, peripheral, or relatively inconsequential matters, as represented by the *Dd* locations. This distinction has important implications for remedial interventions, because it identifies circumstances in which apparently impaired reality testing and consequent poor judgment can be mitigated by encouraging more attention to ordinary and obvious aspects of the person's daily life and less attention to minor and obscure matters of little consequence.

X–%. *X–%* is the reciprocal of the *XA%*, except for rare instances in which a record contains no-form responses (e.g., "blue sky," which is a pure *C* with no form quality code). In these instances, the *X–%* is a somewhat less dependable index of an individual's reality testing than the *XA%*, because no-form responses are not included in the calculation. Used in conjunction with the *XA%*, the *X–%* can nevertheless prove helpful in assessing the capacity of people to perceive their environment and themselves accurately and to exercise good judgment concerning the consequences of their actions. As a reciprocal of the *XA%*, the *X–%* may signify impaired reality testing when it exceeds 0.30.

Xu%. *Xu%* is the percentage of responses with unusual form quality (*FQu*). These are perceptually accurate responses that feature objects not commonly seen in the inkblots, and they are associated with one's commitment to conventionality. *Xu%* falling below 0.10 is likely to indicate an unusually strong commitment to being conventional in what the person chooses to think and do, with strict conformity to rules and regulations. The more elevated *Xu%* is, on the other hand, the more a person is inclined to disregard societal expectations and choose to look, think, and act differently from most other people. It is presently uncertain what the cutoff score should be for an elevated *Xu%*. Exner (2000, p. 189) specified an *Xu%* exceeding 0.25 as the cutoff score for considering a person to be overly individualistic and tending to disregard conventional or socially expected behaviors. However, in the international composite data for 4,704 nonpatient adults from 17 countries reported by Meyer, Erdberg, and Shaffer (2007), the mean *Xu%* was 0.27, with a standard deviation of 0.11, and 68% of the participants exceeded a 0.20 *Xu%*.

These international data appear to show that *Xu%* > 0.25 is quite common among nonpatient adults, which would call for increasing the traditional CS criterion for an elevated *Xu%*. As a suggestion in this regard, adding the *Xu%* standard deviation of 0.11 in the international reference data to its mean of 0.27 would bring the cutoff score for an elevation on this variable to *Xu%* > 0.38. As a further consideration, assessing adults in the twenty-first century should take account of substantial changes that have occurred in the world since the data of the international project were collected. With this in mind, we suggest not using any upper cutoff point for *Xu%*. In cases of *Xu%* > 0.38, the implication would relate to the person's capacity for original and creative thinking.

***Popular* (*P*).** *P* is coded for any of 13 responses that were found in high frequency among nonpatients. The sum of *P* responses in a protocol ordinarily ranges from 4 to 7, which means that *P* > 7 has the same implications as *Xu%* < 0.10 for wanting to resemble other people, and *P* < 4 might have the same implications as an elevated *Xu%*.

Thinking. People adapt best to their surrounding circumstances when they are able to think logically, coherently, constructively, and moderately about the meaning of their experiences and the connections between them. These capabilities are measured on the Rorschach by the weighted sum of six cognitive special scores (*WSum6*), human movement responses (*M*), *Introversive EBper*, *FM+m*, and the *Intellectualization Index* (*INTELL*). Conversely, illogical, incoherent, overly fanciful, and excessively preoccupying ways of thinking are psychological liabilities that typically impair a person's ability to function effectively. Elderly people may at times, such as in certain medical states, show temporarily distorted patterns of thinking that can affect many of their internal experiences and overt behaviors. Clinicians who use the Rorschach should accordingly be cautious in distinguishing between temporarily and chronically impaired patterns of thinking that are identified by the CS thinking variables.

Illogical thinking is measured on the Rorschach by four of the six previously mentioned cognitive special scores: *INCOM* (e.g., "A woman with the head of a chicken"), *FABCOM* (e.g., "Some mice on a merry-go-round"), *ALOG* (e.g., "He must be a coal miner because he's all black"), and *CONTAM* (e.g., "I see a flower and a butterfly here, so I guess it's a butterflower"). Responses coded for any of these four special scores show that circumstantial reasoning is producing an irrational combination of various objects, ideas, and impressions.

Incoherent thinking is demonstrated on the Rorschach by the other two previously mentioned cognitive special scores, *DV* and *DR*. In *DV* responses, disconnected ideas combine to produce strange or redundant verbalizations, as in "A female woman" or "A matched brace of lungs." In *DR* responses, irrelevant statements that do not follow in clear sequence take the form of tangential and sometimes unintelligible ramblings, as in "It's some kind of a butterfly, I like them very much," or "I see rats, and the world would be a better place if there weren't so many of them." *INCOM*, *FABCOM*, *DV*, and *DR* responses are additionally coded for the extent of their deviation from logical and coherent thinking as either Level 1 (relatively mild) or Level 2 (relatively severe), and all six of these cognitive special scores contribute to a *WSum6*.

WSum6. The *WSum6* is the total frequency of the six cognitive special scores, weighted for the degree of mental lapse they identify, and it is a dependable index of thinking disorder. In nonpatient adults, the *WSum6* typically ranges from 6 to 10. The more *WSum6* exceeds 10, the more likely people are to display circumstantial reasoning at times and to think in dissociated ways that are confusing to other people and to themselves as well. A *WSum6* of greater than 17 usually points to clinically significant thought disorder, especially when it includes more than two Level 2 scores. Further information on the nature, coding, and interpretive significance of the cognitive special scores is available in books by Choca (2013, pp. 98–102), Exner (2000, pp. 64–72), Kleiger (2017, pp. 96–100), and Weiner (2003a, pp. 126–128).

Human Movement (M). Constructive thinking consists of using realistic and task-oriented ideation to solve problems and plan deliberate courses of action. Such purposeful thinking about how best to make choices and decisions helps people move through daily life events by design rather than accident and is shown in Human Movement (*M*) responses. *M* responses provide a good index of the capacity to think purposefully, especially when the movement attributed to human figures is active in nature (*Ma*). However, individuals whose *Ma* responses are exceeded in number by their passive human movement responses (*Mp*) are likely to be making excessive use of fantasy in their problem-solving. Accordingly, whereas *Ma* > *Mp* indicates normative capacity for thinking constructively, *Mp* > *Ma* suggests an overly fanciful inclination to deal with situations not by thinking through what could or should be done about them, but instead by imagining how other people or a turn of events will show the way.

The form level of responses involving human movement (*M*) also provides information about the accuracy of perceptions of interpersonal events and a person's ability to form correct impressions of other people. The presence of two or more accurately seen *M* responses (*M+*, *Mo*, or *Mu*) usually identifies adequate capacity for such empathy, whereas individuals with more than one perceptually distorted *M* responses (*M–* > 1) are at risk of misperceiving the nature, motives, and intentions of other people and mistaking the implications of social situations. The more numerous the *M–* responses in a record, the more extensively a person is likely to show faulty perceptions of people and mistaken impressions of interpersonal interactions.

Introversive EBper. *Introversive EBper* describes a proclivity to become preoccupied with one's thoughts at the expense of being open to emotional experience and taking action, and it usually refers to "people who think too much." *EBPer* is coded when *M* substantially exceeds *WSumC*, which is the sum of 0.5 *FC*, 1.0 *CF*, and 1.5 *C*. An *M* that is more than 2.0 points larger than *WSumC* or more than 2.5 points larger when the sum of *M* and *WSumC* exceeds 10 identifies a strong and potentially maladaptive preference for reflective contemplation over affective expression and for thinking about matters instead of doing anything about them.

FM+m. *Fm+m* is associated with worrisome concerns that come unbidden into conscious awareness and cannot be willed away. An *FM+m* score of greater than

6 is a likely index of intrusive ideation and a resulting susceptibility to concentration difficulties.

INTELL. *INTELL* is an index of intellectualization that is calculated by summing twice the number of *AB* and the number of *Art* and *Ay* responses, all of which involve taking some psychological distance from here-and-now reality. An *INTELL* score of greater than 5 usually indicates excessive reliance on intellectualization as a defensive strategy for avoiding or minimizing the emotional components of experience. When occurring together, an *Introversive EBper* and elevation on the *FM+m* and the *INTELL* indices are compelling evidence of a person who tends to think too much.

Affective Experience

Rorschach CS structural variables of affective experience indicate the manner and comfort with which people experience and express their feelings. Good psychological adaptation is fostered by well-developed capacities to process affect sufficiently, pleasurably, and in moderation. A deficiency or impairment in these capacities is likely to result in constricted, negatively toned, and excessive ways of modulating affect.

Modulating Affect Sufficiently. Modulating affect sufficiently involves being able to engage comfortably in emotionally charged situations and being open to exchanging feelings with other people. This capacity for affective engagement and exchange fosters tolerance for having one's feelings aroused and adaptive skills in recognizing and responding to the feelings of others. Sufficient modulation of affect is identified on the Rorschach by an adequate *Affective Ratio* (*Afr*), *Constriction Ratio* (*Const.*), and *Complexity Index* (*Complex.*).

Afr. The *Afr* is calculated by dividing the number of responses given to the last three multicolored cards (VIII–X) by the number of responses given to the first seven black, gray, and red cards (I–VII). In concert with the widely assumed relationship between color and affect, *Afr* is an index of receptivity to emotional stimulation, and people with *Afr* > 0.40 tend to become involved in emotionally arousing situations and to share their feelings with others. The farther their *Afr* falls below 0.40, on the other hand, the more likely people are to feel uneasy in emotion-arousing situations and to keep their feelings to themselves. Because close relationships between people usually involve sharing feelings, low-*Afr* individuals tend to be socially as well as emotionally withdrawn. At the other extreme, individuals with an *Afr* > 0.89 are likely to have more than usual interest in emotional stimulation and exchange.

***Constriction Ratio* (*Const.*).** The *Constriction Ratio* compares the total number of achromatic color responses (*SumC'*) to the weighted sum of color responses (*WSumC*). *SumC'* indicates the extent to which affective experience is being internalized rather than expressed. More specifically, *SumC'* is an indicator of the unpleasant emotions commonly associated with black (as in "a black mood") and gray (as in "a gray day"). Accordingly, the internalized affect suggested by *C'* responses, most of which involve black or gray objects, is generally unpleasant, and a *SumC'* > 2 is usually indicative of sadness and gloom. *WSumC* is an index of the basic capacity to experience and express feelings, aside from whether the person chooses to do so. A *WSumC* of 2.5 or more indicates a person's capacity to become aware of their feelings, whereas a *WSumC* of less than 2.5 suggests lowered capacity to process emotional experience. People whose *SumC'* exceeds their *WSumC* are likely to be emotionally constricted. Their feelings are bottled up and they cannot easily express them, or even recognize their affective state. A low *WSumC* becomes particularly problematic for adjustment when it is exceeded in value by the *SumC'* in a person's record.

***Complexity Index* (*Complex.*).** The *Complexity Index* is a ratio that compares the total number of *Blend* responses in a protocol with the total number of responses (*Blends:R*). A typical protocol contains three or four *Blend* responses that constitute 15%–20% of *R*. Deviations from this normative expectation have implications similar to those of *Lambda*. Relatively numerous *Blend* responses are likely to be associated with multifaceted and sometimes unnecessarily complicated responses to events, whereas relatively few *Blend* responses may reflect overly simplistic ways of engaging in life situations.

Modulating Affect Pleasurably. Modulating affect pleasurably consists of maintaining a positive emotional tone that promotes feeling happy and enjoying oneself. People can ordinarily find pleasure in their lives, provided they can avoid such negative emotions as depression, anxiety, and negativity, each of which can undermine their sense of well-being and turn pleasure into dismay. The presence of these three negative emotions and their interference with a positively toned affective life are captured on the Rorschach by the *Depression Index* (*DEPI*), the *Suicide Constellation* (*S-CON*), the sum of shading responses (*SumShd*), and the number of responses in which both color and shading determinants are used (*Col–Shd Bld*).

As for anxiety, pleasurable modulation of affect is made possible by having sufficient coping resources to meet the demands people face in their lives without becoming unduly upset by them. Being able to minimize their experience of subjectively felt distress fosters a sense of comfort, satisfaction, and well-being. Insufficient coping resources, on the other hand, can result in people becoming anxious, tense, irritable, and unable to tolerate frustration. The adequacy of a person's available coping capacities is measured on the Rorschach by three related indices: the *D-Score* (*D*), the *Adjusted D-Score* (*AdjD*), and the *Adjusted D-Score* minus the *D-Score* (*AdjDMD*). With respect to negativity, this unpleasant affective experience is at times captured on the Rorschach by the frequency of *Space* (*S*) responses.

***DEPI*.** The *DEPI* comprises seven variables that are associated with unpleasant affect, self-critical attitudes, and social disengagement. The presence of any five of these seven variables indicates some depressive tendencies, and more than five strongly suggests either a depressive disorder or a substantial susceptibility to becoming depressed. A *DEPI* < 5 does not rule out the possibility of depression, however, and it should not be considered to do so. Like many other Rorschach indices, *DEPI* rarely produces a false-positive finding, but it is susceptible to generating false-negative results. A low *DEPI* can accordingly be ignored, whereas an elevated *DEPI* is usually solid evidence of a distressing emotional state.

S-CON. The *S-CON* combines 12 variables indicative of impairment in one or more of the cognitive, affective, interpersonal, and self-perception domains of personality functioning. An *S-CON* of 8 or more is associated with suicidal ideation and risk of self-injurious behavior. Additionally, two of these 12 variables—*SumV+FD* > 2 and *Color–Shading Blends* > 0—are particularly likely to characterize suicidality, and their presence makes even an *S-CON* of 7 a cause for concern. Like a low *DEPI*, a low *S-CON* can occur as a false-negative finding, and under no circumstances should it be considered to rule out suicidality. Like an elevated *DEPI*, then, an elevated *S-CON* is rarely a false-positive finding, and its presence is likely to identify an acute and possibly life-threatening emergency that calls for crisis intervention.

SumShd. *SumShd* is the total number of *C'*, *T*, *V*, and *Y* determinants in a record, and it constitutes the right side of the experience base (*eb*). The left side of the *eb* consists of *FM+m*, which was noted in discussing cognitive functioning as being associated with the presence of intrusive ideation. With respect to affective functioning, *SumShd* indicates the intrusion not of worrisome concerns, but of unwelcome and distressing emotions that resist being expelled from conscious awareness. Adults normatively have both some *SumShd* and some *FM+m* in their record, but emotionally well-adjusted persons typically show more of the latter than the former. A *SumShd* greater than *FM+m* usually identifies a maladaptive extent of unpleasant and depressing affect.

Col–Shd Bld. *Col–Shd Bld* is coded for responses with both chromatic (*FC*, *CF*, or *C*) and achromatic or shading (*C'*, *T*, *V*, or *Y*) determinants. People with more than one *Col–Shd Bld* response tend to imbue other people and events in their lives with both pleasant (the color) and unpleasant (the shading) characteristics. This affective ambivalence can cause a person to become persistently unhappy, inclined to spoil potentially positive experiences by finding fault with them, and subject to losing interest in previously enjoyed activities and friendships. In the case of emotionally expressive individuals with a high *Afr* and a large *WSumC*, a *Col–Shd Bld* > 2 may be necessary to identify a maladaptive elevation on this variable.

D-Score. The *D-Score* is a difference score that is calculated by first summing the *M* and *WSumC* to form the *Experience Actual* (*EA*), which is an index of available resources for coping with experience, and then subtracting from it the *Experienced Stress* (*es*), which consists of the previously mentioned left and right sides of the *eb* and represents the psychological demands a person is experiencing. The resulting difference between the *EA* and the *es* normatively ranges from +2.5 to −2.5. For convenience purposes, results within this normative range are given a *D-Score* of 0, and one additional point is assigned for every additional 2.5 points beyond it. Thus, an *EA* minus *es* of +3.0 would yield a *D-Score* of +1, an *EA* minus *es* of −5.5 would yield a *D-Score* of −2, and so on.

A *D-Score* between +1 and −1 shows an adaptive balance between the demands that individuals are experiencing and their psychological resources for coping with these demands. These individuals consequently tend to be self-satisfied and optimistic, feel no urgency to change themselves or their circumstances, and seldom become markedly anxious, tense, or irritable. They are capable of tolerating frustration, persevering in the face of obstacles, controlling their behavior, and refraining from episodes of intense emotionality or impulsive actions.

In contrast, a *D-Score* falling below −1 typically signals a stress overload in which pleasurable affect is being submerged by disturbing worries about unwelcome events in the person's life and feelings of being incapable of doing anything about them. Anxiety, tension, and irritability are hallmarks of *D-Score* < −1, which is also associated with limited tolerance for frustration, concerns about losing self-control, and a negative view of the future. The farther a *D-Score* falls below −1, the more likely a person is to become incapacitated by stress and consequently agitated, distraught, and prone to emotional outbursts and impulsive actions.

A *D-Score* above +1 can also be problematic, but in a reverse way. People with *D-Score* > +1 have ample coping resources and more than adequate capacities to minimize the impact of stressful events on their lives. Their considerable stress tolerance keeps them cool, calm, and collected in troubling or even dangerous circumstances. However, by not allowing events to bother them, they become at risk for ignoring or underestimating the implications of events that should capture their attention and cause them concern. This insensitivity to matters of concern can limit their awareness of any need to modify the kind of person they are or how they are conducting their lives. Instead, *D-Score* > +1 people typically remain set in their ways and seldom seek or respond well to psychological interventions.

AdjD-Score. The *AdjD-Score* is a useful index of the extent to which a person's experienced anxiety is largely situational in nature and not indicative of a persistent experience of stress overload and insufficient coping capacities. The *AdjD* is calculated by subtracting two situational stress scores (*m* > 1 and *Y* > 1) from the *es* to form an *Adjes* and then subtracting this *Adjes* from the *EA*. The resulting *AdjD* thus indicates a person's level of distress beyond what may be attributable to situational factors. Accordingly, a *D-Score* < −1 but an *AdjD* > 0 will usually identify a person who is experiencing situational distress but will resume a customary state of psychological comfort when the situational demands abate.

AdjDMD-Score. The *AdjDMD-Score*, which is obtained by subtracting the *D-Score* from the *AdjD-Score*, provides a further indication of a person's likelihood of experiencing affective or cognitive symptoms of anxiety, particularly when its value is greater than 0.

Space (S). *S* responses occur when respondents do the opposite of what they have been instructed to do. The standard Rorschach instructions ask people to look at the inkblots and say what they might be. If they respond instead to the empty space on a card, they are in effect countermanding the instructions and defining the task in their own terms. Showing some autonomy and self-determination in this way may indicate an adaptive capacity to be one's own person. However, an excessive frequency of *S* responses (*S* > 3) is likely to reflect generalized oppositional tendencies that go beyond adaptive autonomy and are associated with underlying feelings of anger or resentment. Individuals with elevation in *S* typically harbor more than ordinary amounts of such feelings, either toward people in their lives whom they regard as having failed to meet their needs or toward events they view as having prevented them from attaining their goals. It should be noted that an elevated *S* might also reflect feelings of depletion.

Modulating Affect in Moderation. Modulating affect in moderation—the opposite of the previously mentioned tendency of some people to think too much—occurs in people who are considerably more responsive to the murmurs of their heart than to the dictates of their mind. These are people who act mainly according to how they feel, without giving much forethought to the consequences of their behavior. Such minimal modulation of affect is measured on the Rorschach by the *Extratensive EBper*, *FC:CF+C*, and *Pure C* variables.

Extratensive EBper. An *Extratensive EBper* is coded when *WSumC* is more than 2.0 points larger than *M* or more than 2.5 points larger when *EA* > 10, and it identifies a potentially maladaptive preference for affective expression over reflective contemplation and for doing things without thinking about them.

FC:CF+C. With respect to the *FC:CF+C* ratio, *FC* responses—as noted in Chapter 3—are associated with relatively well-modulated and reserved processing of affect in which feelings emerge and dissipate slowly and are deeply felt but mild to moderate in their intensity. *CF* responses, on the other hand, are associated with relatively unmodulated and spontaneous processing of affect in which feelings arise and dissipate quickly but are often quite intense while they last. An *FC* exceeding *CF+C* by more than 2 points (i.e., *FC* > *CF+C* + 2) is likely to indicate tight control of emotional reactivity with relatively low-key and stable processing of affect. Contrariwise, a *CF+C* exceeding *FC* by more than 2 points (i.e., *CF+C* > *FC* + 2) is likely to indicate loose control of emotional reactivity with relatively intense and labile processing of affect.

Pure C. This is the sum of responses in which the percept is based on color only, representing affective intensity and limited control of emotions. The presence of more than one *Pure C* response in a record adds weight to such evidence of volatile affectivity and indicates a propensity for emotional outbursts.

Interpersonal Relatedness

Adaptive interpersonal relatedness consists of being able to: (1) sustain a reasonable level of interest, involvement, and comfort in interacting with other people; (2) anticipate intimacy and security in interpersonal relationships; (3) balance collaboration and acquiescence with competitiveness and assertiveness in relating to other people; and (4) perceive people and social situations accurately and with empathy. Several Rorschach variables are helpful in identifying adequate or impaired capacity in these respects.

Sustaining interpersonal interest, involvement, and comfort. Sustaining interpersonal interest, involvement, and comfort is measured on the Rorschach by the *Coping Deficit Index* (*CDI*), the *Interpersonal Interest* variable (*SumH*), the *Isolation Index*, the *H:(Hd+[H]+[Hd])* ratio, and *Personal* (*PER*) responses.

CDI. *CDI* is a multifactor variable that is coded positive for a low *EA* and four other signs of social difficulty. The previously mentioned *EA* provides a measure of the coping resources on which people can draw in dealing with interpersonal as well as other types of situations. An *EA* of 6 or more usually indicates socially adequate coping resources, whereas *EA* < 6 is likely to identify lowered coping capacities, including interpersonal ineptness. A *CDI* > 3 complements a low *EA* as an indicator of limited capacities for coping effectively with life events, especially those that involve interpersonal interaction.

SumH. *SumH* is the total number of responses having any type of human content, and it indicates the extent of a person's attention to other people. A *SumH* of 2 or more usually reflects at least average interpersonal interest, whereas *SumH* < 2 is likely to indicate limited interest in people.

Isolation Index. *Isolation Index* is calculated by scoring two points for every Nature and Cloud content in a record and one point for every Botany, Geography, and Landscape content, and then dividing their sum by *R*. *Isolation Index* has no particular implications for personality strengths when it is low, but when elevated, as defined by *Isolation Index* > 0.25, it is typically associated with limited involvement in interpersonal and social interactions, particularly in people who live in urban communities. Even when elevated *Isolation Index* people are surrounded by numerous family members or acquaintances, they are unlikely to be sharing companionship and confidences with them or allowing them to play an important part in their lives.

H:(Hd+[H]+[Hd]). The *H:(Hd+[H]+[Hd])* ratio becomes clinically significant when there are fewer *H* responses than (*Hd+[H]+[Hd]*) responses. A finding of *H* < (*Hd+[H]+[Hd]*) suggests susceptibility to discomfort in social situations. Real people can be physically or psychologically harmful to oneself, as in causing one injury, disappointment, embarrassment, or humiliation. Partial and fictitious figures, on the other hand, can do no harm and pose no threat to one's well-being. This distinction between the impact of real as opposed to partial and fictitious figures is likely to account for the association between a Rorschach preference for the latter and social discomfort in real life.

People whose Rorschach protocol includes at least two *H* responses and a total number of *H* responses that exceeds the number of (*Hd+[H]+[Hd]*) responses typically have adequate capacity to identify with and model themselves after other people, which provides a foundation for developing a clear and stable sense of one's identity. A finding of *H* < (*Hd+[H]+[Hd]*), on the other hand, often indicates maladaptive tendencies to identify with partial or fictitious figures that have not been part of an individual's everyday real world.

PER. *PER* is coded for responses in which people inject comments about themselves or their personal experiences. As described in Chapter 3, there are three kinds of *PER* responses. One type consists of a simple and unelaborated justification of a response ("I've seen them on TV"). A second type is a more elaborated reaching out for engagement with the examiner by relating something about themselves ("It's just like my dog that I have at home"). The third type of *PER* response consists of elaborated and self-aggrandizing comments about how much the person knows or has accomplished ("It reminds me of the airplanes I flew when I was a pilot"; "It looks like people dancing, which is something I was pretty good at when I was younger").

The first type of *PER* response is largely unremarkable, unless they are sufficiently numerous to indicate an unusual need for self-justification in interpersonal relationships. The second type, if repetitive, speaks to the possibility of pressing needs to form close relationships with other people through shared experiences. The third type of *PER* response, even occurring just once and more so if recurrent, identifies a view of interpersonal relationships not as occasions for mutual exchange, but rather as self-gratifying opportunities to impress other people with one's importance, talents, and achievements.

Anticipating intimacy and security in interpersonal relationships. Intimacy in interpersonal relationships is a psychological attachment between people who share their private thoughts and feelings. Security in interpersonal relationships consists of freedom from concern about being exploited or taken advantage of in the relationship or about being exposed to the misery of possible rejection. This sense of security encourages people to reach out for intimate attachments, to prefer engaging others up close rather than at arm's length, and to regard intimacy as an opportunity to be cherished rather than a danger to be avoided. Three Rorschach variables that often provide useful information concerning the anticipation of interpersonal intimacy and security are the number of *Texture* responses in a record (*SumT*), the *Hypervigilance Index* (*HVI*), and the presence of *Food* (*Fd*) responses.

SumT. *T* responses indicate a person's capacities for forming close, intimate, and mutually supportive relationships with other people. People who give *T* responses are usually likely to welcome and enjoy being emotionally close to others. In contrast, the absence of *T* responses often identifies a limited capacity to form close and mutually supportive attachments to other people. This implication of $T = 0$ is especially of note when other shading determinants (*C′*, *V*, and *Y*) have been used in formulating responses. In the opposite direction, multiple *T* responses are likely to indicate a need for closeness that is not currently being met in a person's life, and $T > 1$ may be a clue to a person's feeling emotionally deprived, interpersonally unfulfilled, and lonely.

HVI. *HVI* is a multivariable index that is coded as positive when $T = 0$ and is combined with four or more of seven other conditions related to cognitive and interpersonal dimensions of personality functioning. Should *T* be present, five or more of these seven other conditions is sufficient to indicate a positive *HVI*. Individuals with a positive *HVI* tend to be highly alert to potential sources of danger or threat in their environment, usually because they feel unable to trust the motives of others or to depend on the safety of their surroundings. *HVI*-positive people are likely to view close relationships with alarm and to avoid them in favor of keeping their distance from others, guarding carefully the boundaries of their personal space and taking pains to preserve their privacy. They typically approach and assess other people cautiously, often suspiciously, before making any commitments to them.

Fd. *Fd* responses suggest the presence of dependent needs, with security in interpersonal relationships linked to being cared for by other people. However, this inference must be tempered by the number and elaboration of *Fd* responses. A single unelaborated *Fd* response (e.g., "These look like apples") is unlikely to have much interpretive significance. Numerous such unelaborated responses may begin to suggest dependency, but even one elaborated *Fd* response can have such significance, as in "Here I see a tasty apple that I would enjoy eating," or "These parts remind me of a nice breakfast, with the eggs here and the bacon on the sides."

Balancing interpersonal collaboration and acquiescence with competitiveness and assertiveness. The balance people strike between being collaborative and acquiescent or being competitive and assertive in their relationships with others is indicated in the Rorschach by the number of *Cooperative Movement* (*COP*) and *Aggressive Movement* (*AG*) responses, and the ratio of active to passive movement responses (*a:p*).

COP. *COP* responses identify an interest in collaborative engagement with others. Persons with one or two *COP* responses tend to view interactions among people in positive ways and to participate in them willingly. Persons with *COP* > 2 are especially likely to be regarded as likeable and outgoing and to be sought after as a friend or companion. The absence of *COP*, on the other hand, commonly indicates a limited capacity to anticipate and engage in collaborative activities with other people. Unlike the positive interpersonal messages communicated by those who give *COP* responses, individuals with *COP* = 0 typically convey to others a disinterest in or even a distaste for cooperative endeavors. The combination of *COP* = 0 with an elevated *Isolation Index* and a low *SumH* is strongly suggestive of interpersonal avoidance and withdrawal.

AG. *AG* responses identify an expectation that interactions between people are more likely to be competitive and assertive than collaborative and acquiescent. The presence of more than two *AG* responses in a record is associated with a greater than usual likelihood of behaving toward others in a verbally or physically assertive fashion. However, this implication of *AG* > 2 can be offset by the presence of numerous *COP* responses and by a preference for passivity. Of further note, the absence of *AG* responses may on occasion indicate a lack of assertiveness, but *AG* = 0 does not contraindicate an aggressive disposition or violence potential and should not be considered to do so.

a:p. The *a:p* ratio is interpretively significant for interpersonal relatedness when the number of passive movements in a record exceeds the number of active movements by more than one. People who show $p > a + 1$ are likely to be behaviorally passive in their interactions with others. Such persons are typically more comfortable being followers than leaders, are likely to shrink from taking initiative or responsibility, and are inclined to defer to the preferences and wishes of others.

Self-Perception

Self-perception consists of how people view themselves, particularly with respect to their self-esteem, self-awareness, and sense of identity. Being able to maintain a realistic level of self-esteem, a moderate degree of self-awareness, and a stable sense of identity helps people feel good about themselves and behave to their advantage, whereas limitations in these respects can lead to distressing concerns and disadvantageous ways of conducting themselves. Several Rorschach variables help to identify these positive and negative aspects of self-perception.

Maintaining realistic self-esteem. People feel best and act most appropriately when they can maintain a realistic level of self-esteem in which they neither underrate nor overrate their abilities, accomplishments, and personal attractiveness. Maintaining a realistic level of self-esteem thus helps people avoid both underserved self-denigration and unwarranted self-admiration. In addition, people with a realistic level of self-esteem ordinarily strike an adaptive balance between focusing on themselves and attending to the needs and interests of others. The disposition to perceive oneself as a worthy or unworthy person and the inclination to balance self-focusing with attention to others are measured on the Rorschach by *Reflection* responses (*Fr+rF*), the *Egocentricity Index* (*Egoc. Index*), *Vista* (*SumV*) responses, and *Morbid* (*MOR*) responses.

Fr+rF. *Fr+rF* is associated with tendencies to overvalue one's personal worth. People with one or more *Reflection* response in their record (*Fr+rF* > 0) usually have a lofty estimate of their attributes and an inflated sense of their importance and personal appeal. They are inclined to seek attention and admiration from others and to enjoy performing before an audience, which can serve constructive purposes in some lines of work and sometimes make them socially entertaining. On the other hand, people who give *Reflection* responses often exhibit a sense of entitlement, a proclivity for externalizing responsibility, and a degree of selfishness and self-admiration that other people find disagreeable.

***Egocentricity Index* (*Egoc. Index*)**. The *Egoc. Index* is calculated by multiplying the number of *Reflection* responses by 3, adding the number of *Pairs* (two of the same object seen on a card) and dividing this sum by the number of responses. This index measures the balance people strike between focusing on themselves and attending to others. In adults, an *Egoc. Index* ranging from 0.33 to 0.44 indicates an adaptive inclination to attend sufficiently but not excessively both to oneself and to other people. Adults whose *Egoc. Index* falls below 0.33 are usually more attuned to the interests and concerns of other people than to their own needs and preferences, and they tend to be self-sacrificing in their interpersonal relationships. They are also likely to compare themselves unfavorably with other people, whom they regard as being more attractive, more intelligent, or more able than they are, which leads to low self-esteem.

In the opposite direction, an *Egoc. Index* above 0.44 usually identifies a self-centered person who is given more to selfishness than to self-sacrifice and who is often indifferent or oblivious to the happenings in the lives of other people. The interpretive significance of an elevated *Egoc. Index* may be attenuated somewhat if it consists only of *Pairs*, without there being any *Reflection* responses. On the other hand, an elevated *Egoc. Index* with *Reflection* responses often identifies not only heightened self-esteem, but also other characteristics of a narcissistic disposition, including the previously mentioned self-admiration, selfishness, sense of entitlement, and proclivity for externalizing responsibility.

***Vista* (*SumV*)**. In *Vista* (*V*) responses, dark and light nuances in the coloration of the blots are used in creating a three-dimensional perspective with objects seen as being at a distance or behind other objects. Such shading/dimensionality responses are usually associated with self-criticism, diminished self-regard, and sometimes feelings of guilt for having acted in some regrettable way. The more numerous the *V* responses in their record, the more likely people are to view themselves as being unworthy or as having behaved improperly.

MOR. Responses coded with *MOR* describe people or objects seen in the blots as dead, decayed, deformed, destroyed, rusting away, falling apart, or as experiencing dysphoric feelings. Such imagery typically reflects negative attitudes toward one's body and its functions. When *MOR* is greater than 2, a person's self-esteem is usually being diminished by concerns about having a weak, unappealing, or dysfunctional body that is vulnerable to being harmed. It might also reflect pessimistic feeling.

Moderating self-awareness. In addition to maintaining a realistic level of self-esteem, people feel and function best when they have a moderate degree of self-awareness, which consists of recognizing their own needs and motivations and appreciating how their actions affect other people. This aspect of self-perception is measured on the Rorschach by the *Form Dimension* (*FD*) variable

FD. The *FD* variable is coded for three-dimensional perspectives based entirely on form features of the blots, without reference to shading. Most people have one or two *FD* responses in their records, which indicates some capacity for introspection and psychological mindedness. People with *FD* = 0, on the other hand, typically show little affinity for critical self-examination and are unlikely to be introspective or psychologically minded. However, an excessive degree of self-awareness can also be problematic. A finding of *FD* > 2 usually identifies tendencies to be excessively self-aware and markedly self-conscious. People with an elevated *FD* are prone to considerable reflectiveness and may find it difficult to move through their lives without giving a second thought to every idea, feeling, and action.

Forming a stable sense of identity. People with a stable sense of identity have a reasonably clear sense of who they are and what they value, their goals and aspirations, their aptitudes and capacities, and how they are likely to feel, act, and be perceived by others in certain types of situation. The content of this sense of identity ordinarily changes over time as a person moves from being youthful to being elderly, for example, or from being a parent to being a grandparent, from being in the workforce to being retired, and in becoming politically more liberal or conservative. At any point in time and in differing circumstances, however, people with a stable sense of identity remain certain of the kind of person they are and of what they believe in.

Being able to form a clear sense of their identity helps people feel comfortable with themselves and reduces their susceptibility to becoming anxious or depressed. Conversely, a state of identity diffusion, in which people are unsure about the kind of person they are and how they want to live their lives, commonly leads to psychological uneasiness, fragile attachments, fleeting pursuits, and unpredictable behavior. The Rorschach does not directly measure identity stability or diffusion, but it does provide some information about the capacity to identify with and model oneself after real people. This capacity is indicated by the previously mentioned number of whole and real figures seen (*SumH*) and the ratio of this number to the number of partial or fictitious human figures seen (*Hd+[H]+[Hd]*).

Interpretation of Thematic Imagery

As described thus far in the present chapter, what people report seeing in the inkblots provides a structural basis for inferences about their cognitive functioning, affective experience, interpersonal relatedness, and self-perception. As an additional source of information, the thematic imagery in a record often contains clues to a person's underlying needs, attitudes, and concerns. Interpretation of the content themes in a Rorschach protocol begins with identifying those responses that appear particularly rich in thematic imagery. The interpretive process then continues with: (1) considering what these thematically rich responses might signify; (2) drawing on these possibilities to formulate interpretive hypotheses concerning a person's motivations to think, feel, and act in certain ways; and (3) judging the plausibility these thematic interpretations. This part of the interpretive process can be enriched by attention to the sequence in which responses occur, particularly with respect to how they appear to influence each other.

Identifying Responses Rich in Thematic Imagery

Rorschach responses differ in the extent to which their thematic imagery is likely to reveal aspects of a person's inner life; that is, the underlying needs, attitudes, and concerns that motivate their behavior. The responses most likely to be rich in thematic imagery are those that attribute characteristics to a percept that go beyond what can be inferred solely from the stimulus features of the inkblots. Such attributions typically appear in responses that involve form distortion, movement, or some type of embellishment.

With respect to form distortion, the coding of an *FQ–* indicates that the blot does not resemble what it has been said to look like. Hence, the perceived object could not have been based solely on the actual shape of the blot, but it must instead have come from inside the individual and have some special meaning for that person. Likewise, the blots are static and do not move, which means that any actions that are attributed to them have also come from the mind of the person being examined and are likely to say something about that person's inner life. Embellishments include the kinds of content elaborations for which special scores (e.g., *MOR, FABCOM*) are coded, and they also include uncoded elaborations of the characteristics of objects (e.g., seeing people not just as "people," but as "witches," "soldiers," or "fat sloppy men" and seeing animals not just as "animals," but as "friendly dogs" or "dangerous predators").

Formulating Interpretive Hypotheses

As just noted, the identification of responses that provide potentially meaningful imagery leads to the formulation of hypotheses concerning what these images might signify. These imagery-based hypotheses are typically more speculative and embrace more alternatives than interpretations based on the structural variables in a protocol. For example, a low *XA%* indicates with some certainty a propensity for inaccurate perceptions of people and events. In comparison, a response of "A woman with her back turned to me" could indicate some underlying concerns about being rejected by women; or about rejection by some woman in particular (e.g., mother); or about confronting anatomical differences between the sexes, which are less apparent from a rear than a front view; or about something else entirely, the meaning of which is unique to the individual's psyche.

Because of this multiplicity in the possible meanings of thematic images, there is rarely sufficient basis for deciding with certainty what they reveal about the person who reports them. Instead, like symbols in dreams, Rorschach images necessitate some exploration of the alternative possibilities they suggest. For example, images of "angry men" in the blots might indicate identification with angry men or fear of them. Deciding which is the more likely possibility would require additional information from other sources about the person's attitudes and real-life behavior.

To illustrate further the utility of thematic imagery in suggesting how people are inclined to view themselves and other people, consider the possible self-image and interpersonal needs of a woman who saw "Some little birds in a nest, waiting for their mother to feed them." The imagery in this response could indicate that she sees herself as a small and relatively helpless person, that she has strong and perhaps unmet dependent needs to be nurtured and cared for, and that she resents being kept waiting to receive this attention. Another possibility could be that she sees herself providing nourishment to her children.

As one more example of alternative possibilities, consider a man who saw Card I as an *FQ–* "battleship." Does he have an image of himself or other people as big, powerful, indestructible objects that win wars and defeat the enemy, or does being a battleship instead signify to him an oversized, ponderous craft that is easily outflanked by smaller and swifter vessels, has outlasted its usefulness, and should be put in mothballs? Or could it be that a battleship has both meanings to this man because he needs to portray himself as strong and capable but has underlying concerns about becoming inept, outmoded, and put out to pasture?

Judging the Plausibility of Thematic Interpretations

Interpretive hypotheses based on thematic imagery are most likely to be plausible when they are derived from particularly compelling images and limited to conservative inferences about the meanings of these images. The particularly compelling images in a record are those that are repetitive, dramatic, original, and spontaneous.

With respect to repetition, the Rorschach literature has traditionally stressed that recurrent themes in a record say more than occasional themes about a person's inner life (Klopfer et al., 1954, chap. 13; Phillips & Smith, 1953, chap. 6; Schafer, 1954, chap. 5). Drama as a marker of compelling imagery refers to whether a response is delivered in a bland or embellished fashion. For example, consider the difference between the following two structurally similar responses to Card III: "Two people picking up a basket" (a bland response) and "Two big guys struggling with all their might to pick up some heavy object, and I think they are succeeding" (an embellished response). Such dramatic embellishment of an image increases the plausibility of inferences drawn from it.

As for originality, the more a response elaboration differs from how a particular blot or blot detail is commonly seen or described, the more plausible are the interpretive hypotheses it suggests. Spontaneity refers to how early in the response process an image is elaborated. For example, a response to the upper-side details on Card IX of "Sorcerers casting spells at each other" might suggest concerns about aggressive interpersonal interactions, or it might reflect an underlying wish to possess the magical powers of a sorcerer. Whatever the possible implications of this imagery, they are more compelling if the entire image is reported in the initial response than if it emerges only during the inquiry into a bland original response of "Two human figures." Similarly, thematic imagery emerging immediately after the inquiry has begun is more compelling than imagery that does not appear until later in the inquiry, following a request for further information (e.g., "I'm not sure how you're seeing it").

Conservative inferences from thematic imagery are characterized by minimal ambiguity, a ready rationale, and a limited scope. Interpretive hypotheses based on uncertain, remote, and extensive connections between Rorschach images and what is inferred from them are seldom plausible. Regarding ambiguity, some responses are less certainly suggestive of a particular meaning than others. For example, a percept of "weapon" is quite likely to indicate concerns about aggression. Weapons are dangerous and potentially harmful objects that are rarely used for nonaggressive purposes, and there are few if any reasonable alternatives to their relatively unambiguous connection with concerns about aggression.

In contrast, the center detail of Card I being seen as "A woman with her arms up" could signify that she is waving hello, waving goodbye, gesturing in supplication

("Help me"), or gesturing in despair or surrender ("I give up"). Without some elaboration of the response, there is little basis for choosing among these alternative possibilities, and its meaning is ambiguous rather than certain.

As for the rationale of thematic interpretations, their meanings should be readily apparent. The inferred connection just mentioned between seeing numerous weapons and having some concerns about being a victim or perpetrator of violence can easily be understood. Such ease in translating images into personality characteristics enhances the plausibility of the interpretive hypotheses that emerge.

A limited scope in interpretations of thematic imagery consists of restricting them to inferences about a person's underlying needs, attitudes, and concerns at the present moment. A Rorschach image may suggest some reasonable hypotheses about how people may have responded to past events and are likely to behave in future situations. However, as elaborated by Weiner (2003b) with respect to the plausibility of thematic interpretations and clinical decisions in general, those that focus on current personality characteristics are more likely to be dependable than those that address past or future behavioral probabilities.

Sequence Analysis

Sequence analysis is an interpretive process that draws on the manner in which responses follow one another in order to formulate hypotheses concerning issues that cause a respondent concern, how the person typically seeks to cope with or defend against these concerns, and the extent to which these defensive efforts prove successful. To illustrate this process, consider a respondent who, when shown Card II, says, "I don't like this one, there's blood at the top, and these black parts are a couple of ugly-looking birds." With respect to the previously mentioned threefold nature of the Rorschach as a measure of behavior, perception, and association (see Chapter 3), these two successive responses would suggest psychological concern in all three respects.

Specifically, the comment "I don't like this one" is a behavioral manifestation of displeasure with the examination process, as if to say to the examiner, "Why don't you show me nicer pictures?" The association with "blood" suggests concerns about being the perpetrator or victim of physically injurious acts of aggression of being harmed or damaged in some other way. As for perception, the usually disturbing blood response is followed in this example not only by an expression of distaste, but also by an inaccurate percept, the *FQ*– ugly birds. This poor quality of the response following an apparently disturbing one is an instance of poor recovery from its impact, and numerous such instances are likely to identify limited coping capacities and a susceptibility to maladaptive or symptomatic responses to stress.

Sequence analysis can extend between successive cards as well as successive responses, and it often identifies specific types of defenses as well as their adequacy. Suppose in the previous example the respondent were to follow the disturbing imagery of Card II with the following response to Card III: "It looks like two people helping each other to lift a pot, and they have long necks and pointy noses, and there's a butterfly flying in-between them, and there are a couple of monkeys up at the top, in an inverted position." In this response, the person would be visualizing perceptually accurate human and animal figures, describing cooperative movement, and attending to all parts of the blot and some of their details as well. Such a sequence would illustrate the successful Card III deployment of an obsessive–compulsive defensive style in order to recover from the distress invoked by Card II.

Conclusion

This overview of the parameters of Rorschach interpretation demonstrates the value of the inkblot method as a source of information about personality characteristics and its clinical utility in differential diagnosis and treatment, as evidenced in the case illustrations presented in Chapters 8–17 of the present volume. Three features of this interpretive process underlie its value and utility. First, the Rorschach is a performance-based measure in which inferences are drawn from how people respond to a task in reality, not from what they are able and willing to say about themselves. Unlike answers on self-report measures, then, Rorschach responses reveal personality characteristics of individuals independently of whether they recognize these characteristics in themselves and, if so, whether they choose to reveal them to an examiner.

Second, the Rorschach samples both representative and symbolic ways of looking at the world. The Rorschach serves as a representative sample of behavior when the response process closely resembles real-world processes of taking in and processing information. When people look at the blots and form accurate impressions of what they might be, for example, there is good reason to believe that they are likely to perceive people and events accurately in their daily lives. The Rorschach serves as a symbolic sample of behavior when the thematic imagery in responses suggests the possibility of certain attitudes or behavior patterns, as for example when numerous aggressive contents give reason to postulate that the respondent is likely to be an assertive person who regards interpersonal relationships as more likely to be competitive than collaborative.

Third, Rorschach data have implications for a broad range of personality characteristics. These include the previously elaborated connections between the structural data and the cognitive functioning, affective experience, interpersonal relatedness, and self-perception domains of personality and the connection between the content and thematic imagery of responses and a respondent's underlying needs, attitudes, and concerns.

References

Appel, L. (2011). The collapse of potential space in adolescents with psychosomatic disorders. *Rorschachiana: Journal of the International Society for the Rorschach, 32*, 151–182.

Auslander, L. A., Perry, W., & Jeste, D. V. (2002). Assessing disturbed thinking and cognition using the Ego Impairment Index in older schizophrenia patients: Paranoid vs. nonparanoid distinction. *Schizophrenia Research*, *53*, 199–207.

Benedik, E., Coderl, S., Bon, J., & Smith, B. L. (2013). Differentiation of psychotic from non-psychotic psychiatric inpatients: The Rorschach Perceptual Thinking Index. *Journal of Personality Assessment*, *95*, 141–148.

Chaffin, A. G., & Harlow, S. P. (2005). Cognitive learning applied to older adult learners and technology. *Educational Gerontology*, 31, 301–329.

Choca, J. P. (2013). *The Rorschach inkblot test.* Washington, DC: American Psychological Association.

Dao, T. K., & Prevatt, F. (2006). A psychometric evaluation of the Rorschach Comprehensive System's Perceptual Thinking Index. *Journal of Personality Assessment*, *86*, 180–189.

Diener, M. J., Hilsenroth, M. J., Shaffer, S. A., & Sexton, J. E. (2011). A meta-analysis of the relationship between the Rorschach Ego Impairment Index (EII) and psychiatric severity. *Clinical Psychology & Psychotherapy*, *18*, 464–485.

Exner, J. E., Jr. (1988). Problems with brief Rorschach protocols. *Journal of Personality Assessment*, *52*, 649–647.

Exner. J. E., Jr. (2000). *A workbook for the Comprehensive System* (5th ed.). Asheville, NC: Rorschach Workshops.

Exner, J. E., Jr. (2003). *The Rorschach: A comprehensive system. Vol. 1: Basic foundations and principles of interpretation* (4th ed.). Hoboken, NJ: Wiley.

Exner, J. E, Jr., & Weiner, I. B. (1995). *The Rorschach: A comprehensive system: Vol. 3: Assessment of children and adolescents* (2nd ed.). Hoboken, NJ: Wiley.

Hilsenroth, M. J., Eudell-Simmons, E. N., DeFife, J. A., & Charnas, J. W. (2007). The Rorschach Perceptual-Thinking Index (PTI): An examination of reliability, validity, and diagnostic efficiency. *International Journal of Testing*, *7*, 269–291.

Kleiger, J. H. (2017). *Rorschach assessment of psychotic phenomena.* New York, NY: Routledge.

Klopfer, B., Ainsworth, M. D., Klopfer, W. G., & Holt, R. R. (1954). *Developments in the Rorschach technique: Vol. 1. Technique and theory.* New York, NY: World Book.

Kumar, R., & Khess, C. R. J. (2005). Diagnostic efficiency of Schizophrenia Index and Perceptual-Thinking Index in schizophrenia and mania. *Journal of Projective Psychology & Mental Health*, *12*, 115–122.

Meyer, G. J., Erdberg, P., & Shaffer, T. W. (2007). Towards international normative reference data for the Comprehensive System. *Journal of Personality Assessment*, *89*, S201–S216.

Meyer, G. J., Viglione, D. J., Mihura, J. L., Erard, R. E., & Erdberg. P. (2011. *Rorschach Performance Assessment System.* Toledo, OH: Rorschach Performance Assessment System, LLC.

Minassian, A., Cadenhead, K., Sprock, J., & Braff, D. (2003). The use of the Ego Impairment Index across the schizophrenia spectrum. *Journal of Personality Assessment*, *80*, 50–57.

Perry, W., Viglione, D., & Braff, D. (1992). The Ego Impairment Index and schizophrenia: A validation study. *Journal of Personality Assessment*, *59*, 165–175.

Phillip, L., & Smith, J. G. (1953). *Rorschach interpretation: Advanced technique.* New York, NY: Grune & Stratton.

Schafer, R. (1954). *Psychoanalytic interpretation in Rorschach testing.* New York, NY: Grune & Stratton.

Smith, S. R., Baity, M., Knowles, E. S., & Hilsenroth, M. J. (2001). Assessment of disordered thinking in children and adolescents: The Rorschach Perceptual Thinking Index. *Journal of Personality Assessment*, *77*, 447–463.

Tibon-Czopp, S., Appel, L, & Zeligman, R, (2016). Assessing personality patterns of functioning in a decision-making ambiguous task: The Rorschach Reality–Fantasy Scale (RFS-2). *Group Decision and Negotiation*, *25*, 65–75.
Tibon, S., Porcelli, P., & Weinberger, Y. (2005). The Ego Impairment Index and the Reality–Fantasy Scale: Comment on Viglione, Perry, and Meyer (2003). *Journal of Personality Assessment*, *84*, 315–317.
Viglione, D. J., Perry, W., & Meyer, G. (2003). Refinements in the Rorschach Ego Impairment Index incorporating the Human Representation variable. *Journal of Personality Assessment*, *81*, 149–156.
Weiner, I. B. (2003a). *Principles of Rorschach interpretation* (2nd ed.). Mahwah, NJ: Lawrence Erlbaum Associates.
Weiner, I. B. (2003b). Prediction and postdiction in clinical decision making. *Clinical Psychology: Science and Practice*, *10*, 335–338.

PART III

Normative Rorschach Data for Senior Adults

Introduction to Normative Rorschach Data for Senior Adults

Rorschach research has been aimed at enhancing the scientific status of the instrument and thereby promoting conceptually derived and evidence-based assessment practice. Despite the clearly evident benefits of using the Rorschach method in the clinical assessment of both young and older people, it has received mixed reviews and evoked criticisms related to a variety of psychometric issues. As noted in a previous volume regarding Rorschach assessment of adolescents (Tibon-Czopp & Weiner, 2016), the development and initial publication of the Rorschach Comprehensive System (CS; Exner, 1974; Exner & Weiner, 1995) was a turning point in the field by virtue of providing standard guidelines for administration and coding and thus fostering cumulative research and scientific study. Nevertheless, the scientific status of the Rorschach has been questioned over the years by critics who asserted that the reliability and validity of its individual variables had not yet been adequately evaluated. Most challenging in this respect have been the voices of critics who considered Rorschach normative data as outdated and insufficient to warrant using the method in clinical practice for distinguishing between healthy and psychopathological functioning in culturally diverse populations. These criticisms, which were not always just but sometimes warranted, have had the positive effect of stimulating extensive examinations of the instrument that have established the reliability, validity, utility, and cross-cultural applicability of numerous Rorschach variables.

As noted in Chapter 2, the number of Rorschach empirical studies with senior adults as the target population published in the last two decades is relatively small, and most of these studies include only a limited number of participants (e.g., Gross, Newton, & Brooks, 1990). Furthermore, some of these studies provide Rorschach data only about elderly patient samples, and those that do explore Rorschach findings of nonpatient groups frequently focus only on some specific variables or were collected more than 30 years ago.

The discussion in the following three chapters on normative reference data in the elderly addresses the interpretation of CS-based structural variables. In order to generate a full picture of an individual's personality and mental functioning, the interpretation of these variables should be combined with inferences derived from the full range of Rorschach structural, content, and sequential data and with information gleaned from self-report measures and behavioral observations.

Most of the variables presented in Chapters 5–7 are included in the international sample of Meyer, Erdberg, and Shaffer (2007). Also included are two CS combinations of variables (*FM+m* and *Col–Shd Blend*) and four new CS-based indices: *RFS-P*, *RFS-S*, *EII-2*, and *AdjDMD*. *RFS-P* and *RFS-S* are derivations of the *Reality–Fantasy Scale Version 2* (*RFS-2*; Tibon-Czopp, Appel, & Zeligman, 2016) that have been validated as measures of psychotic-like thinking and dissociation proneness, respectively. The *Ego Impairment Index* (*EII-2*; Viglione, Perry, & Meyer, 2003) is a theoretically derived measure of maladaptive functioning that has been validated in a meta-analysis encompassing both adult and adolescent samples (Diener, Hilsenroth, Shaffer, & Sexton, 2011). The *AdjDMD* index (Weiner, 2003) is a measure of anxiety that has been validated in a sample of adolescents (Stokes, Pogge, & Zaccario, 2013). The *EII-2* and the *AdjDMD* can be derived directly from the Rorschach Interpretation Assistance Program (RIAP) Structural Summary. The *RFS-2 Software Version 2.0* can be downloaded from the web. Guidelines for the interpretation of these Rorschach variables are provided in Chapter 4 of the present volume.

Chapter 5 provides Rorschach reference data on a new international sample of nonpatient senior adults collected from Brazil and Portugal, Iran, Israel, Italy, Spain, and the US. Chapter 6 addresses these new international data from a developmental perspective by comparing younger and older groups of nonpatient senior adults. Chapter 7 compares the new senior adult nonpatient data to Rorschach findings obtained from patients with Alzheimer's disease.

References

Diener, M. J., Hilsenroth, M. J., Shaffer, S. A., & Sexton, J. E. (2011). A meta-analysis of the relationship between the Rorschach Ego Impairment Index (EII) and psychiatric severity. *Clinical Psychology & Psychotherapy*, *18*(6), 464–485.

Exner, J. E. (1974). *The Rorschach: A comprehensive system* (Vol. 1). New York, NY: Wiley.

Exner, J. E., Jr., & Weiner, I. B. (1995). *The Rorschach: A comprehensive system: Vol. 3: Assessment of children and adolescents*. New York, NY: Wiley.

Gross, A., Newton, R. R., & Brooks, R. B. (1990). Rorschach responses in healthy community dwelling older adults. *Journal of Personality Assessment*, 55, 335–343.

Meyer, G. J., Erdberg, P., & Shaffer, T. W. (2007). Toward international normative reference data for the Comprehensive System. *Journal of personality assessment*, *89*(Suppl. 1), S201–S216.

Stokes, J. M., Pogge, D. L., & Zaccario, M. (2013). Response character styles in adolescents: A replication of convergent validity between the MMPI-A and the Rorschach. *Journal of Personality Assessment*, *95*(2), 159–173.

Tibon-Czopp, S., Appel, L., & Zeligman, R. (2016). Assessing personality patterns of functioning in a decision-making ambiguous task: The Rorschach Reality–Fantasy Scale (RFS-2). *Group Decision and Negotiation*, *25*(1), 65–75.

Tibon-Czopp, S., & Weiner, I. B. (2016). *Rorschach assessment of adolescents.* New York, NY: Springer.

Viglione, D. J., Perry, W., & Meyer, G. (2003). Refinements in the Rorschach Ego Impairment Index incorporating the human representational variable. *Journal of Personality Assessment, 81*(2), 149–156.

Weiner, I. B. (2003). *Principles of Rorschach interpretation* (2nd ed.). Mahwah, NJ: Lawrence Erlbaum Associates.

CHAPTER 5

International Normative Data for Nonpatients

Normative international reference data serve important purposes in psychological assessment, and the standards for psychological testing include collection of such data as a basic foundation of test construction and evaluation. With respect to clinical decision-making, data obtained from nonpatients from different countries and from different ethnic groups within a country are essential for providing Rorschach norms against which practitioners can compare their patients' protocols. However, as the world becomes global in scope, it is increasingly important to develop a theoretical and empirical understanding of cultural differences in different realms of personality functioning between countries. Understanding these differences has important implications for accurate interpretation of Rorschach findings. Although the heterogeneity of the group of older adults (see Chapter 1) should be taken into consideration when interpreting an individual Rorschach protocol, being able to draw on cross-cultural reference data can help clinicians provide evidence-supported evaluations. These evaluations should successfully distinguish between healthy and psychopathological personality functioning, regardless of the social and cultural background of the person being tested.

Interpreting Rorschach Cross-Cultural Normative Data

Rorschach research on the personality functioning of elderly people in good physical and mental health using the Rorschach has been limited. As noted in Chapter 2, the first suggestions concerning the influence of age on the Rorschach were made by Hermann Rorschach, who described some presumably typical characteristics of aging, including diminished capacity to use inner cognitive and affective resources, constriction and stereotypy of thought, and decrements in perceptual accuracy and intellectual efficiency (Rorschach, 1921/1942). The first research study using the Rorschach to examine personality functioning in the elderly was conducted by Klopfer (1946), who confirmed and elaborated Rorschach's hypotheses. Klopfer's main conclusion was that aging leads to psychopathological manifestations characterized by a deficit in intellectual functions, a loss of links to reality, an inability to fully utilize inner resources, inconsistency of affective reactivity, and difficulty in establishing relationships with others. In Rorschach Comprehensive System (CS) terms, these deficits would be manifested in decreased *R*, *Lambda*, *EA*, *M*, *SumC*, *Afr*, *Sum Shading*, and *Sum Content* and in an increased *X−%*. These initial hypotheses were subsequently confirmed in several studies (Ames, 1960, 1974; Ames, Learned, Metraux, & Walker, 1954; Chesrow, Wosika, & Reinitz, 1949; Davidson & Kruglov, 1952; Grossman, Warshawsky, & Hertz, 1951; Light & Amick, 1956; Prados & Fried, 1947; Shimonaka & Nakazato, 1991).

However, numerous researchers have pointed out that none of these early studies examined the effects on the Rorschach data of such critical considerations as cognitive and behavioral disorders and residential status (e.g., Eisdorfer, 1960; Light & Amick, 1956; Reichlin, 1984). More recent data have in fact demonstrated that the earlier impressions of psychopathological manifestations in the elderly were artifacts of flawed methods, including inattention to such confounding variables as hospitalization, institutionalization, and previously diagnosed mental status impairments (Gross, Newton, & Brooks, 1990; Mattlar, Knuts, & Virtanen, 1985; Pertchik, Shaffer, Erdberg, & Margolin, 2007). The only previous study that provided descriptive data on the CS variables for a group of community-residing nonpatient older adults was the research of Pertchik et al. (2007). In their US-based sample of 52 adults aged 60–80, scores on all of the key CS variables were mostly similar to the scores of adult nonpatients in general.

As noted, the applicability of Rorschach reference data based on US samples to the evaluation of people in other countries has frequently been questioned, but this concern has been somewhat resolved by the previously mentioned international project of Meyer et al. (2007), which presents Rorschach CS data on nonpatient samples of adults, adolescents, and children from many countries. Unlike the child and adolescent samples, the accumulated adult data on 4,704 nonpatients in 21 samples from 17 Western countries have supported the cross-cultural transportability of the CS norms. Because the average scores across the adult samples showed no significant differences in most of the variables, Meyer et al. were able to construct a composite set of norms and cutoff scores that can serve as a benchmark for clinical evaluations virtually anywhere in the world. However, it is important to note that senior adults are markedly underrepresented in the Meyer et al. project. Several of the 21 national samples did not include any elderly participants, and fewer than 2% of the total sample were age 65 or older.

Furthermore, it should be noted that Rorschach assessors presume similar patterns of personality functioning in psychologically healthy people around the world and at all ages, therefore enabling them to use international cross-cultural reference data as a starting point in their evaluation of possible psychopathology. As noted in Chapter 1, however, the homogenous universal premise has been challenged by various authors, particularly with respect to cognitive functioning. Furthermore, despite considerable theorizing on the issue, there are few empirical data concerning the interaction of aging and culture in cognitive functioning.

The following tables present basic Rorschach variables for distinguishing between healthy and psychopathological functioning in four domains: cognitive functioning, affective experience, interpersonal relatedness, and self-perception. As noted in Chapter 4, some of these variables have implications for more than one domain and should be interpreted accordingly. The selected variables provide a basic platform for interpreting the data presented in the eight clusters of the CS Structural Summary. CS structural variables that appear relevant to a case but are not among the selected variables should also be taken into consideration, especially if their values deviate markedly from those found in this new nonpatient sample.

Research findings indicate that many of the traditional cutoff scores for adults are applicable in contemporary assessment of adolescents as well. It remains a major question for clinicians who work with older adults whether these cutoff scores for distinguishing between healthy and psychopathological functioning can be applied to Rorschach protocols of contemporary senior adults. Given that more than 50% of the nonpatient adults in the composite international sample of Meyer et al. (2007) exceeded the traditional cutoff point for three variables (*Xu%* > 0.20, *T* = 0, and *AG* = 0), Tibon-Czopp and Weiner (2016) have suggested that some adjustments of the cutoff scores for these variables should be considered.

However, the cutoff scores presented in this chapter correspond to those suggested by Exner (2003) and based on his most recent reference sample (Exner, 2007), except for the cutoff value for white space, which should be increased from *S* > 2 to *S* > 3. There are also eight variables for which traditional CS tables provide two optional cutoff scores. Based on the international composite reference data reported by Meyer et al. (2007, table 2), the least strict (i.e., most liberal) alternative cutoff scores for these eight variables (as defined by their being exceeded by a higher percentage of nonpatient adults) are used for distinguishing between healthy and psychopathological functioning: *X–%* > 0.30; *D-Score* < –1; *AdjD-Score* < –1; *FC* > (*CF*+*C*) + 2; (*CF*+*C*) > *FC* + 2; *Pure C* > 1; *Afr* < 0.40; and *Pure H* = 0.

As has been noted, clinically useful classification of psychopathological manifestations must begin with an understanding of healthy mental processes that involve a person's overall resources and capacities. Although no profile can encompass the full range of mental functioning, the current chapter provides a handy guide for assessing personality strengths and weaknesses and describing the adequacy of a senior adult's mental functioning. When sufficiently elaborated, the four previously mentioned domains—cognitive, affective, interpersonal, and self-perception—well serve the purposes of capturing the richness and individuality of a person's mental functioning, symptom patterns, and internal subjective experience and of providing a psychodynamic diagnosis (*Psychodynamic Diagnostic Manual*; Lingiardi & McWilliams, 2017). The current chapter focuses on the adequacy of mental functioning rather than on specific psychopathological manifestations, although in cases with severe psychopathological manifestations—whether cognitive or affective—the reference data can also assist in formulating a *Diagnostic and Statistical Manual of Mental Disorders, Fifth*

Edition (*DSM-5*) diagnosis. Case illustrations of this type are included in Part IV of this volume.

When interpreting a Rorschach protocol, practitioners should keep in mind that healthy reactions to various crises may temporarily interrupt the mental functioning of an elderly person. Such reactions typically follow a stable adjustment and are characterized by a relatively brief crisis in which the person might show some temporary decline in coping capacities. The impact of a developmental crisis might be manifested in the person's cognitive functioning, affective experience, interpersonal relatedness, or self-perception, and it can at times be exacerbated by crucial events in the family or among the social groups in which the elderly person is involved. Case illustrations of such circumstances are also included in Part IV. Also to be kept in mind is the evidence cited in Chapter 1 that mentally healthy senior adults usually retain or even improve their major mental capacities with age, which is a finding that helps Rorschach clinicians in distinguishing between normal reactions to crises and psychopathological conditions.

Normative Data for Senior Adults in the Twenty-First Century

As has been noted, the reference values provided in the present chapter integrate data from six nonpatient senior samples—from Brazil and Portugal, Iran, Israel, Italy, Spain, and the US—to create a combined international sample of nonpatient seniors. The Brazilian sample (collected by Lottenberg-Semer and Katz) and the Portuguese sample (Pires, 2007) consisted of 14 and 9 participants, respectively, were combined given that they share the same language. The weighted mean age of the participants in this combined sample of Brazil and Portugal was 66.74. The Iranian sample (collected by Hosseininasab) included 48 participants with a mean age of 71.92. The Israeli sample, which was collected for the purpose of this volume, included 33 participants with a mean age of 70.03. The Italian sample (collected by Brusadelli and Porcelli) included 27 participants with a mean age of 64.85. The Spanish sample (Vázquez Orellana, 2003) included 91 participants with a mean age of 71.98. The US sample (Pertchik, Shaffer, Erdberg, & Margolin, 2007) included 52 participants with a mean age of 68.46. All of the sample participants were community-residing senior adults with no known history of neurocognitive impairments. All samples were collected in the twenty-first century.

In order to examine whether the six samples could be combined into one international sample, we computed T-scores for all the CS variables in each of the six samples. Meyer et al.'s reference data for adults were used as a benchmark for computing these T-scores. It is common practice in evaluating psychological well-being to consider a T-score difference of 10 points (1 SD) or more from a normative mean (M) expectation as likely to reflect at least minor adjustment difficulties, but not to warrant a formal clinical diagnosis. However, a T-score above 65 (M + 1.5 SD) or below 35 (M − 1.5 SD) is considered a marked deviation from normative standards and likely to indicate major adjustment difficulties.

Cross-country comparisons showed that the great majority of the T-scores in all six senior samples were within a fairly narrow range between 40 and 60, with more than half of the scores falling in an even narrower range between 47 and 53. Using a benchmark of T-scores above 65 or below 35, the only markedly deviant cognitive scores were an elevated *DQv/+* and lowered *Popular* scores in the Iranian sample and an elevated Level 1 *DV* score in the US sample. These three deviant scores were country specific and did not characterize any of the other countries. The deviant *DQv/+* in the Iranian sample is most likely attributable to different criteria for coding this specific variable, whereas the lowered *Popular* score most likely represents cultural differences, as demonstrated by Sangro (1997). The elevated Level 1 *DV* in the US sample identifies some mild idiosyncrasies in language usage and not any serious cognitive slippage. Moreover, because this elevation was present only in the US sample, it should not be considered to reflect any general tendency toward word-finding difficulties in the elderly. However, this and other culturally specific differences might warrant further study.

The Iranian sample also had extreme values on two non-cognitive scores, *FD* and *AG*, both of which were markedly elevated (T-scores of 75 and 68, respectively). A somewhat less elevated *AG* score (T-score of 62) was also found in the Israeli sample. The elevation of *AG* responses may indicate aggressive concerns resulting from national trauma (Tibon, Rothschild, & Appel, 2011). Nevertheless, country-specific T-score comparisons show that the Rorschach responses of nonpatient senior adults are basically consistent across cultures, languages, examiners, and recruitment strategies. Generally, community-residing senior adults from different countries and cultures look similar on the full range of CS scores. We created a new set of data by computing weighted average scores across the subsamples, thus giving more weight to larger samples. In instances of a sample with missing information (e.g., *An+Xy* in the Spanish sample), the composite value was based on the remaining samples. The resulting combined sample for our data analysis thus consists of 274 nonpatient senior adults with a weighted mean age of 69.92.

Table 5.1 presents the means, T-scores, and minimum and maximum values of CS variables for the combined international sample of nonpatient seniors (identified as "International Seniors") and compares these data with those in the Meyer et al. (2007) composite international sample of nonpatient adults (identified as "International Adults"). To facilitate clinical inferences regarding cutoff scores for maladaptive or psychopathological functioning, we also provide frequency data for the structural variables described in Chapter 4. Using the same procedures described above, we computed the average proportion of people in the new senior sample in the four domains: cognitive functioning, affective experience, interpersonal relatedness, and self-perception. Table 5.2 provides weighted frequencies for these selected CS variables in the combined sample of nonpatient seniors and compares them with similar proportions in the composite international sample of nonpatient adults.

Table 5.1 Means, T-scores, and minimum and maximum values of CS variables in the combined international sample of nonpatient seniors as compared to the composite international sample of nonpatient adults of Meyer et al. (2007)

	International Seniors				*International Adults*
Variable	*Mean*	*T-score*	*Minimum*	*Maximum*	*Mean*
R	20.33	47	12.00	45.00	22.31
W	7.36	46	0.00	21.00	9.08
D	10.08	50	1.00	25.00	9.89
Dd	2.90	49	0.00	18.00	3.33
S	1.56	46	0.00	13.00	2.49
DQ+	5.72	49	0.00	22.00	6.24
DQo	13.09	48	1.00	33.00	14.68
DQv	0.86	48	0.00	9.00	1.09
DQv/+	0.66	**56**	0.00	15.00	0.29
FQ+	0.15	49	0.00	11.00	0.21
FQxo	10.44	48	0.00	24.00	11.11
FQxu	5.61	49	0.00	22.00	6.20
FQx–	3.76	48	0.00	16.00	4.43
FQxNone	0.21	48	0.00	4.00	0.33
MQ+	0.04	48	0.00	3.00	0.12
MQo	1.69	47	0.00	10.00	2.26
MQu	0.56	49	0.00	5.00	0.69
MQ–	0.45	48	0.00	9.00	0.63
MQNone	0.00	49	0.00	1.00	0.03
SQual–	0.53	47	0.00	5.00	0.87
M	2.71	46	0.00	15.00	3.73
FM	3.84	52	0.00	15.00	3.37
M	1.28	49	0.00	9.00	1.50
FC	1.38	47	0.00	8.00	1.91
CF	0.86	45	0.00	9.00	1.65
C	0.29	49	0.00	5.00	0.34

Table 5.1 (Cont.)

	International Seniors				*International Adults*
Variable	*Mean*	*T-score*	*Minimum*	*Maximum*	*Mean*
Cn	0.00	49	0.00	1.00	0.02
Sum Color	2.54	45	0.00	10.00	3.91
WsumC	1.98	45	0.00	10.50	3.11
SumC'	1.13	46	0.00	9.00	1.75
SumT	0.86	52	0.00	7.00	0.65
SumV	0.41	49	0.00	9.00	0.52
SumY	1.02	48	0.00	14.00	1.34
SumShading	3.40	47	0.00	29.00	4.29
Fr+rF	0.21	48	0.00	8.00	0.41
FD	1.24	52	0.00	16.00	1.02
F	8.79	50	0.00	28.00	8.92
(2)	6.63	49	0.00	25.00	7.04
3r+(2)/R	0.37	49	0.00	1.81	0.38
Lambda	1.31	55	0.00	20.00	0.86
PureF%	0.38	49	0.00	0.95	0.39
FM+m	5.15	51	0.00	22.00	4.87
EA	4.72	**44**	0.00	18.00	6.84
Es	8.57	49	0.00	35.00	9.09
D-Score	−1.21	46	−12.00	3.00	−0.68
AdjD	−0.73	46	−8.00	4.00	−0.20
a (active)	4.86	50	0.00	18.00	4.96
p (passive)	3.11	48	0.00	14.00	3.73
Ma	1.70	48	0.00	11.00	2.09
Mp	1.03	46	0.00	9.00	1.67
Intellect	2.04	49	0.00	21.00	2.35
Zf	11.28	48	1.00	31.00	12.5
Zd	−1.85	47	−21.00	14.00	−0.67

(*continued*)

Table 5.1 (Cont.)

	International Seniors				*International Adults*
Variable	*Mean*	*T-score*	*Minimum*	*Maximum*	*Mean*
Blends	3.15	47	0.00	15.00	4.01
Blends/R	0.16	49	0.00	0.68	0.18
Col–Shd Blends	0.58	50	0.00	4.00	0.60
Afr	0.49	48	0.05	1.14	0.53
Populars	5.16	49	0.00	11.00	5.36
XA%	0.79	50	0.00	1.00	0.79
WDA%	0.80	49	0.00	1.00	0.82
X+%	0.53	51	0.00	0.88	0.52
X–%	0.18	49	0.00	0.70	0.19
Xu%	0.27	50	0.00	0.70	0.27
Isolate/R	0.21	51	0.00	1.06	0.20
H	2.16	49	0.00	16.00	2.43
(H)	0.75	46	0.00	7.00	1.22
Hd	0.99	47	0.00	9.00	1.52
(Hd)	0.27	46	0.00	11.00	0.64
Hx	0.33	49	0.00	10.00	0.41
H+(H)+Hd+(Hd)	4.14	45	0.00	20.00	5.83
(H)+Hd+(Hd)	2.08	45	0.00	12.00	3.36
A	9.36	55	1.00	35.00	7.71
(A)	0.23	47	0.00	3.00	0.42
Ad	1.79	47	0.00	12.00	2.41
(Ad)	0.09	48	0.00	4.00	0.16
An	1.00	49	0.00	9.00	1.16
Art	1.03	49	0.00	7.00	1.22
Ay	0.48	49	0.00	12.00	0.52
Bl	0.20	49	0.00	4.00	0.25
Bt	1.41	50	0.00	9.00	1.41

Table 5.1 (Cont.)

	International Seniors				*International Adults*
Variable	*Mean*	*T-score*	*Minimum*	*Maximum*	*Mean*
Cg	1.41	47	0.00	9.00	1.89
Cl	0.20	50	0.00	4.00	0.18
Ex	0.06	47	0.00	2.00	0.19
Fi	0.29	47	0.00	3.00	0.50
Food	0.61	54	0.00	4.00	0.33
Ge	0.18	49	0.00	3.00	0.26
Hh	0.67	48	0.00	6.00	0.84
Ls	0.78	49	0.00	8.00	0.87
Na	0.76	50	0.00	10.00	0.75
Sc	0.95	49	0.00	6.00	1.11
Sx	0.29	48	0.00	7.00	0.47
Xy	0.16	49	0.00	4.00	0.19
Idiographic	0.82	49	0.00	6.00	0.89
An+Xy	1.29	50	0.00	10.00	1.34
DV	1.02	54	0.00	12.00	0.65
INCOM	0.64	49	0.00	6.00	0.73
DR	0.55	51	0.00	9.00	0.49
FABCOM	0.51	51	0.00	5.00	0.45
DV2	0.03	51	0.00	2.00	0.01
INC2	0.04	48	0.00	2.00	0.10
DR2	0.06	50	0.00	4.00	0.06
FAB2	0.09	50	0.00	2.00	0.08
ALOG	0.13	49	0.00	5.00	0.16
CONTAM	0.00	49	0.00	1.00	0.02
Sum 6 Sp Sc	3.05	51	0.00	15.00	2.75
Lvl 2 Sp Sc	0.22	49	0.00	6.00	0.25

(*continued*)

Table 5.1 (Cont.)

	International Seniors				*International Adults*
Variable	*Mean*	*T-score*	*Minimum*	*Maximum*	*Mean*
WSum6	7.86	50	0.00	47.00	7.63
AB	0.27	49	0.00	7.00	0.32
AG	0.88	54	0.00	8.00	0.54
COP	1.21	51	0.00	8.00	1.07
CP	0.01	49	0.00	1.00	0.02
GHR	2.96	47	0.00	15.00	3.70
PHR	3.03	51	0.00	14.00	2.86
MOR	1.10	49	0.00	8.00	1.26
PER	0.92	52	0.00	14.00	0.75
PSV	0.30	51	0.00	4.00	0.23
PTI Total	0.80	52	0.00	4.00	0.59
DEPI Total	3.94	51	1.00	7.00	3.80
CDI Total	3.25	53	0.00	5.00	2.90
S-CON Total	5.03	52	1.00	10.00	4.67
HVI Total	1.70	**43**	0.00	8.00	2.79
OBS Total (1–5)	1.09	50	0.00	3.00	1.13
WD+	0.19	50	0.00	9.00	0.17
WDo	9.31	46	0.00	24.00	10.69
WDu	4.62	49	0.00	14.00	4.89
WD–	3.11	51	0.00	16.00	2.91
WDNone	0.22	48	0.00	4.00	0.34
EII-2	0.20	54	–2.93	4.58	–0.15
HRV	–0.14	46	–13.00	10.00	0.94
AdjDMD	0.30	n/a	0.00	4.00	n/a
RPS-P	–0.19	n/a	–3.04	1.63	n/a
RFS-S	2.33	n/a	0.00	3.39	n/a

Note: T-scores in bold are significantly elevated or lowered in comparison to the international sample of nonpatient adults (Meyer et al., 2007)

Table 5.2 Frequencies for selected CS variables in the combined international sample of nonpatient seniors: the average proportion of people in four domains of personality—cognitive functioning, affective experience, interpersonal relatedness, and self-perception—as compared to the composite international sample of nonpatient adults

Variables	*Reference Values*	*International Seniors*	*International Adults*
Cognitive functioning			
General indices			
PTI	*PTI* > 3	3%	2%
EII-2	*EII-2* > 0	39%	
RFS-P	*RFS-P* < −0.51	34%	
	RFS-P > +0.65	20%	
RFS-S	*RFS-S* > 2.70	27%	
Attention (processing)			
Lambda	*L* < 0.30	27%	
	L > 0.99	27%	28%
W:D:Dd	*W* > 0.50	17%	
	D < 0.50	44%	
	Dd > 0.15	37%	
Zd	*Zd* > +3	15%	19%
	Zd < −3	35%	29%
DQv	*DQv* > 2	11%	16%
Perception (mediation)			
XA%	*XA%* < 0.70	23%	18%
WDA%	*WDA%* < 0.75	24%	20%
X−%	*X−%* > 0.30	19%	14%
Xu%	*Xu%* > 0.30	35%	
	Xu% < 0.10	7%	
Popular	*P* < 4	**30%**	16%
	P > 7	13%	12%

(*continued*)

Table 5.2 (Cont.)

Variables	*Reference Values*	*International Seniors*	*International Adults*
Thinking (ideation)			
WSum6	*WSum6* > 10	27%	
	WSum6 > 17	10%	
Lvl 2 Sp Sc	*Lv2 Sp Sc* > 0	16%	17%
Mp:Ma	*Mp* > *Ma*	**23%**	32%
Introversive EBper	*EA* < 10:*M* > *WSumC* + 2; *EA* > 10:*M* > *WSumC* + 2.5	**25%**	16%
FM+m	*FM+m* > 6	37%	
INTELL	*2AB+Art+Ay* > 5	13%	11%
Affective experience			
Afr	*Afr* < 0.40	32%	27%
	Afr > 0.89	3%	
WSumC	*WSumC* < 2.5	67%	
Const.	*SumC'* > *WSumC*	21%	
DEPI	*DEPI* = 5 or higher	33%	31%
S-CON	*S-CON* = 8 or higher	8%	4%
Eb	*FM+m* < SumShd	**27%**	35%
Col–Shd Bld	*Col–Shd Bld* > 1	10%	
D-Score	*D-Score* < –1	**38%**	23%
	D-Score > 0	8%	12%
AdjD-Score	*AdjD-Score* < –1	**25%**	13%
	AdjD-Score > 0	12%	19%
AdjDMD	*AdjDMD* > 1	26%	
S	*S* > 3	8%	
Extratensive EBper	*EA* < 10:*WSumC* > *M* + 1.5; *EA* > 10:*WSumC* > *M* + 2	14%	9%
FC:CF+C	*FC* > *CF+C* + 2	12%	13%
	CF+C > *FC* + 2	11%	15%

Table 5.2 (Cont.)

Variables	*Reference Values*	*International Seniors*	*International Adults*
Pure C	*Pure C* > 1	8%	7%
Interpersonal relatedness			
EA	*EA* < 6	66%	
CDI	*CDI* > 3	**44%**	36%
H+(H)+Hd+(Hd)	*H+(H)+Hd+(Hd)* < 2	18%	
Isolation Index	*Isolation Index* > 0.25	33%	
H:Hd+(H)+(Hd)	*H* < *Hd+(H)+(Hd)*	36%	
SumT	*SumT* = 0	48%	57%
	SumT > 1	**24%**	15%
HVI	*HVI Positive*	5%	12%
COP	*COP* = 0	43%	42%
AG	*AG* > 2	**16%**	4%
a:p	*p* > *a* + 1	17%	21%
M–	*M–* > 1	13%	
Fd	*Fd* > 0	45%	
PER	*PER* > 2	8%	
Self-perception			
Fr+rF	*Fr+rF* > 0	**12%**	25%
Egoc. Index	*3r+(2)/R* < 0.33	45%	39%
	3r+(2)/R > 0.44	29%	30%
SumV	*SumV* > 0	36%	
MOR	*MOR* > 2	17%	16%
FD	*FD* = 0	39%	
	FD > 2	28%	

Note: Frequencies in bold are significantly elevated or lowered in comparison to the international sample of nonpatient adults (Meyer et al., 2007)

Implications of the Normative Data

Table 5.1 shows that, if cutoff points of T < 45 or > 55 are applied, deviations of the current international sample of nonpatient seniors from the norms established by the composite adult sample of Meyer et al. (2007) occur only in three variables: *DQv/+*, *EA*, and *HVI Total*, with T-scores of 56, 44, and 43, respectively. However, whereas the lowered *EA* and *HVI Total* commonly characterize seniors in most of the countries, the deviation in *DQv/+* appears to be specific to the Iranian sample. As previously suggested, this deviation might result from different criteria for coding the variable.

The lowered *EA* may indicate a certain decrease in adaptive resources among senior adults. This finding accords with work by Muzio (2006), who found a lowered *EA* in a group of elderly respondents without cognitive impairment. Both *M* and *WSumC*, which are the components of *EA* (see Chapter 4), fall within the range of 0.5 SD in our sample. Nevertheless, since these two variables are at the lower edge of the range (46 and 45, respectively), we can conclude that this slight decrease in adaptive resources is both cognitive and affective. This decrease may be explained by a positive correlation that has been found between human movement and the weighted sum of color responses on the Rorschach and the volume of temporal gray matter in the brain (Ilonen, Salokangas, & Turku Study Group, 2016), which is known to decline in aging (Good et al., 2001). This slight overall decline in available psychological resources, as measured by the Rorschach, might account for the elderly's tendency to slow down their performance as the task becomes more complex, which is usually referred as the "age-related complexity effect" (Salthouse, 1985).

HVI Total is a dimensional variable that, independent of *T*, reflects a cautious and detail-oriented approach to scanning the environment, combined with heightened underlying alertness, suspiciousness, and anger and a need to protect and distance oneself in interpersonal relationships. The somewhat lowered *HVI* on the elderly may indicate relaxing the need to be interpersonally cautious. Indeed, gerontology studies show that people become more positive about their social relationships as they grow older (Carstensen, Fung, & Charles, 2003). It is suggested that, with aging, people prefer to invest in relationships that are emotionally rewarding and significant to them, while becoming less inclined to engage in relationships that are no longer seen as being of consequence. This shifting attitude toward relationships is likely due to a natural change in motivation. Instead of being driven to acquire new knowledge about the self and the social world, older people are motivated to derive emotional meaning from life, to establish intimacy, and to verify their own identity.

On the other hand, the current data provide critical evidence that nonpatient seniors are unlikely—and no more likely than nonpatient adults—to show deviations of more than 5 T-score points in CS markers of cognitive deficiencies and perceptual distortions. These findings differ markedly from the findings of the early studies mentioned previously in this chapter. With respect to the clinical implications of the present findings, and applying the benchmarks of 1 SD (minor adjustment difficulties) and 1.5 SD (major adjustment difficulties), none of the variables in the present senior sample deviates notably from the normative standards among younger adults.

As for cutoff scores, from a comparison between our combined sample of seniors and the Meyer et al. composite sample of adults using Exner's (2007) criteria of 7% difference between frequency of occurrence, 11 variables were found to be substantially different among the elderly: *P* < 4, *Mp* > *Ma*, and *Introversive EBper* within the cognitive functioning domain; *FM+m* < *SumShd*, *D-Score* < –1, and *AdjD-Score* < –1 within the affective domain; *CDI* > 3, *T* = 0, *T* > 1, and *AG* > 2 within the interpersonal domain; and *Fr+rF* > 0 within the self-perception domain.

With respect to *Popular* responses, the data in Table 5.2 show a higher percentage of *P* < 4 (30%) in the senior sample as compared to the adult sample (16%) of Meyer et al. (2007). As noted earlier in this chapter, this variable might be culture dependent. Research findings do in fact show age-related increases in individualistic attitudes in cultures that emphasize individuality, whereas cultures that emphasize social reciprocity and adherence to tradition and conformity are characterized by age-related increases in collectivistic attitudes (Fung & Ng, 2006). Apart from the Iranian sample, the new data were collected in countries that emphasize individuality, which would support an inference that seniors are more loyal to themselves than are younger adults and less committed to societal expectations.

In their thinking, the senior sample shows a lower percentage of *Mp* > *Ma* (23%) than the adult sample (32%). This difference suggests that senior adults are actively engaged in solving their own problems rather than relying on other people or circumstances to solve them. Similar Rorschach findings are reported by Gross, Newton, and Brooks (1990), who concluded that bright and healthy older adults are not necessarily rooted in fantasies and memories of the past, but may instead display more purposeful and deliberate ideational capacities than younger adults. The importance to older people of autonomy and their corresponding reluctance to feel dependent on family members has also been demonstrated by Spitze and Gallant (2004). On the other hand, higher percentages of *Introversive EBper* (25%) in the senior sample than in the adult sample (16%) may reflect a difficulty in shifting between mental sets that is known to accompany normal aging (Coubard et al., 2011; Sorel & Pennequin, 2008).

Within the affective domain, three differences suggest that older people are more susceptible than younger adults to emotional distress: a lower frequency of *FM+m* < *SumShd* (27% as opposed to 35%) and higher frequencies of negative *D-Score* and *AdjD-Score* (38% and 25%, respectively) as compared to those of the combined international sample of adults (23% and 13%, respectively). On the other hand, there is approximately the same frequency of *DEPI* and *S-CON* elevations in the senior sample (33% and 8%, respectively) as in the Meyer et al. sample (31% and 4%, respectively). Moreover, in accord with Kring, Davison, Neale, and Johnson (2007), it is possible that the higher frequencies of negative

D-Score and *AdjD-Score* are not necessarily associated with disruption of a senior's adaptation. Although old age typically includes such stressful life events as the loss of loved ones, progressive health impairment, and disability, most older people will find ways of adapting to this distress without developing depressive disorder.

With respect to interpersonal relatedness, the high percentages of *CDI* > 3 (44%) in our sample as compared to the international combined adult sample (36%) could at least partially result from the lowered *EA*, *AdjD-Score*, and *WsumC* just discussed. Also relevant in this regard is the frequency of *T* > 1 (24%), which differs substantially from the Meyer et al. sample (15%) and suggests that elderly people are somewhat more likely than younger adults to have unmet needs for closeness. This finding approximates data reported by Mattlar (2001), in which 26% of older Finnish participants had *T* > 1. Consistent with these findings is the somewhat lower frequency of *T* = 0 in our sample of seniors (48%) than in the Meyer et al. sample (57%) that might reflect a tendency to be more open to close attachments among older people.

AG > 2 (16%) was also higher in our sample than in the composite international adult sample (4%). Research on the expression of aggressiveness and assertiveness in old age has yielded inconsistent findings that may be related to cultural differences. Some studies have found that elderly people in general have a considerable deficit in their repertoire of assertive social skills, whereas other studies have found that older people experience less discomfort in situations requiring assertiveness than do younger adults, but are nevertheless less likely to respond assertively (Carneiro & Falcone, 2004; Fung & Ng, 2006).

As for self-perception, the senior sample shows a lower percentage of *Reflection* responses (*Fr+rF* > 0 = 12%) than the combined adult sample of Meyer et al. (*Fr+rF* > 0 = 25%). This finding may be explained from a psychodynamic developmental perspective elaborated in Chapter 6. From this perspective, older people become increasingly inclined to accept their faults and limitations and consequently to have a diminished need for self-promotion and self-aggrandizement. During old age, then, defense mechanisms that may be reflected by the *Fr+rF* score, such as grandiosity, may no longer be used to inflate feelings of self-worth. The decline in *Reflection* responses may accordingly identify a shift in self-perception that contributes to a more modest and balanced view of the self.

Conclusion

The current chapter provides contemporary international nonpatient Rorschach data for six samples of community-residing senior adults with no significant neurocognitive impairment (N = 274). The samples were collected in seven countries: a combined sample from Brazil and Portugal, and samples from Iran, Israel,

Italy, Spain, and the US. Comparisons among the samples showed only modest differences. These results demonstrate the cross-cultural applicability of the test and correspond to those of Meyer et al. (2007), who reported a similar convergent trend among international samples of nonpatient adults.

Comparisons of our new international sample of nonpatient seniors with the composite international sample of Meyer et al. (2007) showed similarities between them for most of the key variables. These key variables can therefore serve as a basis for drawing inferences on the personality functioning and subjective experience of senior adults. Thus, the CS reference data for seniors presented in this chapter have important implications for clinical practice with older adults. Using the new data in clinical practice should help ensure that patients are being evaluated relative to a contemporary and broadly generalizable reference standard.

The apparent adult and senior adult stability of most Rorschach scores suggests in turn that most aspects of personality functioning are little if at all altered by age. These findings reveal a healthier psychological profile of the aging personality than what was suggested by earlier studies of the Rorschach. This healthy profile was predicted by Reichlin (1984), who attributed the psychopathological manifestations that seemed to characterize seniors in these early studies to moderator variables that are commonly found in older adults, such as residential status and cognitive deterioration. Indeed, when these variables are adequately controlled, the Rorschach scores of older adults closely resemble those of younger adults. An additional possible reason for the emergence of this healthier Rorschach picture may be improvements in the quality of life enjoyed by older people in the twenty-first century as compared to the previous century, partially as a result of advances in gerontology, public health, and medical science.

Moreover, our Rorschach results accord with numerous gerontological studies showing that personality changes little with increasing age (Ruth & Coleman, 1996; Staudinger, Freund, Linden, & Maas, 1999). These findings contradict common stereotypes of old age, and the facts are that: (1) positive emotions outweigh negative emotions up until very old age; (2) regressive coping styles are relatively rare in the elderly; (3) elderly adults invest more thoughts and actions in current health and family matters than in dying, death, or their past; (4) older adults attain a medium score on measures of optimism and orientation toward the future; (5) the degree of personal life investment does not decrease as much with age as might be expected from biological models of vitality; and (6) age differences in investment consist mainly of changes of content, not of perspective. Taken together, these six facts present a more positive image of the elderly than has often been portrayed.

Differences that have been found between the Rorschach scores of adults and those of senior adults have reflected expected developmental changes from adulthood to old age. The reflection of these expected developmental changes in age-related Rorschach structural variables exemplifies the construct validity of Rorschach assessment. Developmental changes that may call for somewhat different cutoff scores in order to differentiate normal from psychopathological functioning are elaborated in Chapter 6.

References

Ames, L. B. (1960). Age changes in the Rorschach responses of a group of elderly individuals. *Journal of Genetic Psychology, 97*(2), 257–285.

Ames, L. B. (1974). Calibration of aging. *Journal of Personality Assessment, 38*(6), 507–529.

Ames, L. B., Learned, J., Métraux, R. W., & Walker, R. N. (1954). *Rorschach responses in old age.* New York, NY: Brunner/Mazel.

Carneiro, R. S., & Falcone, E. M. D. O. (2004). Um estudo das capacidades e deficiências em habilidades sociais na terceira idade. *Psicologia em Estudo, 9*(1), 119–126.

Carstensen, L. L., Fung, H. H., & Charles, S. T. (2003). Socioemotional selectivity theory and the regulation of emotion in the second half of life. *Motivation and Emotion, 27*(2), 103–123.

Chesrow, E. J., Wosika, P. H., & Reintz, A. H. (1949). A psychometric evaluation of aged white males. *Geriatrics (Basel, Switzerland), 4*(3), 169–177.

Coubard, O. A., Duretz, S., Lefebvre, V., Lapalus, P., & Ferrufino, L. (2011). Practice of contemporary dance improves cognitive flexibility in aging. *Frontiers in Aging Neuroscience, 3,* 13.

Good, C. D., Johnsrude, I. S., Ashburner, J., Henson, R. N., Friston, K. J., & Frackowiak, R. S. (2001). A voxel-based morphometric study of ageing in 465 normal adult human brains. *Neuroimage, 14*(1), 21–36.

Davidson, H. H., & Kruglov, L. (1952). Personality characteristics of the institutionalized aged. *Journal of Consulting Psychology, 16*(1), 5–12.

Eisdorfer, C. (1960). Developmental level and sensory impairment in the aged. *Journal of Projective Techniques, 24,* 129–132.

Exner, J. E., Jr. (2003). *The Rorschach: A comprehensive system: Vol. 1. Basic foundations and principles of interpretation* (4th ed.). New York, NY: Wiley.

Exner, J. E., Jr. (2007). A new US adult nonpatient sample. *Journal of Personality Assessment, 89*(Suppl. 1), S154–S158.

Fung, H. H., & Ng, S. K. (2006). Age differences in the sixth personality factor: Age differences in interpersonal relatedness among Canadians and Hong Kong Chinese. *Psychology and Aging, 21*(4), 810–814.

Good, C. D., Johnsrude, I. S., Ashburner, J., Henson, R. N., Friston, K. J., & Frackowiak, R. S. (2001). A voxel-based morphometric study of ageing in 465 normal adult human brains. *Neuroimage, 14*(1), 21–36.

Gross, A., Newton, R. R., & Brooks, R. B. (1990). Rorschach responses in healthy, community dwelling older adults. *Journal of Personality Assessment, 55*(1–2), 335–343.

Grossman, C., Warshawsky, F., & Hertz, M. (1951). Rorschach studies of personality characteristics of a group of institutionalized old people. *Journal of Gerontology, 6*(4), 97.

Ilonen, T., Salokangas, R. K., & Turku Study Group (2016). The Rorschach Coping Deficit Index as an indicator of neurocognitive dysfunction. *Rorschachiana, 37,* 28–49.

Klopfer, W. G. (1946). Personality patterns of old age. *Rorschach Research Exchange, 10*(4), 145–166.

Kring, A. M., Davison, G. C., Neale, J. M., & Johnson, S. L. (2007). *Abnormal psychology* (10th ed.). Phoenix, AZ: Wiley.

Light, B. H., & Amick, J. H. (1956). Rorschach responses of normal aged. *Journal of Projective Techniques, 20*(2), 185–195.

Lingiardi, V., & McWilliams, N. (Eds.). (2017). *Psychodynamic diagnostic manual: PDM-2.* New York, NY: Guilford Publications.

Mattlar, C. E. (2001). Rorschach profiles of 71 year old Finnish males. Presented at: 2001 Mid-Winter Meeting of the Society for Personality Assessment, Philadelphia, PA.

Mattlar, C. E., Knuts, L. R., & Virtanen, E. (1985). Personality structure on the Rorschach for a group of healthy 71-year-old females and males. *British Journal of Projective Psychology & Personality Study, 30*(1), 3–8.

Meyer, G. J., Erdberg, P., & Shaffer, T. W. (2007). Toward international normative reference data for the Comprehensive System. *Journal of Personality Assessment, 89*(Suppl. 1), S201–S216.

Muzio, E. (2006). *Vers une approche neuropsychologique intégrée de la personnalité à travers le Rorschach en gériatrie et dans la démence de type Alzheimer* (doctoral dissertation). Paris, France: University of Paris.

Pertchik, K., Shaffer, T. W., Erdberg, P., & Margolin, D. I. (2007). Rorschach Comprehensive System data for a sample of 52 older adult nonpatients from the United States. *Journal of Personality Assessment, 89*(Suppl. 1), S166–S173.

Pires, A. A. (2007). Rorschach Comprehensive System data for a sample of 309 adult nonpatients from Portugal. *Journal of Personality Assessment, 89*(Suppl. 1), S124–S130.

Prados, M., & Fried, E. G. (1947). Personality structure of the older age groups. *Journal of Clinical Psychology, 3*(2), 113–120.

Reichlin, R. E. (1984). Current perspectives on Rorschach performance among older adults. *Journal of Personality Assessment, 48*(1), 71–81.

Rorschach, H. (1921/1942). *Psychodiagnostics: A diagnostic test based on perception.* Bern, Switzerland: Hans Huber.

Ruth, J. E., & Coleman, P. (1996). Personality and aging: Coping with management of the self in later life. In J. E. Birren, K.W. Schaie, R. P. Abeles, M. Gatz, & T. A. Salthouse (Eds.), *Handbook of the psychology of aging* (4th ed., pp. 308–322). San Diego, CA: Academic Press.

Salthouse, T. A. (1985). Speed of behavior and its implications for cognition. In J. E. Birren & W. K. Schaie (Eds.), *Handbook of the psychology of aging* (2nd ed., pp. 400–426). New York, NY: Van Nostrand Reinhold.

Sangro, F. M. (1997). Location tables, form quality, and popular responses in a Spanish sample of 470 subjects. *Rorschachiana, 22*(1), 38–66.

Shimonaka, Y., & Nakazato, K. (1991). Aging and terminal changes in Rorschach responses among the Japanese elderly. *Journal of Personality Assessment, 57*(1), 10–18.

Sorel, O., & Pennequin, V. (2008). Aging of the planning process: The role of executive functioning. *Brain and Cognition, 66*(2), 196–201.

Spitze, G., & Gallant, M. P. (2004). "The bitter with the sweet": Older adults' strategies for handling ambivalence in relations with their adult children. *Research on Aging, 26*(4), 387–412.

Staudinger, U. M., Freund, A. M., Linden, M., & Maas, I. (1999). Self, personality, and life regulation: Facets of psychological resilience in old age. In P. B. Baltes & K. U.

Mayer (Eds.), *The Berlin Aging Study: Aging from 70 to 100* (pp. 302–328). New York, NY: Cambridge University Press.

Tibon, S., Rothschild, L., Appel, L., & Zeligman, R. (2011). Assessing effects of national trauma on adaptive functioning of mentally healthy adults: an exploratory Rorschach study. *Psychology*, *2*(9), 953–960.

Tibon-Czopp, S., & Weiner, I. B. (2016). The Rorschach Inkblot Method: Theory. In *Rorschach assessment of adolescents* (pp. 47–63). New York, NY: Springer.

Vázquez Orellana, N. (2003). *La enfermedad de Alzheimer a través del Psicodiagnóstico de Rorschach* (doctoral dissertation). Tarragona, Spain: Rovira i Virgili University.

CHAPTER 6

Developmental Issues

Human orthogenesis, which conceptualizes development as a process occurring across the lifespan, is currently the most prominent theoretical emphasis in the field of developmental psychology. This field of study focuses on age-related changes, normal development, and psychopathological manifestations (Overton, 2010). There is also a strong research focus on various contextual ecological systems that have a substantial impact on development across the lifespan. Accordingly, aging is currently viewed as a relational developmental process that occurs in reciprocal relationships between individuals and their contexts (see Chapter 1).

Lifespan developmental conceptualization is based on a variety of theoretical perspectives that include recognition of multidirectionality in ontogenetic change and consideration of both age-connected and -disconnected developmental factors. These perspectives focus on the dynamic and continuous interplay between growth and decline, historical embeddedness and other structural contextual factors, and the range of plasticity in development. The developing individual is perceived as inherently active, self-creating, self-organizing, self-regulating, nonlinear, complex, and adaptive. This conceptualization reprises and extends Werner's (1948, 1957) orthogenetic principle that developmental changes involve both differentiation and integration.

Basic Developmental Concepts in Aging

Contemporary neuroscience findings and accumulating empirical evidence support the view that personality changes with age occur within a context that is composed of many factors that are biological, social, cultural, and historical. As noted in Chapter 1, Erikson's (1956, 1959) theory delineated eight stages of psychosocial development that continue throughout the life cycle, in which the first five extend from infancy through adolescence and the last three to adulthood. According to Erikson, early adulthood is characterized by a search for intimacy versus experiencing isolation; middle adulthood involves a drive toward generativity while avoiding the perils of stagnation; and late adulthood is marked by searching for a sense of integrity versus falling into despair. Wisdom is the emerging coping strength achievement of old age and normally lends integrity to late life experience, despite declines in bodily and mental functions. As a practical force in the older years, integrity underlies the drive to be vitally involved as caregivers, role models, and guides for others across the generations.

While elaborating Erikson's theory, Cohen (1999) suggested that the ever-extant potential for psychological growth occurs not in spite of old age, but because of it. He defined four developmental phases in adulthood. The first phase, labeled as *midlife reevaluation*, begins in the mid-to-late 30s and typically continues through the mid-60s. This phase involves newfound motivation to reevaluate one's life and make positive changes using what is called "quest energy." Next comes the *liberation phase*, usually occurring between the mid-60s and mid-70s and characterized by a sense of needing to act now, often by engaging in experimental or innovative activities that were not considered in the past. This liberation phase is commonly supported by the new personal freedom and creativity conferred in part by retirement. The *summing-up phase* then occurs in one's late 60s to 90s and is energized by enhanced wisdom and a desire to contribute to the world. The resulting activities in these late years often involve a search for a larger meaning in life. The *encore phase* coming last, from the late 70s to the demise, is characterized by personal reflections and activities that restate, reaffirm, and celebrate the major themes in one's life.

Cohen's optimistic view of human potential in the second half of life is supported by current advances in neuroscience. More specifically, his view is based on four newly established key attributes of the brain: (1) the plasticity of the aging brain, which results in the brain continually resculpting itself in response to experience and learning (Colcombe et al., 2004; Gutchess, 2014; Kramer, Bherer, Colcombe, Dong, & Greenough, 2004); (2) neurogenesis in the aging brain, which means that new brain cells are being formed throughout life (Alvarez-Buylla & García-Verdugo, 2002; Derrick, York, & Martinez, 2000; Galvan & Jin, 2007; Kempermann, Wiskott, & Gage, 2004); (3) decreased reactivity of the amygdala to negative information while maintaining or increasing its reactivity to positive information with age (Mather et al., 2004); and (4) age-related hemispheric asymmetry reductions that may have a compensatory function in the performance of specific tasks (Cabeza, 2002; Cabeza, Anderson, Locantore, & McIntosh, 2002; Reuter-Lorenz et al., 2000; Spreng, Wojtowicz, & Grady, 2010).

These advances are substantiated by accumulating empirical evidence showing that, contrary to common conceptions of personality as a stable structure and in accordance with the newer developmental theories, mean-level changes in traits do occur in meaningful and systematic ways during the life course, including the adult years. Some of this evidence comes from studies that have used the Revised NEO Personality Inventory (NEO PI-R; Costa & McCrae, 1992) to assess personality in terms of the five-factor model of personality (McCrae et al., 1999, 2000). Other studies have used the California Psychological Inventory (CPI; Gough & Bradley, 1996) to assess personality in terms of folk concepts of important interpersonal behaviors (Helson & Kwan, 2000; Labouvie-Vief, Diehl, Tarnowski, & Shen, 2000; Yang, McCrae, & Costa, 1998).

A meta-analysis of longitudinal studies using the NEO PI-R shows that people tend to become more socially dominant, conscientious, and emotionally stable through midlife. Moreover, the period of young adulthood rather than adolescence is the primary period of mean-level personality trait development. Specific traits, such as social vitality, agreeableness, conscientiousness, and openness to experience show continued plasticity beyond age 30 and well into old age (Roberts, Walton, & Viechtbauer, 2006). The main conclusion from this meta-analysis is that personality trait development is not solely a phenomenon of childhood, but of adulthood as well. Furthermore, patterns of personality trait change in adulthood have been found to be intrinsically positive. In this line of research, normative personality change over 40 years of age was found by Helson, Jones, and Kwan (2012) in two longitudinal cohorts with hierarchical linear modeling of CPI data obtained at multiple times between ages 21 and 75. These authors identified period of life and social climate as factors in three personality changes during the adult years: scores on dominance and independence peaked in the middle age of both cohorts, and scores on responsibility were lowest during the peak years of the culture of individualism.

These changes in personality traits during old age have been demonstrated mainly with self-report measures. In contrast to these self-report measures, which elicit information about individuals' conscious understanding of themselves, implicit or performance-based measures of personality, such as the Rorschach, elicit information about cognitive functioning, affective experience, interpersonal relatedness, and self-perception, independently of whether a person being assessed is self-aware of such personality characteristics and open to providing information about them. Hence, utilizing the Rorschach to assess personality change in old age, under the conceptual framework of lifespan development, can make an important contribution to developmental science.

Applying the Rorschach for Assessing Developmental Personality Changes

Various studies have demonstrated the utility of the Rorschach in assessing developmental differences between age groups. As noted by Leichtman (2009), the most influential empirical work with respect to developmental trends shown in Rorschach normative data was conducted in the development of the Rorschach Comprehensive System (CS) age-group reference data for children and adolescents (Exner, 2001; Exner & Weiner, 1995). These Rorschach data have generally confirmed the expected developmental trends in the various domains of personality functioning (Wenar & Curtis, 1991). However, no age-group Rorschach reference data within a population of senior adults have been published prior to the present volume.

Employing the Rorschach for examining developmental personality change in the elderly is important not only for enhancing the theory and clinical utility of the instrument, but also for demonstrating aspects of its construct validity. Such demographic characteristics as a person's age are particularly suitable for assessing the construct validity of an assessment instrument, because they are independently observed variables that have little if any error variance and are completely independent of test findings (Weiner, 2001). Age differences on the Rorschach variables that emerge as predicted by the developmental theory of aging would provide powerful construct validation of the instrument. It should be stressed that developmental changes, whether occurring in childhood, in adolescence, or in adulthood, do not call for corresponding changes in the interpretation of related CS variables. Instead, as elaborated in Chapter 4, it is the implications of Rorschach scores that would be age related, not their interpretation. The presence of values that exceed the CS cutoff points should accordingly be interpreted for senior adults just as they would for any age group, or for any culture or country for that matter.

Rorschach Assessment of Younger and Older Senior Adults

The discussion of developmental trends in the present chapter is based on the international reference data presented in Chapter 5. Participants in four of the six samples that were included in the combined international sample of nonpatient senior adults (Brazil and Portugal, Iran, Israel, and Italy) were divided into two groups: "younger-old" (60–70 years of age) and "older-old" (71–87 years of age). The first group included 86 participants with a mean age of 64.73, and the second group included 45 participants with a mean age of 77.38. To compare these two groups, we computed T-scores for all of the CS variables in each of the groups, using Meyer et al.'s (2007) reference data for adults as a benchmark. Differences of more than 5 T-score points in CS markers between the two age groups, which is equal to 0.5 SD, were considered meaningful. Table 6.1 presents means and T-scores of the CS variables for the two age groups. Table 6.2 provides weighted frequencies for selected CS variables in these groups.

Cognitive Functioning

Comparisons between the two age groups show that, consistent with contemporary and positive views of aging, and similar to the results delineated in Chapter 5, cognitive performance on the Rorschach is mostly similar between the groups. These findings demonstrate that the cognitive functioning of community-residing senior adults with no gross neurocognitive impairments stays relatively stable between the ages of 60 and 87. This cognitive resilience can be understood within multifactorial conceptions of intellectual functioning, more specifically with respect to the dynamic between fluid and crystalized intelligence. As noted in Chapter 1, fluid intelligence, which is the ability to think and reason abstractly and to solve new problems, tends to show age-related declines beginning as early as middle adulthood (Salthouse, 1991). Crystalized intelligence, which consists of the ability to make good use of previously learned knowledge and acquired

Table 6.1 Means and T-scores of CS variables in two age groups

	International Seniors			
	Younger-Old (60–70)		*Older-Old (71–87)*	
	Mean	*T-Score*	*Mean*	*T-Score*
R	20.56	48	21.76	49
W	6.87	45	7.11	46
D	10.90	52	11.27	52
Dd	2.79	48	3.38	50
S	1.56	46	1.16	44
DQ+	6.16	50	7.04	52
DQo	13.01	48	11.89	46
DQv	0.66	47	0.87	49
DQv/+	0.72	56	1.89	74
FQ+	0.17	49	0.07	48
FQxo	10.28	48	9.42	45
FQxu	5.78	49	6.29	50
FQx–	3.95	49	5.27	53
FQxNone	0.22	48	0.11	47
MQ+	0.03	48	0.00	47
MQo	1.65	46	1.96	48
MQu	0.49	48	0.78	51
MQ–	0.41	48	0.93	53
MQNone	0.01	49	0.00	49
SQual–	0.52	47	0.38	46
M	2.64	46	3.67	50
FM	4.50	55	4.82	57
M	1.45	50	1.16	48

(*continued*)

Table 6.1 (Cont.)

	International Seniors			
	Younger-Old (60–70)		*Older-Old (71–87)*	
	Mean	*T-Score*	*Mean*	*T-Score*
FC	1.48	47	1.56	48
CF	0.94	45	0.40	42
C	0.33	50	0.36	50
Cn	0.02	50	0.00	49
Sum Color	2.41	44	2.27	44
WsumC	2.17	46	1.71	44
SumC'	1.30	47	0.93	45
SumT	1.09	55	1.02	54
SumV	0.67	52	0.49	50
SumY	0.81	47	0.56	45
SumShading	3.88	49	3.00	46
Fr+rF	0.23	48	0.20	48
FD	1.85	57	2.18	60
F	7.91	48	8.04	48
(2)	6.09	48	5.20	45
3r+(2)/R	0.34	48	0.29	45
Lambda	1.24	54	0.86	50
PureF%	0.39	50	0.36	48
FM+m	5.95	54	5.98	54
EA	4.81	45	5.38	46
Es	9.84	51	8.98	50
D-Score	−1.66	43	−1.09	47
AdjD-Score	−1.17	42	−0.76	45

Table 6.1 (Cont.)

	International Seniors			
	Younger-Old (60–70)		*Older-Old (71–87)*	
	Mean	*T-Score*	*Mean*	*T-Score*
a (active)	5.41	51	6.22	54
p (passive)	3.27	48	3.53	49
Ma	1.57	47	2.13	50
Mp	1.06	46	1.47	49
Intellect	2.19	49	3.07	53
Zf	11.30	48	12.84	51
Zd	-1.94	47	−3.48	44
Blends	3.98	50	3.09	47
Blends/R	0.23	54	0.15	48
Col–Shd Blends	0.52	49	0.33	47
Afr	0.48	48	0.48	47
Popular	4.62	46	3.51	40
XA%	0.79	50	0.73	45
WDA%	0.81	49	0.75	44
X+%	0.51	49	0.44	44
X–%	0.20	50	0.24	54
Xu%	0.27	50	0.29	52
Isolate/R	0.21	51	0.27	55
H	2.14	48	3.07	53
(H)	0.84	47	0.71	46
Hd	1.05	47	1.20	48
(Hd)	0.22	45	0.02	43
Hx	0.37	50	0.62	52

(continued)

Table 6.1 (Cont.)

	International Seniors			
	Younger-Old (60–70)		*Older-Old (71–87)*	
	Mean	*T-Score*	*Mean*	*T-Score*
H+(H)+Hd+(Hd)	4.24	45	5.00	48
A	9.31	55	10.69	59
(A)	0.23	47	0.24	48
Ad	1.49	45	0.84	42
(Ad)	0.13	49	0.02	47
An	1.30	51	1.09	49
Art	1.07	49	0.89	48
Ay	0.58	51	0.58	51
Bl	0.24	50	0.27	50
Bt	1.31	49	1.98	54
Cg	1.29	47	1.16	46
Cl	0.26	52	0.11	49
Ex	0.03	47	0.04	47
Fi	0.41	49	0.18	46
Food	0.62	54	1.16	63
Ge	0.16	48	0.16	48
Hh	0.76	49	0.69	49
Ls	0.90	50	1.02	51
Na	0.73	50	1.16	54
Sc	0.98	49	1.29	51
Sx	0.47	50	0.40	49
Xy	0.21	50	0.11	48
Idiographic	0.70	48	0.58	47

Table 6.1 (Cont.)

	International Seniors			
	Younger-Old (60–70)		*Older-Old (71–87)*	
	Mean	*T-Score*	*Mean*	*T-Score*
An+Xy	1.51	51	1.20	49
DV	0.69	50	0.91	53
INCOM	0.35	46	0.51	48
DR	0.63	51	0.69	52
FABCOM	0.41	49	0.67	53
DV2	0.01	50	0.07	54
INC2	0.06	49	0.04	48
DR2	0.10	51	0.02	49
FAB2	0.14	52	0.00	47
ALOG	0.13	49	0.07	48
CONTAM	0.01	49	0.00	49
Sum 6 Sp Sc	2.52	49	2.98	51
Lvl 2 Sp Sc	0.31	51	0.13	48
WSum6	7.48	50	7.44	50
AB	0.27	49	0.80	56
AG	1.08	56	1.84	65
COP	1.28	52	1.78	56
CP	0.00	49	0.02	50
GHR	2.86	46	2.67	45
PHR	2.71	49	4.29	56
MOR	1.42	51	1.36	51
PER	0.73	50	0.62	49
PSV	0.28	51	0.33	52

(*continued*)

Table 6.1 (Cont.)

	International Seniors			
	Younger-Old (60–70)		*Older-Old (71–87)*	
	Mean	*T-Score*	*Mean*	*T-Score*
PTI Total	0.77	52	1.02	55
DEPI Total	3.99	51	3.71	49
CDI Total	3.40	54	3.27	53
S-CON Total	5.13	53	4.84	51
HVI Total	1.48	42	1.30	41
OBS Total (1–5)	1.11	50	1.14	50
WD+	0.14	49	0.07	48
WDo	9.73	47	8.89	45
WDu	4.45	49	4.71	49
WD–	3.09	51	4.18	56
WDNone	0.21	48	0.11	47
EII-2	0.10	53	0.44	56
HRV	0.15	47	-1.62	41
AdjDMD	0.49	n/a	0.33	n/a
RPS-P	-0.62	n/a	-0.35	n/a
RFS-S	2.43	n/a	2.33	n/a

Note: Variables in bold show significant difference between the age groups

skills, is often recalled and retained over the years and may even show positive age changes during adulthood given positive cultural and personal circumstances (Baltes, 1993; Staudinger, Cornelius, & Baltes, 1989). Moreover, senior adults may become adept in drawing on their crystallized cognitive mechanics in ways that compensate for their diminished fluid cognitive capacities.

Nevertheless, there are some differences in the cognitive realm between the younger-old and older-old samples, specifically in the mean scores for *DQv/+*, *P*, and *AB*. As noted in Chapter 5, the deviant *DQv/+* comes largely from the Iranian sample and is most likely due to different criteria for coding this specific variable.

Table 6.2 Frequencies for selected CS variables in the two age groups: the average proportions of people in four domains of personality—cognitive functioning, affective experience, interpersonal relatedness, and self-perception

Variables	*Reference Values*	*International Seniors*	
		Younger-Old (60–70)	*Older-Old (71–87)*
Cognitive functioning			
General indices			
PTI	*PTI* > 3	2%	0%
EII-2	*EII-2* > 0	47%	51%
RFS-P	***RFS-P* < −0.51**	24%	46%
	RFS-P > +0.65	18%	15%
RFS-S	***RFS-S* > 2.70**	37%	23%
Attention (processing)			
Lambda	*L* < 0.30	24%	31%
	L > 0.99	26%	27%
W:D:Dd	*W* > 0.50	20%	13%
	D < 0.50	44%	44%
	Dd > 0.15	35%	42%
Zd	*Zd* > +3	12%	11%
	***Zd* < −3**	39%	47%
DQv	*DQv* > 2	9%	11%
Perception (mediation)			
XA%	***XA%* < 0.70**	24%	33%
WDA%	***WDA%* < 0.75**	24%	40%
X−%	***X−%* > 0.30**	22%	31%
Xu%	*Xu%* > 0.30	37%	31%
	Xu% < 0.10	8%	7%

(continued)

Table 6.2 (Cont.)

Variables	*Reference Values*	*International Seniors*	
		Younger-Old (60–70)	*Older-Old (71–87)*
Popular	***P* < 4**	33%	49%
	P > 7	10%	7%
Thinking (ideation)			
WSum6	***WSum6* > 10**	24%	33%
	***WSum6* > 17**	13%	4%
Lvl 2 Sp Sc	*Lv2 Sp Sc* > 0	15%	11%
Mp:Ma	*Mp* > *Ma*	28%	22%
Introversive EBper	***EA* < 10:*M* > *WSumC* + 2;** ***EA* > 10:*M* > *WSumC* + 2.5**	23%	38%
FM+m	*FM+m* > 6	38%	36%
INTELL	*2AB+Art+Ay* > 5	12%	18%
Affective experience			
Afr	*Afr* < 0.40	34%	32%
	Afr > 0.89	4%	2%
WSumC	***WSumC* < 2.5**	64%	73%
Const.	*SumC'* > *WsumC*	22%	18%
DEPI	***DEPI* = 5 or higher**	35%	24%
S-CON	*S-CON* = 8 or higher	9%	7%
Eb	*FM+m* < *SumShd*	21%	18%
Col–Shd Bld	*Col–Shd Bld* > 1	10%	11%
D-Score	*D-Score* < −1	39%	38%
	D-Score > 0	6%	13%
AdjD-Score	*AdjD-Score* < −1	33%	31%
	AdjD-Score > 0	9%	13%

Table 6.2 (Cont.)

Variables	*Reference Values*	*International Seniors*	
		Younger-Old (60–70)	*Older-Old (71–87)*
AdjDMD	***AdjDMD* > 1**	29%	20%
S	*S* > 3	9%	7%
Extratensive EBper	*EA* < 10:*WSumC* > *M* + 1.5; *EA* > 10:*WSumC* > *M* + 2	15%	11%
FC:CF+C	*FC* > (*CF+C*) + 2	17%	16%
	(*CF+C*) > *FC* + 2	9%	4%
Pure C	*Pure C* > 1	6%	9%
Interpersonal relatedness			
EA	*EA* < 6	67%	62%
CDI	***CDI* > 3**	50%	40%
H+(H)+Hd+(Hd)	*H+(H)+Hd+(Hd)* < 2	15%	22%
Isolation Index	***Isolation Index* > .25**	28%	42%
H:Hd+(H)+(Hd)	***H* < *Hd+(H)+(Hd)***	42%	27%
SumT	*SumT* = 0	49%	53%
	SumT > 1	26%	20%
HVI	*HVI Positive*	5%	0%
COP	***COP* = 0**	50%	36%
AG	***AG* > 2**	13%	33%
a:p	*p* > *a* + 1	15%	18%
M–	***M–* > 1**	9%	20%
Fd	***Fd* > 0**	36%	62%
PER	*PER* > 2	9%	7%
Self-perception			
Fr+rF	***Fr+rF* > 0**	15%	7%

(*continued*)

Table 6.2 (Cont.)

Variables	*Reference Values*	*International Seniors*	
		Younger-Old (60–70)	*Older-Old (71–87)*
Egoc. Index	**3r+(2)/R < 0.33**	49%	60%
	3r+(2)/R > 0.44	29%	22%
Sum V	**SumV > 0**	41%	27%
MOR	*MOR* > 2	20%	18%
FD	**FD = 0**	42%	33%
	FD > 2	23%	38%

Note: Variables in bold show significant difference between the age groups

The lowered *Popular* responses may represent the tendency of older adults in the *liberation phase* to behave in accordance with their own feelings and attitudes in response to social expectations as compared to younger adults (Reifman, Klein, & Murphy, 1989). However, this finding appears to be culture dependent (Fung & Ng, 2006). The elevated *AB* responses, that reflect increased use of symbolic thinking, may derive from the desire to find larger meaning of life, characterizing the *summing up* phase. For example, responding to Card II, a 67-year-old woman said, "Hope ... a positive feeling that enables living." Another woman, aged 80, gave the following response to card VI: "The emphasized part symbolizes a personality with self-confidence. It's like you give a child a good base, you become less important for him but he can spread wings."

With respect to deviant cutoff scores within the cognitive realm, the data in Table 6.2 show a substantial difference of more than 7% in the frequencies of the cutoff scores for *RFS-P* < –0.51, *RFS-S* > 2.70, *Zd* < –3, *XA%* < 0.70, *X–%* > 0.30, *P* < 4, *WSum6* > 10, *WSum6* > 17, and *Introversive EBper*. As for *RFS-P*, the higher percentage of *RFS-P* < –0.51 in the older group (46%) than in the younger group (24%) may reflect a developmental shift, with adolescents showing more inclination than adults to adhere to reality (Tibon-Czopp & Weiner, 2016), young adults showing a balance between reality and fantasy (Tibon-Czopp, Appel, & Zeligman, 2016), and older adults showing a greater disposition to exercise fantasy.

In this regard, it may be the case that adolescents, who are in the process of adjusting to reality demands, rely strongly on the external world, whereas senior adults, as they outgrow previous commitments and move into the *liberation phase*, allow themselves to lean increasingly on input from their inner world. However, the tendency to fluctuate between reality and fantasy is lowered as people age, as shown by the lowered frequency of *RFS-S* > 2.7 in the older-old group (23%) as compared to the younger-old group (37%).

In addition, within the attention subdomain of cognitive functioning, Table 6.2 shows a higher percentage of *Zd* < −3 in the older group (47%) than in the younger group (39%). This apparently normal age-related decrease in careful attention (Del Corno & Plotkin, 2017), which leads to processing new information less thoroughly than would be desirable, may point to a progressive deterioration in fluid mechanics. This may also be the case in the perception subdomain, with elevated frequencies of cutoff scores for *XA%* < 0.70, *WDA%* < 0.75, and *X−%* > 0.30 in the older group (33%, 40%, and 41%, respectively) as compared to the younger group (24%, 24%, and 22%, respectively), which taken together point toward a normal age-related decrease in perceptual accuracy (Sara & Faubert, 2000).

With respect to the thinking subdomain of cognitive functioning, *WSum6* > 10 is present in 24% of the younger-old group compared to 33% in the older-old group, but this trend is reversed for *WSum6* > 17, which characterizes 13% of the younger-olds but only 4% of the older-olds. These scores may reflect late-life thinking, which is composed of synthesis, reflection, and wisdom and constitutes a major aspect of late-life creativity (Addams-Price, 1998). The elevation in the frequency of *Introversive EBPer* in older age (38% as compared to 23%), which indicates an increased preference for reflective contemplation over affective expression, can be partially explained by the reduction in *WSumC*, which will be further discussed below.

Affective Experience

Within the affective domain, a significant difference in mean scores between the age groups was found only in *Blends/R*. Participants in the older group show less emotional complexity as compared to participants in the younger group. Indeed, research illustrates that from age 60 onward, individuals tend to show less cognitive–affective complexity (Labouvie-Vief & Medler, 2002). Labouvie-Vief, Diehl, Jain, and Zhang (2007) relate these results to the cognitive decline in fluid capabilities. They offer a theoretical framework in which decreases in complexity can result in compensatory increases in optimization.

Our results further support this hypothesis, as lowered frequencies of both *DEPI* ≥ 5 and *AdjDMD* > 1 in the older group (24% and 20%, respectively) as compared to the younger group (35% and 29%, respectively) were found. These decreases may imply that older seniors experience less subjective distress than younger seniors. In a similar vein, empirical evidence from both cross-sectional and longitudinal studies shows improved emotional experience as people age (Carstensen, Pasupathi, Mayr, & Nesselroade, 2000; Charles, Reynolds, & Gatz, 2001; Gross et al., 1997; Mroczek, 2001). Reviewing results from a series of behavioral studies and conducting a functional magnetic resonance imaging study that showed greater amygdala activation for positive than negative stimuli in older adults but not in younger ones, Mather et al. (2004) suggest that this improvement in emotional experience may be associated with developmental changes in the way emotional information is initially processed and later remembered. Indeed, according to socioemotional selectivity theory (Carstensen, Isaacowitz, & Charles, 1999), as adults age, they increasingly experience an awareness of time being limited and so shift their motivational goals. Goals that focus on the future, such as knowledge acquisition, become less important. Instead, they focus on changes to emotional well-being and meaningful emotional aspects of life. Emotion regulation becomes a higher priority, and older people appear to diminish the processing of negative information that might reduce positive affect. Thus, it might be that changes in priorities across the lifespan may be related to changes in the neural substrates of emotion.

Another difference in the frequency of affective cutoff scores was found in *WSumC* < 2.5, which was elevated in the older group (73%) as compared to the younger one (64%), indicating a lowered capacity to process and express emotional experience in older age. In this respect, it should be noted that findings regarding emotional expressiveness and aging are inconsistent and point toward the possibility that age-related declines in emotional expressivity may be limited primarily to negative as opposed to positive emotions (Gross et al., 1997; Magai, Consedine, Krivoshekova, Kudadjie-Gyamfi, & McPherson, 2006; Pennebaker & Stone, 2003). These results are also in line with the positive affective valence derived from the socioemotional selectivity theory.

Interpersonal Relatedness

Within the interpersonal relatedness domain, significant differences between the age groups were found in the mean scores of *Food*, *AG*, *PHR*, and *HRV*, and in the frequencies of *CDI* > 3, *Isolation Index* > 0.25, *H* < *Hd+(H)+(Hd)*, *COP* = 0, *AG* > 2, *M–* > 1, and *Fd* > 0. The findings suggest that as people age, not only their need to be engaged in satisfying interpersonal relationship is similar to that of younger senior adults, they also cope more effectively with life events, especially those that involve interpersonal interaction (as shown by the decreased frequency of *CDI* > *3* from 50% in the younger group to 40% in the older group), feel more comfortable in social situations (as shown by the decreased frequency of *H* < *Hd+(H)+(Hd* from 42% in the younger group to 27% in the older group), have exacerbated dependency needs (as shown by the elevated frequency of *Fd* > *0* from 36% in the younger group to 62% in the older group), show elevated interest in collaborative engagement with others (as shown by the decreased frequency of *COP* = *0* from 50% in the younger group to 36% in the older group), and behave toward others in a more assertive fashion (as shown by the elevated frequency of *AG* > *2* from 13% in the younger group to 33% in the older group). On the other hand, they may limit their involvement in interpersonal and social interactions (as shown by the elevated frequency of *Isolation Index* > 0.25 from 28% in the younger group to 42% in the older group) and have more faulty perceptions of people (as shown by the elevated frequency of *M–* > 1 from 9% in the younger group to 20% in the older group). These seemingly contradicting results are also evident in other empirical studies and may be explained in light of the socioemotional selectivity theory, which suggests that although the size of older people's social networks is reduced, an increasingly large percentage of their total network is occupied by emotionally close social partners. It has been suggested that such differences are not due to age, but to differences in the perception of future time (Carstensen, Isaacowitz, & Charles, 1999).

Indeed, research shows that older adults more readily sever superficial or unsatisfying relationships in order to spend their time with people they care about and with whom they feel comfortable and able to freely express their true selves. In accord with lifespan theories, the older-old cope at least as effectively as their younger counterparts—despite the likelihood that they will face physical ills or losses of one sort or another—by regulating their emotions through influencing the interpersonal situations they will experience. Moreover, people become better at adapting to their conditions as they get older. Regardless of their health status, older people typically are better prepared—in terms of both satisfaction with life and coping capacities—to face the vicissitudes of aging (Hamarat, Thompson, Steele, Matheny, & Simons, 2002; Staudinger, Marsiske, & Baltes, 1995).

Self-Perception

With respect to the self-perception domain, no differences were found between the groups in variables mean scores. However, differences were found in the frequencies of cutoff scores of $Fr+rF > 0$, $3r+(2)/R < 0.33$, $SumV > 0$, $FD = 0$, and $FD > 2$. The older group showed a lower percentage of reflection responses ($Fr+rF > 0$ = 7%) as compared to the adult sample ($Fr+rF > 0$ = 15%). This trend starts even earlier as reflected in the percentage of this score in Meyer et al.'s (2007) reference data for adults of 25%. This finding may be explained in light of Erikson's developmental theory (1959). According to this theory, older persons increasingly accept their faults and limitations and correspondingly have a diminished need for self-promotion and self-aggrandizement. During old age, defense mechanisms that may be reflected by the *Fr+rF* score such as grandiosity may no longer be used to inflate feelings of self-worth. Thus, the decline in this score may reflect a specific shift in self-conceptions that contributes to a more modest and balanced view of the self.

However, the increased frequency of $3r+(2)/R < 0.33$ in the older group (60%) as compared to the younger one (49%) may imply a lower self-esteem in old age. Nevertheless, the handful of studies that examined age differences in self-esteem in old age failed to produce a consensual portrait of age differences. Some of the findings show a decrease in self-esteem (Ranzijn et al., 1998; Robins, Trzesniewski, Tracy, Gosling, & Potter, 2002; Tiggemann & Lynch, 2001), some demonstrate that self-esteem remains stable (Brandtstadter, Wentura, & Greeve, 1993; Ryff, 1989), and some even report an increase in self-esteem (Gove, Ortega, & Style, 1989). These inconsistencies may be driven by differences in the definition and measure of the structure, as well as diversity in the sociodemographic characteristics of the samples. While reduced self-esteem in aging is thought to be related to an increase in the risk of potential losses with advancing age, this increased risk may be countered by the considerable resourcefulness and adaptive flexibility of many aging people. Our results may shed some light on these conflicting viewpoints by showing a shift in the balance between self-focusing and attending to others, which may reflect the developmental need to give back as a means of finding a larger meaning in life, characterizing the *summing-up* phase.

This interpretation gains strength when combining the decreased frequency in the older group of *SumV* > 0 (27% versus 41%) and *FD* = 0 (33% versus 42%) with the increased frequency of *FD* > 2 (38% versus 23%), which indicates that introspection becomes more central and positive as people age. Indeed, research on the aging self has identified life review as a potentially relevant activity involved in the construction, maintenance, and transformation of the self (Haber, 2006). In this respect, life review is seen as a highly complex process of self-regulation encompassing the reconstruction, explanation, and evaluation of the past. The effective use of life review as a protective mechanism or resource of the self is considered by developmental theories that conceptualize an individual's life review as a rich resource for the restoration of psychological balance in current late-life circumstances, especially in the face of death. Thus, when experiences of aging have a negative impact on a person's current sense of self, reviewing past experiences can redefine one's current sense of self in light of past achievements (Cohen, 1999; Molinari & Reichlin, 1985). Indeed, successful aging was found in "noticeable" life reviewers as compared to "slight" life reviewers (Wong & Watt, 1991).

Conclusion

The current chapter presents major features of the developmental process in old age as they emerge from the Rorschach. Contemporary reference samples of nonpatient senior adults divided into two age groups of younger-old (60–70) and older-old (71–87) closely resemble each other and the composite adult sample of Meyer et al. (2007) in their Rorschach data. There are nevertheless some differences in the Rorschach structural scores that reflect expected developmental changes in old age.

In the cognitive realm, the Rorschach scores reflect the predicted decrease in processing new information carefully (*Zd*) and perceiving novel stimuli accurately (*XA%*, *WDA%*, and *X–%*), which point to a normative age-related decrease in fluid intelligence. However, as people age, they tend to express their attitudes more freely (*P*), use symbolic thinking as part of their search for meaning in life (*AB*), and enjoy increased cognitive inner freedom (*RFS-P*). Within the affective domain, the results show the predicted decrease in emotional complexity (*Blends/R*) and expressiveness (*WSumC*) along with less subjective distress (*DEPI* and *AdjDMD*). Within the interpersonal relatedness domain, while limiting their involvement in social interactions (*Isolation Index*) and having more faulty perceptions of people (*M–*), older seniors feel more comfortable in social situations (*H* < *Hd+[H]+[Hd]*) that can fulfill their exacerbated dependency needs (*Fd*). Furthermore, they show elevated interest in collaborative engagement with people (*COP*) and tend to behave in a more assertive fashion (*AG*), leading to coping more effectively with interpersonal conditions (*CDI*). Finally, within the self-perception domain, as people age, they show a shift in the balance between self-focusing (*Fr+rF*) and attending to other people (*3r+(2)/R* < 0.33). In addition, they are more involved in positive introspection (*SumV* and *FD*), maybe as part of the process of life review, which in turn can promote psychological and physical health.

The normative age changes, as shown in this chapter, are consistent with the theoretical conceptualization of personality development in old age. The concepts of lifespan and functional plasticity that focus on processes of growth and decline are thus validated by the empirical data. However, our results lack representation of the oldest-old senior adults. Research findings on this age group demonstrate that the fourth age entails a level of biocultural incompleteness, vulnerability, and unpredictability that is distinct from the positive views of the third age (Baltes & Smith, 2003). Further research is needed in order to confirm these findings. Nevertheless, our results place the Rorschach as productive at promoting positive human development across the lifespan for diverse people around the world.

References

Addams-Price, C. (1998). *Creativity and successful aging*. New York, NY: Springer.

Alvarez-Buylla, A., & García-Verdugo, J. M. (2002). Neurogenesis in adult subventricular zone. *Journal of Neuroscience*, *22*(3), 629–634.

Baltes, P. B. (1993). The aging mind: Potential and limits. *The Gerontologist*, *33*(5), 580–594.

Baltes, P. B., & Smith, J. (2003). New frontiers in the future of aging: From successful aging of the young old to the dilemmas of the fourth age. *Gerontology*, *49*(2), 123–135.

Brandtstadter, J., Wentura, D., & Greve, W. (1993). Adaptive resources of the aging self: Outlines of an emergent perspective. *International Journal of Behavioral Development*, *16*(2), 323–349.

Cabeza, R. (2002). Hemispheric asymmetry reduction in older adults: The HAROLD model. *Psychology and Aging*, *17*(1), 85–100.

Cabeza, R., Anderson, N. D., Locantore, J. K., & McIntosh, A. R. (2002). Aging gracefully: Compensatory brain activity in high-performing older adults. *Neuroimage*, *17*(3), 1394–1402.

Carstensen, L. L., Isaacowitz, D. M., & Charles, S. T. (1999). Taking time seriously: A theory of socioemotional selectivity. *American Psychologist*, *54*(3), 165–181.

Carstensen, L. L., Pasupathi, M., Mayr, U., & Nesselroade, J. R. (2000). Emotional experience in everyday life across the adult life span. *Journal of Personality and Social Psychology*, *79*(4), 644–655.

Charles, S. T., Reynolds, C. A., & Gatz, M. (2001). Age-related differences and change in positive and negative affect over 23 years. *Journal of Personality and Social Psychology*, *80*(1), 136–151.

Cohen, G. D. (1999). Human potential phases in the second half of life: Mental health theory development. *The American Journal of Geriatric Psychiatry*, *7*(1), 1–7.

Colcombe, S. J., Kramer, A. F., McAuley, E., Erickson, K. I., & Scalf, P. (2004). Neurocognitive aging and cardiovascular fitness. *Journal of Molecular Neuroscience, 24*(1), 9–14.

Costa, P. T., & McCrae, R. R. (1992). Normal personality assessment in clinical practice: The NEO Personality Inventory. *Psychological Assessment, 4*(1), 5–13.

Del Corno, F., & Plotkin, D. (2017). Profile of mental functioning for the elderly—ME axis. In V. Lingiardi & N. McWilliams (Eds.), *Psychodynamic Diagnostic Manual* (2nd ed., pp. 755–776). New York, NY: Guilford Press.

Derrick, B. E., York, A. D., & Martinez, J. L., Jr. (2000). Increased granule cell neurogenesis in the adult dentate gyrus following mossy fiber stimulation sufficient to induce long-term potentiation. *Brain Research, 857*(1–2), 300–307.

Erikson, E. H. (1956). The problem of ego identity. *Journal of the American Psychoanalytic Association, 4*, 56–121.

Erikson, E. H. (1959). Growth and crises of the healty personality. *Psychological Issues, 1*, 50–100.

Exner, J. E. (2001). *A Rorschach workbook for the Comprehensive System* (5th ed.). Asheville, NC: Rorschach Workshops.

Exner, J. E., & Weiner, I. B. (1995). *The Rorschach: A comprehensive system (assessment of children and adolescents)* (2nd ed., Vol. 3). New York, NY: Wiley.

Fung, H. H., & Ng, S. K. (2006). Age differences in the sixth personality factor: Age differences in interpersonal relatedness among Canadians and Hong Kong Chinese. *Psychology and Aging, 21*(4), 810–814.

Galvan, V., & Jin, K. (2007). Neurogenesis in the aging brain. *Clinical Interventions in Aging, 2*(4), 605–610.

Gough, H. G., & Bradley, P. (1996). *California Personality Inventory Manual.* Palo Alto, CA: Consulting Psychologists.

Gove, W. R., Ortega, S. T., & Style, C. B. (1989). The maturational and role perspectives on aging and self through the adult years: An empirical evaluation. *American Journal of Sociology, 94*(5), 1117–1145.

Gross, J. J., Carstensen, L. L., Pasupathi, M., Tsai, J., Götestam Skorpen, C., & Hsu, A. Y. (1997). Emotion and aging: Experience, expression, and control. *Psychology and Aging, 12*(4), 590–599.

Gutchess, A. (2014). Plasticity of the aging brain: new directions in cognitive neuroscience. *Science, 346*(6209), 579–582.

Haber, D. (2006). Life review: Implementation, theory, research, and therapy. *International Journal of Aging and Human Development, 63*(2), 153–171.

Hamarat, E., Thompson, D., Steele, D., Matheny, K., & Simons, C. (2002). Age differences in coping resources and satisfaction with life among middle-aged, young-old, and oldest-old adults. *Journal of Genetic Psychology, 163*(3), 360–367.

Helson, R., Jones, C., & Kwan, V. S. (2002). Personality change over 40 years of adulthood: Hierarchical linear modeling analyses of two longitudinal samples. *Journal of Personality and Social Psychology, 83*(3), 752–766.

Helson, R., & Kwan, V. S. (2000). Personality development in adulthood: The broad picture and processes in one longitudinal sample. *Advances in Personality Psychology, 1*, 77–106.

Kempermann, G., Wiskott, L., & Gage, F. H. (2004). Functional significance of adult neurogenesis. *Current Opinion in Neurobiology, 14*(2), 186–191.

Kramer, A. F., Bherer, L., Colcombe, S. J., Dong, W., & Greenough, W. T. (2004). Environmental influences on cognitive and brain plasticity during aging. *Journals of Gerontology Series A: Biological Sciences and Medical Sciences, 59*(9), M940–M957.

Labouvie-Vief, G., Diehl, M., Tarnowski, A., & Shen, J. (2000). Age differences in adult personality: Findings from the United States and China. *Journals of Gerontology Series B, 55*(1), 4–17.

Labouvie-Vief, G., Diehl, M., Jain, E., & Zhang, F. (2007). Six-year change in affect optimization and affect complexity across the adult life span: A further examination. *Psychology and Aging, 22*(4), 738–751.

Labouvie-Vief, G., & Medler, M. (2002). Affect optimization and affect complexity: Modes and styles of regulation in adulthood. *Psychology and Aging, 17*(4), 571–588.

Leichtman, M. (2009). Concepts of development and the Rorschach: The contributions of Paul Lerner and John Exner in historical context. *Journal of Personality Assessment, 91*(1), 24–29.

Magai, C., Consedine, N. S., Krivoshekova, Y. S., Kudadjie-Gyamfi, E., & McPherson, R. (2006). Emotion experience and expression across the adult life span: Insights from a multimodal assessment study. *Psychology and Aging, 21*(2), 303–317.

Mather, M., Canli, T., English, T., Whitfield, S., Wais, P., Ochsner, K., … Carstensen, L. L. (2004). Amygdala responses to emotionally valenced stimuli in older and younger adults. *Psychological Science, 15*(4), 259–263.

McCrae, R. R., Costa, P. T., de Lima, M. P., Simões, A., Ostendorf, F., Angleitner, A., … Chae, J. H. (1999). Age differences in personality across the adult life span: parallels in five cultures. *Developmental Psychology, 35*(2), 466–477.

McCrae, R. R., Costa, P. T., Jr., Ostendorf, F., Angleitner, A., Hřebíčková, M., Avia, M. D., … Saunders, P. R. (2000). Nature over nurture: Temperament, personality, and life span development. *Journal of Personality and Social Psychology, 78*(1), 173–186.

Meyer, G. J., Erdberg, P., & Shaffer, T. W. (2007). Toward international normative reference data for the Comprehensive System. *Journal of Personality Assessment, 89*(Suppl. 1), S201–S216.

Molinari, V., & Reichlin, R. E. (1985). Life review reminiscence in the elderly: A review of the literature. *International Journal of Aging and Human Development, 20*(2), 81–92.

Mroczek, D. K. (2001). Age and emotion in adulthood. *Current Directions in Psychological Science, 10*(3), 87–90.

Overton, W. F. (2010). Life-span development: Concepts and issues. In *The handbook of life-span development* (pp. 1–29). Hoboken, NJ: Wiley.

Pennebaker, J. W., & Stone, L. D. (2003). Words of wisdom: Language use over the life span. *Journal of Personality and Social Psychology, 85*(2), 291–301.

Ranzijn, R., Keeves, J., Luszcz, M., & Feather, N. T. (1998). The role of self-perceived usefulness and competence in the self-esteem of elderly adults: Confirmatory factor analyses of the Bachman revision of Rosenberg's Self-Esteem Scale. *Journals of Gerontology Series B: Psychological Sciences and ocial Sciences, 53*(2), 96–104.

Reifman, A., Klein, J. G., & Murphy, S. T. (1989). Self-monitoring and age. *Psychology and Aging, 4*(2), 245–246.

Reuter-Lorenz, P. A., Jonides, J., Smith, E. E., Hartley, A., Miller, A., Marshuetz, C., & Koeppe, R. A. (2000). Age differences in the frontal lateralization of verbal and spatial working memory revealed by PET. *Journal of Cognitive Neuroscience, 12*(1), 174–187.

Roberts, B. W., Walton, K. E., & Viechtbauer, W. (2006). Patterns of mean-level change in personality traits across the life course: A meta-analysis of longitudinal studies. *Psychological Bulletin, 132*(1), 1–25.

Robins, R. W., Trzesniewski, K. H., Tracy, J. L., Gosling, S. D., & Potter, J. (2002). Global self-esteem across the life span. *Psychology and Aging, 17*(3), 423–434.

Ryff, C. D. (1989). In the eye of the beholder: Views of psychological well-being among middle-aged and older adults. *Psychology and Aging, 4*(2), 195–210.

Salthouse, T. A. (1991). Mediation of adult age differences in cognition by reductions in working memory and speed of processing. *Psychological Science, 2*(3), 179–183.

Sara, M., & Faubert, J. (2000). Aging, perception, and visual short-term memory for luminance-defined form. *Ophthalmic and Physiological Optics, 20*(4), 314–322.

Spreng, R. N., Wojtowicz, M., & Grady, C. L. (2010). Reliable differences in brain activity between young and old adults: a quantitative meta-analysis across multiple cognitive domains. *Neuroscience & Biobehavioral Reviews, 34*(8), 1178–1194.

Staudinger, U. M., Cornelius, S. W., & Baltes, P. B. (1989). The aging of intelligence: Potential and limits. *Annals of the American Academy of Political and Social Science, 503*(1), 43–59.

Staudinger, U. M., Marsiske, M., & Baltes, P. B. (1995). Resilience and reserve capacity in later adulthood: Potentials and limits of development across the life span. *Developmental Psychopathology, 2*, 801–847.

Tibon-Czopp, S., Appel, L., & Zeligman, R. (2016). Assessing personality patterns of functioning in a decision-making ambiguous task: The Rorschach Reality–Fantasy Scale (RFS-2). *Group Decision and Negotiation, 25*(1), 65–75.

Tibon-Czopp, S., & Weiner, I. B. (2016). The Rorschach Inkblot Method: Research. In *Rorschach assessment of adolescents* (pp. 65–95). New York, NY: Springer.

Tiggemann, M., & Lynch, J. E. (2001). Body image across the life span in adult women: The role of self-objectification. *Developmental Psychology, 37*(2), 243–253.

Weiner, I. B. (2001). Advancing the science of psychological assessment: The Rorschach Inkblot Method as exemplar. *Psychological Assessment, 13*, 423–432.

Wenar, C., & Curtis, K. M. (1991). The validity of the Rorschach for assessing cognitive and affective changes. *Journal of Personality Assessment, 57*(2), 291–308.

Werner, H. (1948). *Comparative psychology of mental development.* New York, NY: International Universities Press.

Werner, H. (1957). The concept of development from a comparative and organismic view. In D. B. Harris (Ed.), *The concept of development* (pp. 215–148). Minneapolis, MN: University of Minnesota Press.

Wong, P. T., & Watt, L. M. (1991). What types of reminiscence are associated with successful aging? *Psychology and Aging, 6*(2), 272–279.

Yang, J., McCrae, R. R., & Costa, P. T., Jr. (1998). Adult age differences in personality traits in the United States and the People's Republic of China. *Journals of Gerontology Series B: Psychological Sciences and Social Sciences, 53*(6), 375–383.

CHAPTER 7

Patients with Alzheimer's Disease

The collection of normative reference data is a basic foundation of the construction, standardization, and evaluation of any assessment tool. While nonpatient reference data are an essential part of a clinical decision-making process, wherein the data can be compared against test results, data obtained from samples of patients with various kinds of disorders are also needed to assist in drawing conclusions about specific features of impairment. By combining patient and nonpatient Rorschach data, personality dysfunction and patterns of psychological disturbance can be identified by noting how the data resemble those of patients with certain symptoms and difficulties together with determining how much their Rorschach protocols differ from those of nonpatients (Weiner, 2001). Multiple samples may also be helpful in enabling clinicians to establish cutoff points for distinguishing between healthy and psychopathological scores for a specific disorder on Rorschach variables. Having both patient and nonpatient reference data is particularly important in seniors, since clinicians need to differentiate between scores that characterize a normal aging process versus scores that delineate psychopathological manifestations.

Cognitive and Emotional Symptoms in Alzheimer's Disease

Alzheimer's disease is a chronic progressive neurodegenerative disorder and one of the most common mental health problems in the elderly. A recent report of the Alzheimer's Association (2018) reveals that 1 in 10 people aged 65 and older has Alzheimer's disease. The percentage of people with Alzheimer's disease increases with age: 3% of people aged 65–74, 17% of people aged 75–84, and 32% of people aged 85 and older. In most regions of the world, the age-standardized prevalence for those aged 60 or more varies within a narrow band of 5%–7%, with a higher prevalence in Latin America (8.5%) and a distinctively lower prevalence (2%–4%) in the four sub-Saharan African regions (Prince et al., 2013). With an aging population and the fact that age is the greatest risk factor for Alzheimer's disease, this disorder could reach epidemic proportions.

The specific criteria that guide the application of Alzheimer's disease diagnosis vary somewhat according to whether one uses guidelines established by the National Institute of Neurological and Communicative Disorders and Stroke and the Alzheimer's Disease and Related Disorders Association (NINCDS-ADRDA; McKhann et al., 1984) or by the *Diagnostic and Statistical Manual of Mental Disorders, Fifth Edition* (*DSM-5*; American Psychiatric Association, 2013). The two are similar, however, in their focus on cognitive decline in an individual that cannot otherwise be accounted for. The clinical diagnosis thus requires a decline in memory combined with degradation in at least one other cognitive domain, such as language, abstract reasoning, visuospatial skills, or executive functioning (Loewenstein, 2013).

Alzheimer's disease affects people in different ways, and people with the disorder differ in how they experience its symptoms and progress through its stages. As a consequence, differences between typical age-related cognitive changes and early signs of Alzheimer's dementia can be subtle. Nevertheless, three general stages have been identified in the typically slow progression of Alzheimer's disease: mild (early stage), moderate (middle stage), and severe (late stage). The pace at which symptoms advance from one stage to another varies among people and reflects the degree of damage to neurons in different parts of the brain. Difficulty remembering recent conversations, names, or events as well as apathy and depression are quite often early symptoms. Later-developing symptoms include impaired communication, disorientation, confusion, poor judgment, behavioral changes, and, ultimately, difficulty speaking, swallowing, and walking. Contemporary data show that changes in the brain related to Alzheimer's disease begin years before any signs of the disorder appear. This time period is referred to as preclinical Alzheimer's disease. It is thus clear that psychological functions other than memory might be impaired before a person's symptoms meet the criteria of Alzheimer's diagnosis. Prominent among these are symptoms of higher-order cognitive functions such as reasoning and executive functions, but there are also non-cognitive symptoms such as those manifested in personality disturbances (Sperling et al., 2011).

Although often neglected in the assessment process, the emotional symptoms of Alzheimer's disease are currently recognized as important and intrinsic aspects of the disease. For many years, the relevance of these symptoms was not adequately investigated, because they were considered only a secondary consequence of cognitive decline. Nevertheless, these emotional symptoms have relevant diagnostic, prognostic, and therapeutic implications, and they may provide useful clues for the clinical diagnosis of dementia subtypes (Bozeat, Gregory, Ralph, & Hodges, 2000; Hargrave, Geck, Reed, & Mungas, 2000). Emotional symptoms may occur in up to 90% of Alzheimer's patients (Piccininni, Di Carlo, Baldereschi, Zaccara, & Inzitari, 2005), appearing not only in the severe stages, but also in the mild phases of the condition, sometimes preceding cognitive dysfunction and the onset of the overt disorder (Rubin & Kinscherf, 1989). Moreover, the occurrence of these symptoms may affect cognitive functioning and thus exacerbate a patient's disability. On the other hand, treatment of patients' emotional symptoms may help to improve their cognitive symptoms, which would warrant conducting a careful and systematic evaluation of the emotional aspects of Alzheimer's disease.

There is no single test for assessing Alzheimer's disease. Instead, clinicians use a variety of approaches and tools to help make the diagnosis. These include: (1) obtaining a medical and family history from the individual, including a psychiatric history and a history of cognitive and behavioral changes; (2) asking a family member to provide information about changes in thinking skills and behavior; (3) conducting cognitive tests and physical and neurologic examinations; (4) having the individual undergo blood tests and brain imaging to rule out other potential causes of dementia symptoms, such as a tumor or certain vitamin deficiencies; and (5) in some circumstances, using brain imaging to determine whether the individual has high levels of β-amyloid, which is a hallmark of Alzheimer's disease and normal levels of which would suggest that Alzheimer's disease is not the cause of the observed dementia.

Rorschach Assessment of Patients with Alzheimer's Disease

Rorschach assessment can enhance understanding of the Alzheimer's disease global spectrum, help in identifying the typical psychological profile during the different stages of the disease, and assist in developing treatment plans that will bolster the afflicted person's sense of well-being. Given the Rorschach's impressive empirical research database in the fields of both personality and neuropsychological assessment (Muzio, 2016), it can make a substantial contribution to the diagnosis, management, and treatment of Alzheimer's disease. The Rorschach can provide a characterization of cognitive deficits and emotional functioning that includes delineation of areas of weakness that can contribute to functional impairments, now and in the future. Additionally, the Rorschach can enable follow-up assessments that can track the extent to which a patient's symptoms improve, worsen, or remain the same over time or in response to interventions.

Moreover, because such neuropsychological deficits as poor episodic memory are a consistent feature of early-emerging Alzheimer's disease but also overlap with cognitive impairments in such other disorders as depression (Swainson et al., 2001), utilizing the Rorschach in forming a differential diagnosis can be quite advantageous. While cross-sectional research illustrates the high comorbidity between depression and Alzheimer's disease, longitudinal research has demonstrated that depressive symptoms may actually be an early sign or risk factor for subsequent cognitive decline and dementia (Bieliauskas & Drag, 2013). Such non-cognitive symptoms as agitation, insomnia, weight loss, and loss of interest are also shared by both disorders. This overlap of certain symptoms creates a risk of false diagnosis of depression in cases of Alzheimer's disease, as well as difficulties in identifying a real depression in Alzheimer's disease patients.

The subjective experience of people with Alzheimer's disease is widely varied, based on premorbid history, the etiology of the disorder, and the stage of the illness. Nevertheless, the disorder itself often prevents clinicians from developing a substantive sense of a person's customary thoughts, feelings, and behavioral tendencies. Because patients with Alzheimer's disease may have lost some of their capacity for insight and their facility with language, they can find it difficult to conceptualize and describe their inner psychic lives. They may nevertheless still experience significant emotional and behavioral concerns that call for psychological intervention. Appreciation of the person's subjective experience can augment more traditional medical evaluation and identify opportunities for such therapeutic intervention that might not otherwise be considered. An implicit assessment method like the Rorschach can provide salient information about personality constructs whether or not people have accurately conceptualized these constructs, considered how they describe them, and are self-aware and openly willing to provide information relevant to these constructs (Ganellen, 2007).

Although the Rorschach has been widely used in the study of neurological populations, only a few peer-reviewed Rorschach studies have directly studied Alzheimer's patients as a distinct group, and these few studies have usually focused on the cognitive aspects of the disease (Kimoto et al., 2017; Muzio, Andronikof, David, & Di Menza, 2001; Perry, Poteratt, Auslander, Kaplan, & Jeste, 1996; Silva & Webbe, 2006). In order to enable clinicians to utilize the Rorschach in assessing Alzheimer's disease patients, it is essential to develop reference data for all of the Rorschach Comprehensive System (CS) variables in an Alzheimer's disease population.

The discussion of CS reference norms for Alzheimer's disease patients in the present chapter combines data from two Alzheimer's disease patient samples: one from France (Muzio, 2006) and the other from Spain (Vázquez Orellana, 2003). The French sample included 112 participants with a mean age of 78.57. The Spanish sample included 91 participants with a mean age of 72.03. All of the participants were diagnosed as having clinically mild to moderate Alzheimer's dementia. Using the same procedures described in Chapter 5, we created the new set of data by computing weighted average scores across the subsamples. The combined sample thus contains 203 participants with a weighted mean age of 75.64. Although this sample may not represent Alzheimer's disease patients in non-Western cultures, we believe that preliminary presentation of some contemporary reference data for evaluating Alzheimer's disease patients can provide clinicians with interpretive guidelines to use at present.

A comparison between the two subsamples showed the same trends in all of the variables except for the special scores of *DV2*, *DR2*, *ALOG*, and *CONTAM*, which were elevated only in the French sample. The elevation in these scores caused relatively high *Level 2* and *WSum6* scores in the French sample. A question remains as to whether these relatively small variations between the countries are due to differences in participants' cognitive functioning or to different criteria for coding these special scores. Despite these potential influences, the between-sample differences are modest, which further supports the cross-country transportability of the Rorschach method used for creating the combined nonpatient international sample of senior adults.

The reference data of the Alzheimer's disease sample were compared to the international senior sample presented in Chapter 5. We have also computed T-scores for all of the CS variables, using Meyer et al.'s (2007) reference data for adults as a benchmark. Table 7.1 presents means, T-scores, and minimum and maximum scores of the CS variables for the combined sample of patients with Alzheimer's disease as compared to the combined international sample of nonpatient seniors (International Seniors). Deviations are noted in bold when the value of a variable exceeds a cutoff point of 5 (T < 45 or > 55), which is equal to 0.5 SD below or above the mean value of this variable in the Meyer et al. composite international sample. Table 7.2, which is based solely on the French sample, compares weighted frequencies for selected CS variables in the combined sample of Alzheimer's patients with the international sample of nonpatient seniors.

Cognitive Functioning

Table 7.1 shows that, if cutoff points of T < 45 or > 55 are applied, deviations of the current sample of Alzheimer's disease patients from both the international senior sample and the norms established by the composite adult sample of Meyer et al. (2007) occur mostly in the cognitive domain. This is not surprising, as cognitive impairment is the hallmark feature of Alzheimer's disease and is associated with numerous cognitive changes. As elaborated in Chapter 4, cognitive functioning is measured by the Rorschach using both general indices and individual variables that are divided into three subdomains of attention (processing), perception (mediation), and thinking (ideation).

The general cognitive indices of *PTI Total* and *EII-2* are elevated with T-scores of 56 and 57, respectively. However, although Alzheimer's disease patients show inaccurate perception and disordered thinking, the great majority do not cross the threshold of a schizophrenia-spectrum or other psychotic disorder, as shown by the low frequency of *PTI* > 3 (8%). Nevertheless, *EII-2* > 0, which exists in 68% of Alzheimer's disease patients as compared to 39% in international seniors, implies deficits in ego functions of reality testing, reasoning, and quality of object relations. Apparently, neurological changes gradually weaken the ego of patients with Alzheimer's disease, and neurologically mediated functions that correspond to frontal executive functions start to deteriorate (*Psychodynamic Diagnostic Manual*; Lingiardi & McWilliams, 2017). The degradation is also manifested in the *RFS-S* index score, in which 71% of Alzheimer's disease patients deviate from the normative cutoff score as compared to 27% of international seniors. This finding, suggesting lability in thinking and forming impressions, reflects the cognitive fluctuations typical of Alzheimer's disease (Trachsel, Hermann, & Biller-Andorno, 2015).

Within the attention subdomain, deviations occur in *R*, *DQ+*, *Lambda*, *Pure F%*, *Zf*, *Blends*, and *PSV*, with T-scores of 43, 41, 66, 58, 41, 41, and 64, respectively. Perry et al. (1996), who found similar deviations, related them to the phenomena of aphasia, amnesia, and apraxia frequently observed in Alzheimer's disease patients.

Table 7.1 Means, T-scores, and minimum and maximum values of CS variables in the combined sample of Alzheimer's disease patients as compared to the international sample of nonpatient seniors

	Alzheimer's Disease Patients				*International Seniors*
Variable	*Mean*	*T-score*	*Minimum*	*Maximum*	*Mean*
R	17.16	**43**	8.00	50.00	20.33
W	6.81	45	0.00	24.00	7.36
D	8.41	47	1.00	24.00	10.08
Dd	1.94	46	0.00	21.00	2.90
S	0.85	**42**	0.00	18.00	1.56
DQ+	3.01	**41**	0.00	12.00	5.72
DQo	12.86	47	2.00	43.00	13.09
DQv	1.20	51	0.00	18.00	0.86
DQv/+	0.09	47	0.00	4.00	0.66
FQ+	0.04	47	0.00	2.00	0.15
FQxo	8.68	**44**	1.00	20.00	10.44
FQxu	3.58	**43**	0.00	17.00	5.61
FQx–	4.56	50	0.00	20.00	3.76
FQxNone	0.28	49	0.00	6.00	0.21
MQ+	0.01	48	0.00	2.00	0.04
MQo	0.87	**42**	0.00	5.00	1.69
MQu	0.13	**44**	0.00	3.00	0.56
MQ–	0.25	46	0.00	3.00	0.45
MQNone	0.00	49	0.00	1.00	0.00
SQual–	0.38	46	0.00	8.00	0.53
M	1.29	**41**	0.00	8.00	2.71
FM	3.04	48	0.00	14.00	3.84
M	0.57	**44**	0.00	7.00	1.28
FC	0.68	**43**	0.00	5.00	1.38
CF	0.58	**43**	0.00	8.00	0.86
C	0.26	49	0.00	4.00	0.29

Table 7.1 (Cont.)

	Alzheimer's Disease Patients				*International Seniors*
Variable	*Mean*	*T-score*	*Minimum*	*Maximum*	*Mean*
Cn	0.01	49	0.00	2.00	0.00
Sum Color	1.51	**41**	0.00	9.00	2.54
WsumC	1.31	**42**	0.00	8.00	1.98
SumC'	0.54	**43**	0.00	8.00	1.13
SumT	0.46	48	0.00	3.00	0.86
SumV	0.34	48	0.00	5.00	0.41
SumY	0.76	46	0.00	9.00	1.02
SumShading	2.09	**44**	0.00	14.00	3.40
Fr+rF	0.02	46	0.00	1.00	0.21
FD	0.19	**43**	0.00	5.00	1.24
F	9.74	52	1.00	35.00	8.79
(2)	6.80	49	0.00	18.00	6.63
3r+(2)/R	0.39	51	0.00	0.92	0.37
Lambda	2.41	**66**	0.05	15.00	1.31
Pure F%	0.53	**58**	0.04	0.93	0.38
FM+m	4.36	48	0.00	19.00	5.15
EA	2.65	**39**	0.00	12.00	4.72
Es	5.74	**43**	0.00	22.00	8.57
D-Score	−0.87	49	−7.00	3.00	−1.21
AdjD-Score	−0.64	46	−5.00	3.00	−0.73
a (active)	3.33	45	0.00	14.00	4.86
p (passive)	1.62	**42**	0.00	11.00	3.11
Ma	0.86	**43**	0.00	6.00	1.70
Mp	0.43	**42**	0.00	5.00	1.03
Intellect	0.78	**44**	0.00	11.00	2.04
Zf	8.00	**41**	1.00	25.00	11.28

(continued)

Table 7.1 (Cont.)

	Alzheimer's Disease Patients				*International Seniors*
Variable	*Mean*	*T-score*	*Minimum*	*Maximum*	*Mean*
Zd	–1.56	48	–17.00	18.00	–1.85
Blends	1.24	**41**	0.00	9.00	3.15
Blends/R	0.07	**42**	0.00	0.57	0.16
Col-Shd Blends	0.18	45	0.00	3.00	0.58
Afr	0.52	49	0.20	1.22	0.49
Populars	3.94	**42**	0.00	11.00	5.16
XA%	0.72	**43**	0.00	1.00	0.79
WDA%	0.74	**43**	0.00	1.00	0.80
X+%	0.52	50	0.09	0.93	0.53
X–%	0.26	**57**	0.00	0.81	0.18
Xu%	0.19	**43**	0.00	0.61	0.27
Isolate/R	0.17	48	0.00	0.94	0.21
H	1.11	**43**	0.00	7.00	2.16
(H)	0.36	**43**	0.00	4.00	0.75
Hd	0.79	46	0.00	8.00	0.99
(Hd)	0.18	45	0.00	4.00	0.27
Hx	0.11	47	0.00	4.00	0.33
H+(H)+Hd+(Hd)	2.44	**40**	0.00	11.00	4.14
A	8.70	53	0.00	21.00	9.36
(A)	0.14	46	0.00	4.00	0.23
Ad	2.05	48	0.00	14.00	1.79
(Ad)	0.06	48	0.00	5.00	0.09
An	0.75	47	0.00	16.00	1.00
Art	0.47	45	0.00	6.00	1.03
Ay	0.15	46	0.00	3.00	0.48
Bl	0.09	47	0.00	6.00	0.20
Bt	1.45	50	0.00	11.00	1.41

Table 7.1 (Cont.)

	Alzheimer's Disease Patients				*International Seniors*
Variable	*Mean*	*T-score*	*Minimum*	*Maximum*	*Mean*
Cg	0.99	45	0.00	6.00	1.41
Cl	0.20	50	0.00	6.00	0.20
Ex	0.02	46	0.00	1.00	0.06
Fi	0.08	45	0.00	4.00	0.29
Food	0.37	51	0.00	6.00	0.61
Ge	0.15	48	0.00	3.00	0.18
Hh	0.25	**44**	0.00	7.00	0.67
Ls	0.34	45	0.00	16.00	0.78
Na	0.18	45	0.00	4.00	0.76
Sc	0.39	45	0.00	6.00	0.95
Sx	0.16	47	0.00	5.00	0.29
Xy	0.01	47	0.00	1.00	0.16
Idiographic	0.90	50	0.00	7.00	0.82
An+Xy	0.92	47	0.00	16.00	1.29
DV	0.61	50	0.00	4.00	1.02
INCOM	0.47	47	0.00	4.00	0.64
DR	0.85	54	0.00	7.00	0.55
FABCOM	0.49	50	0.00	5.00	0.51
DV2	0.08	55	0.00	3.00	0.03
INC2	0.22	54	0.00	3.00	0.04
DR2	0.46	**63**	0.00	8.00	0.06
FAB2	0.18	53	0.00	5.00	0.09
ALOG	0.35	54	0.00	5.00	0.13
CONTAM	0.27	**66**	0.00	5.00	0.00
Sum 6 Sp Sc	3.98	55	0.00	17.00	3.05
Lvl 2 Sp Sc	0.95	**61**	0.00	8.00	0.22

(continued)

Table 7.1 (Cont.)

	Alzheimer's Disease Patients				*International Seniors*
Variable	*Mean*	*T-score*	*Minimum*	*Maximum*	*Mean*
WSum6	14.82	**59**	0.00	91.00	7.86
AB	0.08	47	0.00	5.00	0.27
AG	0.47	49	0.00	5.00	0.88
COP	0.41	**44**	0.00	5.00	1.21
CP	0.04	51	0.00	3.00	0.01
GHR	1.46	**40**	0.00	6.00	2.96
PHR	2.07	47	0.00	10.00	3.03
MOR	0.57	45	0.00	6.00	1.10
PER	0.38	47	0.00	7.00	0.92
PSV	1.03	**64**	0.00	12.00	0.30
PTI Total	1.52	**60**	0.00	5.00	0.80
DEPI Total	3.51	48	1.00	7.00	3.94
CDI Total	3.72	**57**	0.00	5.00	3.25
S-CON Total	4.84	51	1.00	9.00	5.03
HVI Total	1.10	**40**	0.00	7.00	1.70
OBS Total (1–5)	0.51	**43**	0.00	3.00	1.09
WD+	0.04	48	0.00	2.00	0.19
WDo	9.38	46	2.00	19.00	9.31
WDu	3.40	45	0.00	13.00	4.62
WD–	4.14	55	0.00	14.00	3.11
WDNone	0.18	48	0.00	3.00	0.22
EII-2	0.76	**60**	–1.18	4.73	0.20
HRV	–0.63	45	-9.00	6.00	–0.14
AdjDMD	0.33	n/a	0.00	4.00	0.30
RPS-P	–0.25	n/a	–3.86	2.41	–0.19
RFS-S	2.88	n/a	1.94	3.78	2.33

Note: T-scores in bold are significantly elevated or lowered in comparison to the international sample of nonpatient adults (Meyer et al., 2007)

Table 7.2 Frequencies for selected CS variables in the French sample of Alzheimer's disease patients: the average proportion of people in four domains of personality—cognitive functioning, affective experience, interpersonal relatedness, and self-perception—as compared to the international sample of nonpatient seniors

Variables	*Reference Values*	*Alzheimer's Disease Patients*	*International Seniors*
Cognitive functioning			
General indices			
PTI	*PTI* > 3	8%	3%
EII-2	*EII-2* > 0	68%	39%
RFS-P	*RFS-P* < −0.51	35%	34%
	RFS-P > +0.65	24%	20%
RFS-S	*RFS-S* > 2.70	71%	27%
Attention (processing)			
Lambda	*L* < 0.30	6%	27%
	L > 0.99	**62%**	27%
W:D:Dd	*W* > 0.50	21%	17%
	D < 0.50	45%	44%
	Dd > 0.15	33%	37%
Zd	*Zd* > +3	**5%**	15%
	Zd < −3	**45%**	35%
DQv	*DQv* > 2	17%	11%
Perception (mediation)			
XA%	*XA%* < 0.70	**43%**	23%
WDA%	*WDA%* < 0.75	**50%**	24%
X−%	*X−%* > 0.30	**38%**	19%
Xu%	*Xu%* > 0.30	19%	35%
	Xu% < 0.10	17%	7%
Populars	*P* < 4	**29%**	**30%**
	P > 7	6%	13%

(*continued*)

Table 7.2 (Cont.)

Variables	*Reference Values*	*Alzheimer's Disease Patients*	*International Seniors*
Thinking (ideation)			
WSum6	*WSum6* > 10	**62%**	27%
	WSum6 > 17	**45%**	10%
Lvl 2 Sp Sc	*Lvl 2 Sp Sc* > 0	**51%**	16%
Mp:Ma	*Mp* > *Ma*	**15%**	**23%**
Introversive EBper	*EA* < 10:*M* > *WSumC* + 2; *EA* > 10:*M* > *WSumC* + 2.5	9%	**25%**
FM+m	*FM+m* > 6	24%	37%
INTELL	*2AB+Art+Ay* > 5	**3%**	13%
Affective experience			
Afr	*Afr* < 0.40	21%	32%
	Afr > 0.89	4%	3%
WSumC	WSumC < 2.5	76%	67%
Const.	*SumC'* > *WSumC*	14%	21%
DEPI	*DEPI* = 5 or higher	**21%**	33%
S-CON	*S-CON* = 8 or higher	3%	8%
Eb	*FM+m* < *SumShd*	31%	**27%**
Col–Shd Bld	*Col–Shd Bld* > 1	3%	10%
D-Score	*D-Score* < −1	**38%**	**38%**
	D-Score > 0	**3%**	8%
AdjD-Score	*AdjD-Score* < −1	**31%**	25%
	AdjD-Score > 0	17%	12%
AdjDMD	*AdjDMD* > 1	17%	26%
S	*S* > 3	9%	8%
Extratensive EBper	*EA* < 10:*WSumC* > *M* + 1.5; *EA* > 10:*WSumC* > *M* + 2	16%	14%
FC:CF+C	*FC* > *(CF+C)* + 2	**5%**	12%
	(CF+C) > *FC* + 2	**6%**	11%

Table 7.2 (Cont.)

Variables	*Reference Values*	*Alzheimer's Disease Patients*	*International Seniors*
Pure C	*Pure C* > 1	5%	8%
Interpersonal relatedness			
EA	*EA* < 6	81%	66%
CDI	*CDI* > 3	**68%**	**44%**
H+(H)+Hd+(Hd)	*H+(H)+Hd+(Hd)* < 2	37%	18%
Isolation Index	*Isolation Index* > .25	21%	33%
H:Hd+(H)+(Hd)	*H* < *Hd+(H)+(Hd)*	46%	36%
SumT	*SumT* = 0	51%	48%
	SumT > 1	19%	**24%**
HVI	*HVI Positive*	**0%**	5%
COP	*COP* = 0	**60%**	43%
AG	*AG* > 2	5%	**16%**
a:p	*p* > *a* + 1	**6%**	17%
M–	*M–* > 1	4%	13%
Fd	*Fd* > 0	23%	45%
PER	*PER* > 2	3%	8%
Self-perception			
Fr+rF	*Fr+rF* > 0	**3%**	**12%**
Egoc. Index	*3r+(2)/R* < 0.33	**26%**	45%
	3r+(2)/R > 0.44	**52%**	29%
SumV	SumV > 0	28%	36%
MOR	*MOR* > 2	9%	17%
FD	*FD* = 0	81%	39%
	FD > 2	3%	28%

Note: Frequencies in bold are significantly elevated or lowered in comparison to the international sample of nonpatient adults (Meyer et al., 2007)

Another perspective for interpreting these scores would suggest that Alzheimer's disease patients invest relatively low psychic energy in processing information (low *R*) and use an economic strategy of exploring the environment that involves narrowing the frame of reference and preferring simple solutions even to complex problems (high *Lambda*, and *Pure F%*, low *Blends*). Such a strategy may serve as a way of defending against difficulties in shifting attention (high *PSV*) and integrating experiences, ideas, and feelings (low *DQ+*, and *Zf*).

This narrowing of attention can result in the loss of important features of the environment and a decrease in the quality and effectiveness of the person's information processing. Such an economic strategy may also influence the value of certain other Rorschach variables that could be lowered by a restricted protocol. Whatever the case, the facts are that 62% of Alzheimer's disease patients show $L > 0.99$, compared to only 27% of international seniors and 28% of international adults, and $Zd < -3$ is found in 45% of Alzheimer's disease patients but only in 35% of international seniors and 29% of international adults. There is nevertheless accumulating evidence for a breakdown in attentional processes even in psychologically healthy older adults (see Table 5.1), but it is more prominent among patients with Alzheimer's disease. These processes include aspects of visual attention, divided attention, task switching, and selective attention (for a review, see Balota & Faust, 2001). Moreover, Tse, Balota, Yap, Duchek, and McCabe (2010) suggest that much of the difficulty with episodic memory in Alzheimer's disease may be caused by deficits in these attentional mechanisms.

Within the perception subdomain, deviations occur in *FQxo*, *FQxu*, *Popular*, *X–%*, and *Xu%* with T-scores of 44, 43, 42, 57, and 44, respectively. In addition, the frequencies of the cutoff scores of $XA\% < 0.70$, $WDA\% < 0.75$, and $X\text{–}\% > 0.30$ are highly elevated with the values of 43%, 50%, and 38%, respectively, as compared to both international seniors (23%, 24%, and 19%, respectively) and international adults (18%, 20%, and 14%, respectively). This suggests that Alzheimer's disease patients may experience difficulty in interpreting or translating what they perceive accurately (low *X–%*, and *XA%*) and conventionally (low *Popular*, high *Xu%*), and are particularly vulnerable to errors of judgment in the impressions they form even of unambiguous and commonly occurring situations (low *WDA%*). These findings are consistent with behavioral data showing higher-level visual processing impairments among patients with Alzheimer's disease (Kurylo, Corkin, Rizzo, & Growdon, 1996; Mendez, Mendez, Martin, Smyth, & Whitehouse, 1990) and also with a neuropathological distribution that corresponds to the ventral visual stream involved in shape perception and the dorsal visual stream involved in spatial localization (Arnold, Hyman, Flory, Damasio, & Van Hoesen, 1991; Brun & Englund, 1981; Corkin et al., 1991; Hof, Bouras, Constantinidis, & Morrison, 1989; Hof & Morrison, 1990).

This decline in object perception is a significant predictor of instrumental functional dependence in Alzheimer's disease patients in such daily activities as food preparation, driving, and medication management, as distinct from memory, executive function, and semantic knowledge abilities, and it highlights the importance of assessing perceptual processes before making inferences about a person's functional abilities (Jefferson, Barakat, Giovannetti, & Glosser, 2006). Lowered perceptual accuracy also plays a role in such well-known Alzheimer's disease phenomena as failing to recognize the faces of familiar people and misjudging distances when reaching for things.

Within the thinking subdomain, deviations occur in *M* and its derivations *MQo*, *MQu*, *Ma*, and *Mp*, with T-scores of 41, 42, 44, 43, and 42, respectively; in the special scores of *DR2* and *CONTAM*, with T-scores of 63, and 66, respectively, resulting in *Level 2* and *WSum6* T-scores of 61 and 59, respectively; and in *m* and *Intellect*, with T-scores of 44 and 44, respectively. In addition, the frequencies of all the traditional cutoff scores in this domain (*WSum6* > 17, *Level 2* > 0, *Mp* > *Ma*, *Introversive EBper*, *FM+m* > 6, and *INTELL* > 5) are highly deviant from the international seniors' frequencies of these scores. It should be noted that the finding of elevation in some of the special scores characterizes the French sample but not the Spanish sample of patients. The difference between the two samples from two different countries could be attributable to ambiguities in the scoring criteria for the special scores (Perry et al., 1996). Generally, Alzheimer's disease patients tend to rely less on thinking than nonpatients and to experience difficulty in initiating active and deliberate ideational activity (low *M*). As a consequence, they may be inclined to respond to new situations with either puzzlement or impulsivity.

This inference has received support in a series of recent studies (Andos et al., 2015; Giromini, Viglione, Zennaro, & Cauda, 2017; Pineda, Giromini, Porcelli, Parolin, & Viglione, 2011; Porcelli, Giromini, Parolin, Pineda, & Viglione, 2013; Porcelli & Kleiger, 2016) that have demonstrated a link between *M* responses and the embodied simulation mechanism mediated by the mirror neuron system (MNS), which is a neurological network involved in such higher-level cognitive functions as action understanding and planning, perspective-taking, and empathy (Ferrari, Bonini, & Fogassi, 2009; Gallese, Keysers, & Rizzolatti, 2004; Iacoboni, 2009; Oberman, Pineda, & Ramachandran, 2007; Rizzolatti & Craighero, 2004; Rizzolatti, Fogassi, & Gallese, 2001).

Most striking in this respect is the progressive weakening of the MNS in the neurodegenerative process of Alzheimer's disease, which has been demonstrated only recently by Farina et al. (2017). These research findings have the potential to shed light on many of the phenomena related to Alzheimer's disease. Most importantly, they allow for interpretation of Alzheimer's disease in light of the action–perception coupling hypothesis. This hypothesis postulates that a part of cognition results from the coupling between action and perception representations, and it corresponds to implicit action simulation instead of explicit recall of abstract symbols (Boulenger et al., 2008; Jeannerod, 1994, 2001, 2006; Jeannerod, Arbib, Rizzolatti, & Sakata, 1995; Pulvermüller & Fadiga, 2010). More research is needed to reveal whether the impairment in executive functions, together with such typical Alzheimer's disease patient behaviors as indifference, loss of interest, and passivity or perplexity in the face of new situations, are at least partly a result of MNS deterioration.

Affective Experience

In the affective domain, patients with Alzheimer's disease have substantially lowered scores on *S*, *FC*, *CF*, *Sum Color*, *WSumC*, *SumC'*, *SumShading*, and *Blends/R*, with T-scores of 42, 43, 43, 41, 42, 43, 44, and 42, respectively. These deviations indicate that, although Alzheimer's disease patients are as willing as most people to become involved in emotionally arousing situations and share their feelings with others (*Afr*), they have difficulty integrating emotional signals and emotional stimuli in their efforts to solve problem and make decisions (low *FC*, *CF*, *Sum Color*, and *WSumC*). Possibly as a result, they tend to avoid complexity (low *Blends/R*) and limit their conscious awareness of distressing emotions (low *S*, *SumC'*, and *SumShading*).

However, there is as yet no neuropsychosocial model of emotional awareness that incorporates the influence of both neuropsychological impairments and psychosocial responses in Alzheimer's disease (Clare, 2010), which makes unclear the extent to which these present findings on emotionality reflect a psychological process of defense or a neurobiological deficit. Nevertheless, the neurological basis of color responses has been demonstrated in a study by Ilonen et al. (2016) in which color responses correlated positively with relative temporal gray matter volume. Decreased gray matter volume in the temporal hippocampus, which is often detected in Alzheimer's disease (Schuff et al., 2009), has been associated with various learning and memory problems (Lezak, Howieson, Loring, & Fischer, 2004). Our results also accord with the disconnection between the cortex and the limbic system that is characteristic of Alzheimer's disease and is associated in particular with a decrease in cholinergic innervation between the limbic system and the cerebral cortex (Callen, Black, & Caldwell, 2002). This disconnection prevents Alzheimer's disease patients from using emotional cues in ways that would substantially improve their decision-making and problem-solving.

It is important to note that, although high rates of depression are usually found in Alzheimer's disease, the frequencies of *DEPI* > 4 and *D-Score* < −1, which indicate a distressing emotional state, were not elevated in our sample of Alzheimer's disease patients. Evidence from a broad range of sources (for a review, see Olin et al., 2002) suggests that there may be a form of depression that is specific to Alzheimer's disease and not detected by usual measures of depression. How such a specific manifestation of this depressive experience might be reflected in the Rorschach is a question for further investigation.

Interpersonal Relatedness

In the interpersonal relatedness domain, deviant scores in Alzheimer's disease patients occur in *EA*, *es*, *H*, *(H)*, *H+(H)+Hd+(Hd)*, *COP*, *GHR*, *CDI Total*, and *HVI Total*, with T-scores of 39, 43, 43, 43, 40, 44, 40, 57, and 40, respectively. In addition, 81% of Alzheimer's disease patients have an *EA* < 6 and 64% have a *CDI* > 3, as compared to 66% and 44%, respectively, in nonpatient international seniors. These deviations indicate that Alzheimer's disease patients are likely to have limited coping capacities for dealing with interpersonal situations (low *EA*), which can lead to their restricting attention to other people (low *H*, *(H)*, and *H+[H]+Hd+[Hd]*), feeling uncomfortable in social situations and in interactions with others (high *CDI Total*), and experiencing difficulty in forming and maintaining rewarding interpersonal relationships (low *COP*, and *GHR*). They may consequently strike others as being interpersonally avoidant and withdrawn, even though they retain the fundamental human needs for connection and nurturance (*SumT*).

It is of note that no clear conclusion can be drawn concerning whether the depletion of coping resources in Alzheimer's disease is secondary to the neurodegenerative illness or a reflection of premorbid personality characteristics. Several studies have found correlations between a lower degree of social activity and a higher risk of Alzheimer's disease (for a review, see Fratiglioni, Paillard-Borg, & Winblad, 2004). Other studies have related loss of social contacts with loss of motivation, with both being premorbid features in these patients (Bauer, Stadtmüller, Qualmann, & Bauer, 1995). Nevertheless, Ilonen, Salokangas, and the Turku Study Group (2016) found a significant link between the *CDI* and limited cognitive capacity. They concluded that the *CDI* has some neurocognitive components and, when lowered, it may reflect deterioration associated with neurocognitive dysfunction. More specifically, in this regard, each of the *EA*, *COP*, and *H* components of the *CDI* was also lowered in our Alzheimer's disease sample and thus found to be related to neurocognitive capacity. It accordingly appears that both sufficient resources for solving problematic situations in daily living and an ability to perceive whole and realistic humans as being in positive interpersonal interactions are based on basic neurocognitive capacities that are impaired in Alzheimer's disease.

The reduced frequency of *M* responses in Alzheimer's disease patients, which was discussed in considering the cognitive domain, also has a bearing on interpersonal functioning. Specifically, their reduced *M* may indicate that Alzheimer's disease patients have limited awareness of their own needs and concerns and those of other people, with particular deficiencies in their capacities for mentalization and empathy (Le Bouc et al., 2012; Mihura, Meyer, Dumitrascu, & Bombel, 2013). However, more research is needed in order to determine whether these deficits are a result of memory problems, of difficulties in abstraction, reasoning, and the ability to make inferences, or of the previously described MNS deficiency.

Self-Perception

In the self-perception domain of personality functioning, there is a deviation in *FD*, with a T-score of 43, which indicates lowered capacity for introspection in Alzheimer's disease patients. Indeed, 81% of Alzheimer's disease patients have *FD* = 0, whereas only 39% of international seniors show this score. In addition, only 3% of Alzheimer's disease patients have *Fr+rF* > 0, compared to 12% of international seniors, but 52% have an elevated *Egocentricity Index* of more than 0.44, compared to 29% of international seniors. It thus appears that Alzheimer's disease patients tend to focus their attention more on themselves than on other people. However, this self-focusing tendency most likely results from a lowering of cognitive and emotional resources and does not involve the self-admiration that characterizes narcissism. Taken together, these Rorschach reference data show that self-perception is the least damaged of the four domains of personality functioning in Alzheimer's disease patients.

In a similar line of research, Gil et al. (2001) found that patients with Alzheimer's disease show a heterogeneous impairment of self-consciousness. The most disturbed aspects were awareness of cognitive deficiencies, moral judgment, and prospective memory, while the least disturbed were awareness of identity and mental representation of the body. Furthermore, consciousness of identity was sound, regardless the severity of dementia. Fargeau et al. (2010) have also observed that the social self dimension was often more impaired in Alzheimer's disease patients than were other self dimensions. Interviews of early Alzheimer's disease patients have shown that they were involved in the same process of identity preservation as are most people (Beard, 2004). These results also accord with Sabat's (2001) conception of Alzheimer's disease patients as unique human beings striving to maintain selfhood and self-esteem.

Conclusion

Understanding and effectively treating Alzheimer's disease have become some of the most important challenges for psychological research and clinical practice in the twenty-first century. Since psychotherapeutic interventions directed at patients with Alzheimer's disease can have positive effects, the Rorschach can serve as an important tool for both assessment and therapy for these patients. The present chapter provides Rorschach data on patients diagnosed with Alzheimer's disease from France and Spain. Comparison between these patients and two composite samples of international nonpatient adults (Meyer et al., 2007) and senior adults (see Chapter 5) points out substantial differences. As would be expected, most of these differences are demonstrated in the cognitive domain of personality functioning and indicate neuropsychological deficits that characterize patients with Alzheimer's disease. These include lowered capacities to perceive people and events accurately and conventionally (*XA%*, *WDA%*, *X–%*, *Popular*), to think logically and coherently (*WSum6*, *Level 2*), and to initiate active and deliberate ideational activity (*M*). Perhaps as a consequence, they show a narrowed frame of reference (*R*, *Lambda*, *Pure F%*, *Blends*), with a resulting negative effect on the quality of their information processing (*DQ+*, *Zd*). Taken together, they show deficits in ego functioning (*EII-2*) as well as lability in thinking and forming impressions (*RFS-S*).

Apart from these cognitive differences, we found some deviations in the affective, interpersonal, and self-perception domains of personality functioning. Affectively, patients with Alzheimer's disease are willing to become involved in emotionally arousing situations (*Afr*), but their limited coping resources (*EA*) detract from their ability to integrate affective and ideational information in dealing with various situations (*WSumC, M*). Within the interpersonal relatedness realm, although patients with Alzheimer's disease have the same needs for connection and nurturance as nonpatients (*SumT*), they have limited capacities for mentalization and empathy (*M*). As a result they may feel uncomfortable in social situations and have difficulty recognizing and expressing their own needs and those of others (*CDI*). Least influenced by their disorder is their self-perception, with Alzheimer's disease patients resembling nonpatients except for a slightly lowered capacity for introspection (*FD*). Our results are in accord with current neuropsychological knowledge regarding Alzheimer's disease, and add a new perspective for understanding the disease. This new perspective may expand our understanding of the subjective experience of patients with Alzheimer's disease. Increased understanding can in many ways enable clinicians to provide high-quality care for these patients, particularly with respect to the emotional and social aspects of their disorder.

References

Alzheimer's Association (2018). 2018 Alzheimer's disease facts and figures. *Alzheimer's & Dementia, 14*(3), 367–429.

American Psychiatric Association (2013). *Diagnostic and statistical manual of mental disorders* (5th ed.). Arlington, VA: Author.

Ando, A., Salatino, A., Giromini, L., Ricci, R., Pignolo, C., Cristofanelli, S., ... Zennaro, A. (2015). Embodied simulation and ambiguous stimuli: The role of the mirror neuron system. *Brain Research, 1629*, 135–142.

Arnold, S. E., Hyman, B. T., Flory, J., Damasio, A. R., & Van Hoesen, G. W. (1991). The topographical and neuroanatomical distribution of neurofibrillary tangles and neuritic plaques in the cerebral cortex of patients with Alzheimer's disease. *Cerebral Cortex, 1*(1), 103–116.

Balota, D. A., & Faust, M. (2001). Attention in dementia of the Alzheimer's type. *Handbook of Neuropsychology, 6*, 51–80.

Bauer, J., Stadtmüller, G., Qualmann, J., & Bauer, H. (1995). Premorbid psychological processes in patients with Alzheimer's disease and in patients with vascular dementia. *Zeitschrift fur Gerontologie und Geriatrie, 28*(3), 179–189.

Beard, R. L. (2004). In their voices: Identity preservation and experiences of Alzheimer's disease. *Journal of Aging Studies, 18*(4), 415–428.

Bieliauskas, L. A., & Drag, L. L. (2013). Differential diagnosis of depression and dementia. In *Handbook on the neuropsychology of aging and dementia* (pp. 257–270). New York, NY: Springer.

Bozeat, S., Gregory, C. A., Ralph, M. A. L., & Hodges, J. R. (2000). Which neuropsychiatric and behavioural features distinguish frontal and temporal variants of frontotemporal dementia from Alzheimer's disease? *Journal of Neurology, Neurosurgery & Psychiatry, 69*(2), 178–186.

Boulenger, V., Silber, B. Y., Roy, A. C., Paulignan, Y., Jeannerod, M., & Nazir, T. A. (2008). Subliminal display of action words interferes with motor planning: A combined EEG and kinematic study. *Journal of Physiology—Paris, 102*(1–3), 130–136.

Brun, A., & Englund, E. (1981). Regional pattern of degeneration in Alzheimer's disease: Neuronal loss and histopathological grading. *Histopathology*, *5*(5), 549–564.

Callen, D. J., Black, S. E., & Caldwell, C. B. (2002). Limbic system perfusion in Alzheimer's disease measured by MRI-coregistered HMPAO SPET. *European Journal of Nuclear Medicine and Molecular Imaging*, *29*(7), 899–906.

Clare, L. (2010). Awareness in people with severe dementia: Review and integration. *Aging and Mental Health*, *14*(1), 20–32.

Corkin, S., Kurylo, R., Dolan, R., Hyman, B. T., Arriagada, P. V., McKee, A., ... Growdon, J. H. (1991). Brain behavior correlates for audition and vision in a very mild case of Alzheimer's disease. In *21st annual meeting of the Society for Neuroscience abstracts* (Vol. *13*, pp. 147–148). Washington, DC: Society for Neuroscience.

Fargeau, M. N., Jaafari, N., Ragot, S., Houeto, J. L., Pluchon, C., & Gil, R. (2010). Alzheimer's disease and impairment of the self. *Consciousness and Cognition*, *19*(4), 969–976.

Farina, E., Baglio, F., Pomati, S., D'Amico, A., Campini, I. C., Di Tella, S., ... Pozzo, T. (2017). The mirror neurons network in aging, mild cognitive impairment, and Alzheimer's disease: a functional MRI study. *Frontiers in Aging Neuroscience*, *9*, 371.

Ferrari, P. F., Bonini, L., & Fogassi, L. (2009). From monkey mirror neurons to primate behaviours: Possible "direct" and "indirect" pathways. *Philosophical Transactions of the Royal Society of London B: Biological Sciences*, *364*(1528), 2311–2323.

Fratiglioni, L., Paillard-Borg, S., & Winblad, B. (2004). An active and socially integrated lifestyle in late life might protect against dementia. *Lancet Neurology*, *3*(6), 343–353.

Gallese, V., Keysers, C., & Rizzolatti, G. (2004). A unifying view of the basis of social cognition. *Trends in Cognitive Sciences*, *8*(9), 396–403.

Ganellen, R. J. (2007). Assessing normal and abnormal personality functioning: Strengths and weaknesses of self-report, observer, and performance-based methods. *Journal of Personality Assessment*, *89*(1), 30–40.

Gil, R., Arroyo-Anllo, E. M., Ingrand, P., Gil, M., Neau, J. P., Ornon, C., & Bonnaud, V. (2001). Self-consciousness and Alzheimer's disease. *Acta Neurologica Scandinavica*, *104*(5), 296–300.

Giromini, L., Viglione, D. J., Jr., Zennaro, A., & Cauda, F. (2017). Neural activity during production of Rorschach responses: An fMRI study. *Psychiatry Research: Neuroimaging*, *262*, 25–31.

Hargrave, R., Geck, L. C., Reed, B., & Mungas, D. (2000). Affective behavioural disturbances in Alzheimer's disease and ischaemic vascular disease. *Journal of Neurology, Neurosurgery & Psychiatry*, *68*(1), 41–46.

Hof, P. R., Bouras, C., Constandinidis, J., & Morrison, J. H. (1989). Balit's syndrome in Alzheimer's disease: Specific disruption of the occipito-parietal visual pathway. *Brain Research*, *493*(2), 368–375.

Hof, P. R., & Morrison, J. H. (1990). Quantative analysis of a vulnerable subset of pyramidal neurons in Alzheimer's disease: II. Primary and secondary visual cortex. *Journal of Comparative Neurology*, 301(1), 55–64.

Iacoboni, M. (2009). Imitation, empathy, and mirror neurons. *Annual Review of Psychology*, *60*, 653–670.

Ilonen, T., Salokangas, R. K., & Turku Study Group (2016). The Rorschach Coping Deficit Index as an indicator of neurocognitive dysfunction. *Rorschachiana*, *37*, 28–40.

Jeannerod, M. (1994). The hand and the object: the role of posterior parietal cortex in forming motor representations. *Canadian Journal of Physiology and Pharmacology*, *72*(5), 535–541.

Jeannerod, M. (2001). Neural simulation of action: a unifying mechanism for motor cognition. *Neuroimage, 14*(1), S103–S109.

Jeannerod, M. (2006). *Motor cognition: What actions tell the self.* New York, NY: Oxford University Press.

Jeannerod, M., Arbib, M. A., Rizzolatti, G., & Sakata, H. (1995). Grasping objects: The cortical mechanisms of visuomotor transformation. *Trends in Neurosciences, 18*(7), 314–320.

Jefferson, A. L., Barakat, L. P., Giovannetti, T., Paul, R. H., & Glosser, G. (2006). Object perception impairments predict instrumental activities of daily living dependence in Alzheimer's disease. *Journal of Clinical and Experimental Neuropsychology, 28*(6), 884–897.

Kimoto, A., Iseki, E., Ota, K., Murayama, N., Sato, K., Ogura, N., & Arai, H. (2017). Differences in responses to the Rorschach test between patients with dementia with Lewy bodies and Alzheimer's disease—From the perspective of visuoperceptual impairment. *Psychiatry Research, 257*, 456–461.

Kurylo, D. D., Corkin, S., Rizzo, J. F., III, & Growdon, J. H. (1996). Greater relative impairment of object recognition than of visuospatial abilities in Alzheimer's disease. *Neuropsychology, 10*(1), 74–81.

Le Bouc, R., Lenfant, P., Delbeuck, X., Ravasi, L., Lebert, F., Semah, F., & Pasquier, F. (2012). My belief or yours? Differential theory of mind deficits in frontotemporal dementia and Alzheimer's disease. *Brain, 135*(10), 3026–3038.

Lezak, M. D., Howieson, D. B., Loring, D. W., & Fischer, J. S. (2004). *Neuropsychological assessment.* New York, NY: Oxford University Press.

Lingiardi, V., & McWilliams, N. (Eds.) (2017). *Psychodynamic diagnostic manual: PDM-2.* New York, NY: Guilford Publications.

Loewenstein, D. (2013) Assessment of Alzheimer's disease. In L. Ravdin & H. Katzen (Eds.), *Handbook on the neuropsychology of aging and dementia* (pp. 271–283). New York, NY: Springer.

McKann, G., Drachman, D., Folstein, M., Katzman, R., Price, D. M., & Stadlan, E. M. (1984). Clinical diagnosis of Alzheimer's disease. *Neurology*, 34, 939–944.

Mendez, M. F., Mendez, M. A., Martin, R., Smyth, K. A., & Whitehouse, P. J. (1990). Complex visual disturbances in Alzheimer's disease. *Neurology, 40*(3 Pt 1), 439–439.

Meyer, G. J., Erdberg, P., & Shaffer, T. W. (2007). Toward international normative reference data for the Comprehensive System. *Journal of Personality Assessment, 89*(Suppl. 1), S201–S216.

Mihura, J. L., Meyer, G. J., Dumitrascu, N., & Bombel, G. (2013). The validity of individual Rorschach variables: Systematic reviews and meta-analyses of the comprehensive system. *Psychological Bulletin, 139*(3), 548–605.

Muzio, E. (2006). *Vers une approche neuropsychologique intégrée de la personnalité à travers le Rorschach en gériatrie et dans la démence de type Alzheimer* (doctoral dissertation). Paris, France: University of Paris.

Muzio, E. (2016). Inkblots and neurons. *Rorschachiana, 37*, 1–6.

Muzio, E., Andronikof, A., David, J. P., & Di Menza, C. (2001). Contribution of the Rorschach test (Comprehensive System) to psychometric assessment in geriatrics: the example of dementia of the Alzheimer's type. *Revue de Geriatrie, 26*(2), 121–132.

Oberman, L. M., Pineda, J. A., & Ramachandran, V. S. (2007). The human mirror neuron system: A link between action observation and social skills. *Social Cognitive and Affective Neuroscience, 2*(1), 62–66.

Olin, J. T., Schneider, L. S., Katz, I. R., Meyers, B. S., Alexopoulos, G. S., Breitner, J. C., … Krishnan, K. R. R. (2002). Provisional diagnostic criteria for depression of Alzheimer disease. *American Journal of Geriatric Psychiatry, 10*(2), 125–128.

Perry, W., Potterat, E., Auslander, L., Kaplan, E., & Jeste, D. (1996). A neuropsychological approach to the Rorschach in patients with dementia of the Alzheimer type. *Assessment, 3*(3), 351–363.

Piccininni, M., Di Carlo, A., Baldereschi, M., Zaccara, G., & Inzitari, D. (2005). Behavioral and psychological symptoms in Alzheimer's disease: Frequency and relationship with duration and severity of the disease. *Dementia and Geriatric Cognitive Disorders, 19*(5–6), 276–281.

Pineda, J. A., Giromini, L., Porcelli, P., Parolin, L., & Viglione, D. J. (2011). Mu suppression and human movement responses to the Rorschach test. *Neuroreport, 22*(5), 223–226.

Porcelli, P., Giromini, L., Parolin, L., Pineda, J. A., & Viglione, D. J. (2013). Mirroring activity in the brain and movement determinant in the Rorschach test. *Journal of Personality Assessment, 95*(5), 444–456.

Porcelli, P., & Kleiger, J. H. (2016). The "feeling of movement": Notes on the Rorschach human movement response. *Journal of Personality Assessment, 98*(2), 124–134.

Prince, M., Bryce, R., Albanese, E., Wimo, A., Ribeiro, W., & Ferri, C. P. (2013). The global prevalence of dementia: a systematic review and metaanalysis. *Alzheimer's & Dementia, 9*(1), 63–75.

Pulvermüller, F., & Fadiga, L. (2010). Active perception: sensorimotor circuits as a cortical basis for language. *Nature Reviews Neuroscience, 11*(5), 351.

Rizzolatti, G., & Craighero, L. (2004). The mirror-neuron system. *Annual Review of. Neuroscience, 27*, 169–192.

Rizzolatti, G., Fogassi, L., & Gallese, V. (2001). Neurophysiological mechanisms underlying the understanding and imitation of action. *Nature Reviews Neuroscience, 2*(9), 661–670.

Rubin, E. H., & Kinscherf, D. A. (1989). Psychopathology of very mild dementia of the Alzheimer type. *American Journal of Psychiatry, 146*(8), 1017–1021.

Sabat, S. R. (2001). *The experience of Alzheimer's disease: Life through a tangled veil.* Oxford, UK: Blackwell.

Schuff, N., Woerner, N., Boreta, L., Kornfield, T., Shaw, L. M., Trojanowski, J. Q., … Weiner, M. W. (2009). MRI of hippocampal volume loss in early Alzheimer's disease in relation to ApoE genotype and biomarkers. *Brain, 132*(4), 1067–1077.

Silva, D. M., & Webbe, F. M. (2006). A neuropsychological interpretation of differences on the Rorschach among patients with possible dementia of the Alzheimer's type. *Archives of Clinical Neuropsychology, 21*(6), 514–515.

Sperling, R. A., Aisen, P. S., Beckett, L. A., Bennett, D. A., Craft, S., Fagan, A. M., … Park, D. C. (2011). Toward defining the preclinical stages of Alzheimer's disease: Recommendations from the National Institute on Aging–Alzheimer's Association workgroups on diagnostic guidelines for Alzheimer's disease. *Alzheimer's & Dementia, 7*(3), 280–292.

Swainson, R., Hodges, J. R., Galton, C. J., Semple, J., Michael, A., Dunn, B. D., … Sahakian, B. J. (2001). Early detection and differential diagnosis of Alzheimer's disease and depression with neuropsychological tasks. *Dementia and Geriatric Cognitive Disorders, 12*(4), 265–280.

Trachsel, M., Hermann, H., & Biller-Andorno, N. (2015). Cognitive fluctuations as a challenge for the assessment of decision-making capacity in patients with dementia. *American Journal of Alzheimer's Disease & Other Dementias, 30*(4), 360–363.

Tse, C. S., Balota, D. A., Yap, M. J., Duchek, J. M., & McCabe, D. P. (2010). Effects of healthy aging and early stage dementia of the Alzheimer's type on components of response time distributions in three attention tasks. *Neuropsychology, 24*(3), 300–315.

Vázquez Orellana, N. (2003). *La enfermedad de Alzheimer a través del Psicodiagnóstico de Rorschach* (doctoral dissertation). Tarragona, Spain: Rovira i Virgili University.

Weiner, I. B. (2001). Considerations in collecting Rorschach reference data. *Journal of Personality Assessment, 77*(1), 122–127.

Zlot, S. I. (1995). Psychological distress and cognitive impairment in neurological inpatients: Its prevalence and its recognition by residents. *International Journal of Psychiatry in Medicine, 25*(2), 203–213.

PART IV

Applying Rorschach Assessment of Senior Adults: Case Illustrations

Introduction to Case Illustrations

In this part of the volume, we address the diagnostic and therapeutic applications of Rorschach assessment in senior adults. The following 10 chapters present case illustrations of both older adults with impaired personality functioning and those who show normal-range functioning. The case illustrations are drawn from five countries—Brazil, Iran, Israel, the UK, and the US—and they are representative of the younger group of senior adults (aged 65–72). Four of the cases concern elderly individuals with diagnosable functional impairments: a 72-year-old American man diagnosed with dementia (Chapter 8); a 65-year-old American man with bipolar disorder (Chapter 9); a 65-year-old American man with Korsakoff's syndrome (Chapter 10); and a 65-year-old Israeli woman with an acute depressive reaction (Chapter 11).

Six of the cases concern elderly people who are functioning mostly in the normal range, but have nevertheless been susceptible to various types of symptoms and subjective distress: a 65-year-old-Iranian woman with a traumatic stress condition (Chapter 12); a 75-year-old British man with manic defenses (Chapter 13); a 65-year-old British man with a medical condition and somatization (Chapter 14); a 67-year-old British man traumatized in childhood (Chapter 15); a 65-year-old Brazilian woman with fibromyalgia and alexithymia (Chapter 16); and a 67-year-old British man with obsessive–compulsive personality (Chapter 17). In light of the age-related similarities reported in Chapter 5, the inferences drawn from the Rorschach responses of these senior adults are identical to what would be inferred from the records of younger adults.

CHAPTER 8

Dementia "Old Miners" or "Happy Clowns?"

Dementia, which is currently classified in the *Diagnostic and Statistical Manual of Mental Disorders, Fifth Edition* (*DSM-5*; American Psychiatric Association, 2013) as Major Neurocognitive Disorder, consists of a progressive deterioration of memory and language skills together with diminished capacities for such executive functions as planning, problem-solving, and decision-making. This decline in cognitive abilities typically detracts from the quality of a person's daily life, diminishes opportunities for pleasurable social interactions, and limits the possibilities of occupational activity (Nilsson & Ohta, 2014; Smith & Farias, 2018).

In part V of the *Psychodynamic Diagnostic Manual* (*PDM*-2), Del Corno and Plotkin (2017) elaborate as follows the characteristic patterns of cognitive, affective, and interpersonal functioning in major neurocognitive disorder and the subjective experience of declining mental capacities as the disorder progresses from its early to middle stages. With respect to their cognitive functioning, note Del Corno and Plotkin, elderly people with major neurocognitive disorder may, as their disorder progresses, show not only memory loss and diminished language and executive skills, but also impaired reality testing, poor impulse control, and disordered thinking. As specific consequences of the cognitive decline, individuals with dementia may come to misperceive the implications of events, the likely outcomes of their actions, and the intentions of other people, which taken together can result in their exercising poor judgment and even on occasion forming paranoid delusions; they may be inclined to make hasty decisions and translate their feelings into actions without adequate forethought; and they may be prone to instances of illogical, incoherent, and overly concrete thinking.

In their affective functioning, patients with dementia often have difficulty modulating their feelings and avoiding becoming overly emotional. Especially in situations that are affect arousing, they are subject to being overwhelmed by strong emotions they cannot temper. Interpersonally, major neurocognitive disorder does not necessarily detract from a person's preexisting level of interest in other people and capacity to form close and mutually supportive relationships with them. However, their conversations with other people can be discomfiting, especially when they have difficulty keeping in mind the topic being discussed or cannot recall words they meant to use.

As their dementia progresses, people with this condition also become increasingly likely to have changed roles in their family and friendship relationships. For example, a person who has taken care of others becomes a person who must be taken care of; a former breadwinner becomes a person who no longer contributes to the family income; a person who took the lead in family decision-making is no longer capable of doing so; and a person who has shared responsibilities for household management can no longer do his or her share.

With respect to the subjective experience of declining mental capacities, the most disturbing internal consequence of developing dementia is a disrupted sense of identity. A stable self-identity consists of knowing who and what one is—one's strengths and shortcomings, one's hopes and dreams, and one's convictions and beliefs. With dawning awareness of cognitive decline, increased dependence on others, and limited control of their destiny, persons with major neurocognitive disorder may ask themselves, "Who is this person, whom I don't recognize and who is not like me?" This uncertainty and these ruminations often generate anxiety, fear, anger, and depression, and it is also likely to take a toll on the person's self-regard. People with this disorder often seek ways of countering such disturbing affect. These include avoiding or simplifying their responses to situations that might expose their cognitive and communication difficulties; attempting to bolster their self-regard by gathering information and expanding their knowledge of certain subjects, and a philosophical resignation to it being what it is.

Background Information

The present case illustrates the detection of a previously unsuspected cognitive decline. He is a 72-year-old man who was evaluated in the course of a personal injury lawsuit that he has brought against a physical rehabilitation facility. With just a ninth-grade education, he had been able to start and run a successful painting contracting business, from which he had retired several years earlier. He is married and has several grown children, and he has no known history of psychological disorder. When seen for a psychological examination, he was able to give a valid 28-response Rorschach, but was unable to perform subtests of the Wechsler Abbreviated Scale of Intelligence (WASI-2), nor could he complete the Minnesota Multiphasic Personality Inventory-2—Restructured Form (MMPI-2-RF) without having the items read to him, because he was unable to remember where on the answer sheet he should put his responses. He was subsequently referred for more thorough neuropsychological testing, which resulted in his being diagnosed with moderate dementia of unspecified origin. He had entered this facility following a fall in which he suffered a hip fracture. He alleges that he was physically abused by one of the staff nurses in the facility who had also, according to his report, humiliated him by telling other staff and patients that he had the smallest penis she had ever seen. Tables 8.1 and 8.2 present the Structural Summary and Sequence of Scores for his Rorschach protocol.

Table 8.1 Structural Summary

			Affect	Interpersonal
***R* = 28**	***L* = 2.50***			
***EB* = 2:2**	***EA* = 4.0***	***EBPer* = 1.0**	***FC:CF+C* = 2:1**	***COP* = 1 *AG* = 0**
***eb* = 4:0**	*es* = 4	***D* = 0**	***Pure C* = 0**	*GHR:PHR* = 2:2
	Adjes = 4	***AdjD* = 0**	***Const.* = 0:2**	***a:p* = 3:3**
			***Afr* = 0.47**	***Fd* = 1***
***FM* = 4**	***SumC'* = 0**	***SumT* = 0**	***S* = 0**	***SumT* = 0**
***m* = 0**	***SumV* = 0**	***SumY* = 0**	***Complex.* = 1:28**	***Human Content* = 4**
			CP = 0	***Pure H* = 4**
				PER* = 2
				***Isolation Index* = 0.04**
	Cognitive Functioning			Self-Perception
Thinking (Ideation)		Perception (Mediation)	Attention (Processing)	
***a:p* = 3:3**	*Sum6* = 1	***XA%* = 0.75**	*Zf* = 7	***Egoc. Index* = 0.43**
***Ma:Mp* = 2:0**	***Lv2* = 0**	***WDA%* = 0.78**	***W:D:Dd* = 7:20:1**	***Fr+rF* = 0**
***INTELL* = 0**	***WSum6* = 3**	***X–%* = 0.25**	*W:M* = 7:2	***Sum V* = 0**
***MOR* = 0**	***M–* = 1**	*S–* = 0	***Zd* = +2.5**	***FD* = 0***
	Mnone = 0	***P* = 5**	*PSV* = 1	*An+Xy* = 0
		X+% = 0.64	*DQ+* = 3	***MOR* = 0**
		***Xu%* = 0.11**	***DQv* = 0**	***H:(H)+Hd+ (Hd)* = 4:0**
***PTI* = 0**	***DEPI* = 2**	***CDI* = 4***	***S-CON* = 1**	***HVI* = No** *OBS* = No
***FM+m* = 4**	***Col–Shd* = 0**			
RFS-P* = 1.07	***RFS-S* = 2.79***	***EII-2* = –0.56**	***AdjDMD* = 0**	

Note: The format of the two sections of the table is derived from the Rorschach Interpretation Assistance Program (RIAP). The scores in bold (upper section) are those of the basic variables used for distinguishing between healthy and psychopathological personality functioning as presented in Chapter 4. Noted with asterisks (*) are scores that exceed the normative range (see Chapter 5)

Interpretation of Rorschach Data

As previously noted and shown in his Structural Summary, he was able to give a valid Rorschach with 28 responses. The length of this record would suggest that he was comfortable in the Rorschach situation and fully cooperative with its procedures. Striking, however, is his elevated *Lambda* of 2.50, which identifies an extremely narrow frame of reference and reluctance to engage in novel or unfamiliar activities. As noted in Chapter 4 and confirmed in Chapter 5, senior

Table 8.2 Sequence of Scores

Card	*Resp.*								*RFS-2*
I	1	*Do*	*FMp–*	2	*A*			*PER*	–4
	2	*Do*	*Fo*	2	*Ad*				3
	3	*Do*	*FMao*		*A*			*PER*	1
II	4	*Do*	*Fu*	2	*Hh*				2
	5	*Do*	*Fo*		*A*	*P*			4
	6	*W+*	*Fo*	2	*H, Cg*		*ZW*	*DR, PHR*	3
III	7	*Do*	*Fo*		*A*				3
	8	*Ddo*	*F–*		*A*				–3
	9	*Do*	*Fu*	2	*Bt*				2
	10	*Do*	*Fo*		*A*				3
IV	11	*Do*	*FMpo*		*A*				1
	12	*Do*	*Fo*		*Ad*				3
	13	*Do*	*Fo*		*Ad*				3
V	14	*Wo*	*FMpo*		*A*	*P*	*ZW*		1
	15	*Do*	*F–*		*A*				–3
VI	16	*Wo*	*F–*		*A*		*ZW*		–3
	17	*Wo*	*Fu*		*A*		*ZW*		2
VII	18	*Do*	*Fo*	2	*A*				3
	19	*W+*	*Mao*	2	*Cg, H*		*ZW*	*COP, GHR*	0
VIII	20	*Wo*	*FC–*		*A*		*ZW*		–3
	21	*Do*	*Fo*	2	*A*	*P*			4
	22	*Do*	*Fo*		*A*	*P*		*PSV*	4
IX	23	*Do*	*FCo*	2	*Fd*				2
	24	*Do*	*Fo*	2	*H*			*GHR*	3
	25	*Do*	*Fo*		*A*				3

Table 8.2 (Cont.)

Card	*Resp.*								*RFS-2*
X	26	*W+*	*Ma.CF–*		*H, Hx*		*ZW*	*PHR*	–5
	27	*Do*	*Fo*	2	*A*	*P*			4
	28	*Do*	*F–*	2	*A*				–3

Note: The *RFS-2* column refers to the score of each response on the *Reality–Fantasy Scale Version 2.0*

adults tend to show a somewhat higher *Lambda* than younger people, perhaps because their minds are less open to new interests and perspectives. However, his using only pure form determinants in more than 70% of his responses (20 of 28) is unusual among the elderly, though common in patients with Alzheimer's disease (see Chapter 7).

The content and wording of his responses provide further evidence of an impoverished mental life and minimal communication skills. As shown in his Sequence of Scores, 21 of his 28 responses were animals or animal details, and most of these responses consisted of just one or two words, delivered with little pause between them and without any close examination of the blots. For example, on Card III, his four responses were "Fish," "Horse," "Palm trees," and "Butterfly" with no additional words; on Card IV, Responses 11 and 12 were "A dog" and "A bear"; and on Card V, he said, "A bat and a deer." Additional evidence of his limited capacity for fanciful thinking appears in his elevated *RFS-P* of 1.07 and *RFS-S* of 2.79, which indicate concrete thinking, defined as a collapse of fantasy into reality, and dissociative proneness with minimal awareness of inner thoughts and feelings, respectively (see Chapter 4).

Also noteworthy in this regard is this man's elevated *CDI* of 4, which indicates limited ability to cope effectively with life demands. However, despite having an *EA* of only 4, which further indicates limited coping resources, he has a *D-Score* of zero, which indicates freedom from subjectively felt distress. His having limited coping resources but not feeling distressed is attributable to his having an *es* of only 4. He thus appears to avoid experiencing felt distress, despite his limited coping resources, by minimizing his exposure to demands that would be difficult for him to meet. Moreover, all of his four *es* responses are *FM*, which usually are not associated with felt discomfort, and there are no *m*, *C'*, or shading responses to suggest disturbing thoughts or feelings. This combination of a low *EA* with a low *es* and a resulting *D-Score* of 0, particularly in the context of a high *Lambda* record, typifies people with limited coping capacities who avoid becoming upset by limiting their exposure to situations that would exceed their capabilities to manage effectively.

Turning to this man's cognitive functioning, the attention variables in his record fall largely within normal limits. His location choices are nevertheless unusual, with 20 of his 28 responses given to *D* locations. As also noted in Chapter 4 and confirmed in Chapter 5 (Table 5.1), senior adults are somewhat less likely than younger people to give *W* responses, but not to the extent in this record. Similarly of note is the presence of a *PSV* (perseveration), which typically indicates an attempt to avoid cognitive missteps by repeating what is already familiar. Perseverative responses are likely to be pathological when they occur between cards, as in saying that the people being seen on Card III are the same people that were seen on Card II. In the present instance, however, the *PSV* occurs within the same card and is largely unremarkable, consisting just of *D Fo Popular* animal percepts in Responses 21 and 22 on Card VIII.

This man is somewhat below average in his ability to perceive people and events realistically, as shown by an *X–%* of 0.25. However, this finding does not exceed the cutoff score of *X–%* > 0.30 that identifies impaired reality testing. His five *Popular* (*P*) responses indicate normal-range recognition of conventional modes of response and provide further evidence of his generally adequate reality testing. There is also no evidence of disordered thinking in his record. His *WSum6* of only 3 is consistent with his being able to think logically and coherently, and his only critical special score is a mild *DR* in Response 3, where he saw "old miners," and on inquiry said, "They used to be able to go shoveling." In accord with there being few indications of impaired reality testing or disordered thinking in his record, neither his *PTI* nor his *EII-2* is elevated.

The affective cluster in this man's protocol is notable in three respects, each of which reflects his high *Lambda* style and low *EA*. First, he shows limited channels for expressing emotion, with a *WSumC* of just 2. Second, his somewhat low *Affective Ratio* (*Afr*) of 0.47 suggests some aversion to emotionally charged situations and an inclination to avoid or withdraw from social interactions. Third, his *Complexity Index* of 1:28, with just one blend response among his 28 responses, reflects a preference to simplify his emotional as well as his cognitive life experiences.

Despite the simplification that characterizes his Rorschach responses, he gave evidence of some retained interest in other people and some anticipation of collaborative relationships with them, as shown by his four *Pure H* responses and one *COP* response. There are nevertheless some possible reasons for concern in this regard. Having as many or more *PHR* as *GHR* responses often points to a history of problematic interpersonal relationships, and his ratio is 2:2.

The one *Fd* and two *PER* responses in this protocol must also be interpreted cautiously. Food responses are often considered evidence of some dependent needs, but a single food response, especially when unelaborated, may not warrant such an inference. His *Fd* in Response 23 consisted of two apples that were described only as round and red, with nothing further said about them, such as how they might taste or how enjoyable they would be to eat. As for the *PER* responses, which are often elaborations intended to impress other people with how much the person knows or has accomplished, these were simple and unelaborated. Accordingly, neither the *Fd* nor the *PER* responses appear to warrant any inferences.

As for his self-perception, this man's *Egocentricity Index* of 0.43 is within normal limits and gives no indication that he compares himself unfavorably to other people. To the contrary, the absence of any *V* or *MOR* responses, both of which suggest negative and critical attitudes toward oneself, may be evidence of his perceiving himself in a favorable light. Also with a positive implication, his previously noted four *Pure H* responses, with no human detail or imaginary figure responses, are often indications that the person has established a stable sense of identity. The only negative finding among his self-perception variables is the *FD* = 0, which indicates that he is little given to introspection and, consistent with the previously noted *RFS* indications of minimal awareness of inner thoughts and feelings, does not pay much attention to the kind of person he is.

Even in a record as constricted as this one, there is often some revealing thematic imagery that casts light on how respondents view themselves, other people, and the world around them. Two dramatically different images in this man's record are notable in this respect. The first of these is the previously mentioned *DR* in Response 6 of the "old miners" who "used to be able to go shoveling." Perhaps he is identifying here with these miners and seeing himself as an aged person who is no longer capable of doing what he once did. In contrast, his image in Response 26 was of "happy clowns" who are "dancing around and having fun." It may be that the happy clowns represent a wish for how things could be, whereas the old miners represent how things really are. The "happy clowns" response might also be seen as a defensive effort to ward off appearing of feeling depressed by literally showing a happy face to the world.

Conclusion

This 72-year-old man was residing in a physical rehabilitation facility following a hip fracture and was suing the facility for alleged physical abuse and public humiliation by the nursing staff. In a psychological examination related to this personal injury suit, he gave a valid 28-response Rorschach, but had considerable difficulty responding to cognitive tasks on the WASI-2. He was subsequently referred for more thorough neuropsychological testing, which resulted in his being diagnosed with moderate dementia of unspecified origin.

His Rorschach protocol, despite its length, was most notable for its constriction and simplicity. He had an elevated *Lambda* of 2.11; 21 of his 28 responses were animals or animal details; most of his responses consisted of just one or two words; 20 of his 28 responses were given to *D* locations; his *Complexity Index* was 1:28; and his elevated *RFS* scores and *FD* = 0 identified minimal capacity for awareness of his inner thoughts and feelings. He additionally gave evidence of limited coping resources, with an elevated *CDI* of 4. He was nevertheless able to pair a low *EA* of

4 with an equally low *es* of 4 and thereby show a *D-Score* of 0. Taken together, this combination of findings indicates the absence of subjectively felt distress achieved by limiting exposure to demands that would be difficult to manage. Consistent with this avoidance of distress is his somewhat low *Afr*, indicating an inclination to avoid or withdraw from emotionally charged situations.

In his ability to perceive people and events accurately he is somewhat below average, but not to the extent that would indicate impaired reality testing or inability to recognize conventional modes of response. There was likewise no evidence of disordered thinking in his record, with his *PTI* and *EII-2* both within normal limits. With respect to the quality of his object relationships, the findings were mixed. On the positive side were four *Pure H* responses, one *COP* response, and a normal-range *Isolation Index* (0.04) and *Egocentricity Index* (0.43). Less adaptive were the previously noted low *Afr* and *FD* = 0, and the presence of as many *PHR* as *GHR* responses. As a final note, the thematic imagery in his record suggests that he has some concerns about aging, against which he defends in part by attempting to show a happy face to the world.

These Rorschach findings illustrate the constricted and impoverished mental life that is likely to characterize dementia, together with defensive efforts to limit the manifestations of memory and communication difficulties. The constriction, simplification, and avoidance in this man's record, with its prominence of *D* locations, animal contents, and mostly unelaborated two-word responses, is a case in point. As such, the Rorschach results would not appear to have much bearing on the personal injury lawsuit in this case. On the one hand, there are no indications of the kind of impaired reality testing or disordered thinking that would lead him to imagine or manufacture the complaints of his lawsuit. Conversely, however, there are also no indications in the test data of any anxiety, distress, fearfulness, or other psychological ill effects that could be attributed to the misconduct he alleges.

References

American Psychiatric Association (2013). *Diagnostic and statistical manual of mental disorders* (5th ed.). Arlington, VA: Author.

Del Corno, F., & Plotkin, D. (2017). Symptom patters in the elderly. Part V in V. Lingiardi & N. McWilliams (Eds.), *Psychodynamic diagnostic manual* (2nd ed., pp. 751–888). New York, NY: Guilford Press.

Nilsson, L.-G., & Ohta, N. (Eds.) (2014). *Dementia and memory.* New York, NY: Psychology Press.

Smith, G. E., & Farias, S. T. (2018). *APA handbook of dementia.* Washington, DC: American Psychological Association.

CHAPTER 9

Bipolar Disorder
"A Broken Heart, Ruptured in Some Way"

As described in the *Diagnostic and Statistical Manual of Mental Disorders, Fifth Edition* (*DSM-5*; American Psychiatric Association, 2013), bipolar disorder consists of alternating states of depression and hypomania. Depression is characterized among other symptoms by sadness, lethargy, pessimism, feelings of worthlessness, difficulty concentrating, and insomnia. In contrast, hypomania is characterized by good spirits, abundant energy, and grandiose self-admiration, frequently combined with racing thoughts, pressured speech, impulsivity, and distractibility (Fountoulakis, 2015; Lehman & Forester, 2017).

Bipolar disorder usually presents in young adulthood, but may persist into old age. Community and population-based surveys indicate a marked decline in the prevalence of bipolar disorder in late life. Specifically, bipolar disorder is only an eighth as likely to be present in the over-65 age group than in young adults aged 18–29. There is also some evidence that bipolar disorder tends to be less intense in seniors than in younger adults and that older individuals with this disorder are less frequently symptomatic than younger ones. Older bipolar patients have a later age of onset of illness than younger individuals on average, and later onset of mania is associated with more cognitive impairments. These may include abnormalities in attention, working memory, executive function, verbal memory, and processing speed, and they may have a significant impact on disability.

However, it is not clear whether such cognitive impairments are a cause or an effect of the bipolar states. Older adults with bipolar disorder generally have multiple chronic medical conditions that are sometimes related to metabolic syndromes. A question remains as to whether these syndromes are due to long-term use of psychotropic medications or whether older adults with bipolar disorder have an inherent increased risk of medical problems. Substance abuse—a significant and disabling comorbidity in younger individuals—is considerably less common in older cohorts (Depp & Jeste, 2004; Depp et al., 2007; Gildengers et al., 2009; Lingiardi & McWilliams, 2017, pp. 829–830).

Mania can occur for the first time at ages over 50 years, in which case the bipolar disorder is customarily termed "late onset." Compared to early-onset bipolar disorder, the late-onset form is more likely than the early-onset form to result from—or at least to be associated with—medical/neurological conditions or to be triggered by medication use. Individuals with late-onset bipolar disorder have typically shown better premorbid functioning and less family history of bipolar disorder than those with the early-onset type (Lingiardi & McWilliams, 2017, p. 829).

Aging itself is associated with substantial psychological changes that may have a positive influence on susceptibility to bipolar disorder and its course. In particular, such age-related changes as decreased emotional reactivity, more effective coping with interpersonal conditions, and a more modest and balanced view of the self, as noted in Chapter 6, may serve as protective factors for some older people who have or are developing a bipolar disorder.

Background Information

The person in this case is a 65-year-old American college-educated and recently retired businessman who consulted a psychiatrist with complaints of dissatisfaction with his life and a dismal outlook on the future, and he also said that at one point in his life he had been diagnosed with bipolar disorder. He is currently experiencing racing thoughts, difficulty concentrating, and bedtime insomnia. He was referred for a psychological examination to clarify his diagnostic status and identify aspects of his personality style and functioning relevant to planning treatment for him. He was relaxed and affable during the examination but showed some pressure of speech as he rapidly and energetically gave a 41-response Rorschach. Tables 9.1 and 9.2 present the Structural Summary and Sequence of Scores for his Rorschach protocol.

Interpretation of Rorschach Data

Prominent in this man's Rorschach protocol is his high *Lambda* of 2.73. Such a markedly elevated *Lambda* usually identifies a narrow frame of reference and detachment from thoughts and feelings, and it usually portends a bland and unrevealing set of Rorschach responses. Similarly in this regard, his elevated *RFS-P* of 0.95 suggests a limited capacity for awareness of internal experience. Despite his apparent closed-mindedness, however, he produced not only a long record, but also one that provides considerable information about his psychological adjustment, coping style, and personal concerns. Also surprising in his summary scores is an unusual difference between his normal *PTI* of 0 and his elevated *EII-2* of 1.16. Both of these scales are measures of disordered thinking and impaired reality testing, and ordinarily they are closely correlated. As noted in Chapter 4, however, the *EII-2* but not the *PTI* takes into account the *PHR* being equal to or more numerous than the *GHR* and also the frequency of such disturbing contents as *Anatomy*, *Blood*, *Sex*, and *Morbid*. In this man's protocol, the *GHR:PHR* ratio is 2:8, and 21 of his 41 responses are coded for one or more of these four contents, which taken together point to considerable underlying concern about interpersonal relationships and his own bodily functioning.

Table 9.1 Structural Summary

			Affect	Interpersonal
***R* = 41**	***L* = 2.73***			
***EB* = 3.0:4.5**	***EA* = 7.5**	***EBPer* = 1.5**	***FC:CF+C* = 3:3**	***COP* = 0* *AG* = 2**
***eb* = 2:0**	*es* = 2	***D* = 2***	***Pure C* = 0**	*GHR:PHR* = 2:8
	Adjes = 2	***AdjD* = 2***	***Const.* = 0:4.5**	***a:p* = 2:3**
			***Afr* = 0.86**	***Fd* = 1***
***FM* = 1**	***SumC'* = 0**	***SumT* = 0**	***S* = 1**	***SumT* = 0**
***m* = 1**	***SumV* = 0**	***SumY* = 0**	***Complex.* = 1:41**	***Human Content* = 10**
			CP = 0	***Pure H* = 2**
				PER* = 2
				***Isolation Index* = 0.07**
	Cognitive Functioning			Self-Perception
Thinking (Ideation)		Perception (Mediation)	Attention (Processing)	
***a:p* = 2:3**	*Sum6* = 1	***XA%* = 0.76**	*Zf* = 10	***Egoc. Index* = 0.27***
***Ma:Mp* = 2:1**	***Lv2* = 0**	***WDA%* = 0.73***	***W:D:Dd* = 7:23:11***	***Fr+rF* = 0**
***INTELL* = 4**	***WSum6* = 0**	***X−%* = 0.24**	*W:M* = 7:3	***SumV* = 0**
MOR* = 4	***M−* = 0**	*S−* = 0	***Zd* = −5.5***	***FD* = 1**
	Mnone = 0	***P* = 9***	*PSV* = 1	*An+Xy* = 12
		X+% = 0.49	*DQ+* = 5	***MOR* = 4***
		***Xu%* = 0.27**	***DQv* = 3***	***H:(H)+Hd+ (Hd)* = 2:8***
***PTI* = 0**	***DEPI* = 4**	***CDI* = 2**	***S-CON* = 5**	***HVI* = No** *OBS* = No
***FM+m* = 2**	***Col-Shd* = 0**			
RFS-P* = 0.95	***RFS-S* = 2.61**	***EII-2* = 1.16***	***AdjDMD* = 0**	

Note: The format of the two sections of the table is derived from the Rorschach Interpretation Assistance Program (RIAP). The scores in bold (upper section) are those of the basic variables used for distinguishing between healthy and psychopathological personality functioning as presented in Chapter 4. Noted with asterisks (*) are scores that exceed the normative range (see Chapter 5)

On the other hand, his *D-Score* of +2 gives evidence of more than adequate psychological coping resources to meet the demands in his life and substantial capacity to remain calm and untroubled even in circumstances that would make most people anxious, fearful, or otherwise upset. On a less positive note, a positive *D-Score* is usually associated with insensitivity to the feelings and concerns of other people, limited recognition of the actual danger posed by certain circumstances, and disinterest in considering any personal needs for change.

Table 9.2 Sequence of Scores

Card	*Resp.*								*RFS-2*
I	1	*Wo*	*Fo*		*A*	*P*	*ZW*		4
	2	*Wo*	*Fo*		*A*	*P*	*ZW*	*PSV*	4
	3	*Ddo*	*Fu*		*Ad*				2
	4	*Do*	*Fu*	2	*Ad*				2
	5	*Ddo*	*F–*		*Hd, Sx*			*PHR*	–3
II	6	*D+*	*FMpo*	2	*A*	*P*	*ZA*		1
	7	*D+*	*mp.CF–*		*An, Bl*		*ZA*	*MOR, AB*	–4
	8	*Do*	*F–*		*Hd, Sx*			*PHR*	–3
	9	*Ddo*	*F–*		*An, Sx*				–3
	10	*Ddo*	*Fo*		*An, Sx*				3
III	11	*Do*	*F–*	2	*An*				–3
	12	*Do*	*FCo*		*An*				2
	13	*Do*	*Mao*	2	*H, Cg, Sx*	*P*		*GHR*	0
IV	14	*Wo*	*FDo*		*(H)*	*P*	*ZW*	*MOR, PHR*	2
	15	*Do*	*F–*		*Ad*				–3
V	16	*Wo*	*Fo*		*A*		*ZW*		3
VI	17	*Wo*	*Fo*		*Ad*	*P*	*ZW*	*PER*	4
	18	*Do*	*Fo*		*Art*				3
	19	*Ddo*	*Fu*		*Ad*				2
VII	20	*Wv*	*Fo*		*Cl*				5
	21	*D+*	*Mp+*	2	*Hd*	*P*	*ZD*	*GHR*	–1
	22	*DdSv*	*Fu*		*Ge*				2
VIII	23	*W+*	*FCu*		*Art, Ad*		*ZW*		1
	24	*Do*	*F–*		*An*				–3
	25	*Ddo*	*Fu*		*An, Sx*				2
	26	*Do*	*Fo*	2	*A*	*P*			4
	27	*Ddo*	*Fo*		*An*				3
	28	*Do*	*F–*		*Hd, Sx*			*PHR*	–3
	29	*Ddv*	*CFu*		*Id*				–1
IX	30	*Ddo*	*Fu*		*Hd, Sx*			*PHR*	2
	31	*Ddo*	*Fu*		*Hd, Sx*			*PHR*	2
	32	*Do*	*Fo*		*An*				3
	33	*D+*	*Mao*	2	*H, Cg*		*ZD*	*AG, MOR, PHR*	0

Table 9.2 (Cont.)

Card	*Resp.*								*RFS-2*
X	34	*Do*	*Fo*	2	*A*	*P*			4
	35	*Do*	*Fo*		*An*				3
	36	*Do*	*Fu*		*An*				2
	37	*Do*	*Fo*	2	*A*				3
	38	*Do*	*Fu*		*Hd*			*PHR*	2
	39	*Do*	*F–*		*An, Sx*				–3
	40	*Do*	*FCo*	2	*Fd*				2
	41	*Do*	*CF–*	2	*(Ad)*			*MOR, PER*	–3

Note: The *RFS-2* column refers to the score of each response on the *Reality–Fantasy Scale Version 2.0*

Also calling for further consideration, however, is the manner in which he achieves his +2 *D-Score*. With just an average *EA* of 7.5, he has a small *es* of only 2. Both of these *es* determinants are on the movement (*FM*+*m*) side of the *eb*, with scores of 0 for the achromatic and shading determinants that are usually associated with unwelcome and unpleasant affects. Hence, some parts of this man's Rorschach data suggest considerable underlying concerns, and some parts of the data suggest considerable avoidance of such concerns. Lest contradictory inferences appear to question the dependability of the test results, clinicians should keep in mind that the Rorschach is never wrong. It presents representative samples of behavior, and should parts of the data point in different directions, it falls to the clinician to account for these differences.

In this instance, it is reasonable to conclude that this man presents opposite faces to the world, depending on the circumstances, and that the Rorschach is capturing both underlying concerns and somewhat successful defenses against them. On the surface, his *eb* imbalance suggests that he is a man who seldom allows anything to bother him, which may account in part for his ease and affability during an examination that many people find anxiety-provoking. Also relevant in this regard are his above-average Affective Ratio (*Afr*) of 0.86, which suggests an openness to engagement in affect-arousing situations, and his *FC*:*CF*+*C* ratio of 3:3, which identifies adaptive capacities to experience and express his feelings in both measured and spontaneous ways.

With further respect to the Structural Summary, the attention variables in this protocol deviate from normative expectation in three respects. His *W*:*D*:*Dd* ratio of 7:23:11 indicates inordinate attention to peripheral or irrelevant features of events. As noted in Chapter 4, adults typically give a sixth or fewer of their responses to *Dd* locations, and Table 5.1 shows a *Dd* frequency of 14% in nonpatient senior adults. This man's 11 *Dd* responses constitute more than 25% of his 41-response record, which suggests that he is easily distracted by relatively unimportant and peripheral considerations in dealing with his daily life experiences. Added to this distractibility are a lack of precision in focusing his attention (*DQv* = 3) and evidence in his *Zd* = –5.5 that he is an *underincorporator*, which is a person who tends to draw conclusions hastily, without paying sufficient attention to information that should be considered, and who is consequently more likely to be careless than careful and impulsive than reflective.

This man's *WDA%* of 0.73 and *X–%* of 0.24 indicate that he occasionally has some difficulty perceiving people and events accurately. However, these scores do not rise to the level that would constitute evidence of impaired reality testing. Moreover, his nine *Popular* responses indicate that he is fully capable of recognizing and endorsing conventional ways of seeing the world and behaving in it. He similarly appears able to think logically and coherently, with *WSum6* of 0, but two other scores in his thinking cluster merit mention. The four *Morbid* responses are suggestive of generally pessimistic thinking, and the four *INTELL* responses indicate some reliance on intellectualization as a way of warding off unpleasant feelings.

However, his adaptability to the testing situation does not appear to carry over into his real-life object relationships. The Rorschach correlates of his interpersonal functioning indicate limited ability to anticipate or form close and mutually supportive attachments with other people (*COP* = 0) and a likely history of social ineptness and ill-advised interpersonal behaviors that other people find disagreeable (the previously mentioned *GHR:PHR* = 2:8). Both the *Fd* = 1 and the *PER* = 2 are also asterisked in Table 9.2 to indicate that they are normatively unusual. However, the *Fd* response was an unelaborated "Eggs" in Response 40, and the *PER* responses in Responses 17 and 41 consisted only of "I've seen them before." These responses are not sufficiently dramatic to warrant inferring dependent needs (as are numerous elaborated *Food* responses) or narcissistic self-admiration (as are multiple "showing-off" *Personal* responses that relay how much the person knows and has accomplished).

As a further indicator of probable interpersonal difficulties, this man's ratio of *H* responses to *(H)+Hd+(Hd)* responses is 2:8. Such an imbalance in human contents, with much more attention to partial and imaginary human figures than to real and physically whole human beings, often points to social discomfort. Real and fully functional people can be harmful, rejecting, or in other ways cause a person to feel awkward, embarrassed, or disappointed. Partial and fictitious figures, on the other hand, cannot generate any such discomfiting effects and are less likely to make a person feel uneasy than having to deal with real and live people who have all of their parts in place.

This man appears to have difficulty feeling comfortable with himself as well as with other people. His *Egocentricity Index* of 0.27 falls below the normal range and suggests low self-esteem and a proclivity to compare himself unfavorably to other people. Compounding this tendency to denigrate himself are indications of particularly negative attitudes toward his body, which he seems to perceive as inadequate, damaged, or vulnerable to being harmed. The indications in this regard are the presence of the four previously mentioned *Morbid* responses and their compelling thematic imagery: "A broken heart, ruptured in some way" on Card II; "A monster with deformed arms and a small head" on Card IV; "A disfigured fellow with deformed arms" on Card IX; and "An animal in a slaughterhouse with their skin and legs removed" on Card X. As a further reflection of his probable concerns about being vulnerable to harm, his final response to Card X was "There's a lot of pincers in these, and if you're not careful they might pinch you." As for disturbing contents, the Sequence of Scores shows that 18 of this man's 41 responses included one or more disturbing contents, with one *Blood* and several *Anatomy* and *Sex* responses.

Particularly striking in this man's thematic imagery are the numerous *Sex* responses, which included three breasts with nipples, four vaginas, and "A shaft of a penis with the scrotum here" (which was not the good-form penis response to the top detail of Card VI, but instead a poor-form penis response to the upper red detail on Card II). The presence of these *Sex* responses is strongly suggestive of a sexual preoccupation.

Conclusion

This 65-year-old American retired businessman was referred by a psychiatrist for clarification of his diagnostic status and assistance in treatment planning. He complained to the psychiatrist of dissatisfaction with his life and a dismal outlook on the future, together with racing thoughts, difficulty concentrating, and bedtime insomnia, and he also said that at one point in his life he had been diagnosed with bipolar disorder. His Rorschach did not demonstrate disordered thinking or impaired reality testing, but it was a complex mixture of hypomanic and depressive features and of indications of pressing underlying concerns and strong defenses against being troubled by them.

Suggestive of hypomania, he was affable and relaxed during the testing and rapidly, energetically, and with enthusiasm delivered a 41-response record. Along with pressured speech, he gave evidence of impulsivity and distractibility, with a *Zd* of –5.5 and more than 25% of his responses given to *Dd* locations. Suggestive of depression were a low *Egocentricity Index* of 0.27 and four *Morbid* responses, which taken together point to low self-esteem, a negative body image, and pessimistic thinking. Particularly striking with respect to its implications for depression was a *Morbid* response of "A broken heart, ruptured in some way."

In addition to these suggestions of hypomania and depression, he gave numerous indications of problematic interpersonal relationships. As evidenced by a *COP* of 0, far more numerous *PHR* than *GHR* responses, and far more *Hd+(H)+(Hd)* than *H* responses, he does not anticipate or reach out for close and mutually supportive relationships with other people and, despite superficial appearances to the contrary, he seems likely to be uncomfortable and inept in social situation.

As for his concerns and defenses, 18 of this man's 41 responses included one or more of the three disturbing contents of *Anatomy*, *Blood*, and *Sex*. Of these, the

Sex responses of three breasts, four vaginas, and a penis strongly suggest a sexual preoccupation. Although the Rorschach findings cannot speak to the nature and origin of this sexual preoccupation, it is reasonable to speculate that this energetic 65-year-old man is having concerns about actual or anticipated declines in his ability to perform sexually. Despite these and whatever other concerns he may have, however, he is a well-defended man who typically avoids distress by maintaining a narrow frame of reference, with a *Lambda* of 2.73, and manages to keep disturbing thoughts and feelings out of his conscious awareness, with an *es* of only 2, neither of which involved achromatic color or shading. He showed an average range *EA* of 7.5, but with only the two *es* responses, he has a *D-Score* of +2, which points to considerable stress tolerance, but also to a reluctance or unwillingness to consider making any personal changes.

With respect to treatment planning, this disinterest in change is likely to foster a resistance to psychotherapy that will have to be addressed before any substantial progress can be made in the treatment. Softening such resistance usually requires therapists to expand their patients' frame of reference by causing them to examine events they had previously been able to ignore, to worry about how they should behave in situations they would previously have managed with aplomb, and to feel anxious and upset in circumstances where they would previously have remained calm and untroubled. However, therapists should be cautioned that such attacks on a resistive patient's entrenched defensive style must be mounted slowly and gently, lest they do more harm than good. In the case of bipolar disorder, for example, abrupt stripping away of hypomanic defenses may result in a patient falling into a deep depression.

References

American Psychiatric Association (2013). *Diagnostic and statistical manual of mental disorders* (5th ed.). Arlington, VA: Author.

Depp, C. A., & Jeste, D. V. (2004). Bipolar disorder in older adults: a critical review. *Bipolar Disorders, 6*(5), 343–367.

Depp, C. A., Moore, D. J., Sitzer, D., Palmer, B. W., Eyler, L. T., Roesch, S., … Jeste, D. V. (2007). Neurocognitive impairment in middle-aged and older adults with bipolar disorder: Comparison to schizophrenia and normal comparison subjects. *Journal of Affective Disorders, 101*(1–3), 201–209.

Fountoulakis, K. N. (2015). *Bipolar disorder: An evidence-based guide to manic depression.* New York, NY: Springer-Verlag.

Gildengers, A. G., Mulsant, B. H., Begley, A., Mazumdar, S., Hyams, A. V., Reynolds, C. F., III … Butters, M. A. (2009). The longitudinal course of cognition in older adults with bipolar disorder. *Bipolar Disorders, 11*(7), 744–752.

Lehman, S. W., & Forester, B. P. (Eds.) (2017). *Bipolar disorder in older age patients.* Cham, Switzerland: Springer International Publishing.

Lingiardi, V., & McWilliams, N. (2017). *Psychodynamic diagnostic manual* (2nd ed.). New York, NY: Guilford Press.

CHAPTER 10

Korsakoff's Syndrome "Reminds Me of My Life"

Korsakoff's syndrome is a pervasive memory disorder resulting from extensive thiamine deficiency usually associated with chronic severe alcoholism and characterized by amnesia for both past and current events. This recall is usually temporally graded, with remaining memory being somewhat better for childhood than adult events (Race & Verfaellie, 2012). As described in Chapter 1, the recall of personally experienced events is labeled *episodic* memory and differs from *semantic* memory, which is recall of language usage and the meaning of concepts. Korsakoff's syndrome invariably diminishes episodic memory, especially for autobiographical events, but it may or may not also impair semantic memory (Kopelman, Thomson, Guerrini, & Marshall, 2009).

Korsakoff patients are prone to filling in gaps in their memory with confabulations, especially in talking about their personal past and present lives (Borsutzky, Fujiwara, Brand, & Markowitsch, 2008). Two types of confabulation exist in different stages of the syndrome: spontaneous confabulations, which generally involve grandiose content and usually disappear within weeks after the development of the syndrome; and provoked confabulations, in which the erroneous memories that are communicated are generally plausible and can often be found in the chronic stage of the syndrome. With further respect to their cognitive functioning, Korsakoff patients typically show impairments in such executive processes as response inhibition, response generation, working memory updating, planning, and concept shifting, as well as a lack of reflective abilities, such as deficits in perspective-taking and lack of insight into their illness.

In their affective functioning, patients with Korsakoff's syndrome may at times be emotionally flat and affectively detached, but they are frequently irritable or euphoric as well, and they usually remain affectively unstable throughout the rest of their lives. They can easily be provoked into intense emotions and suspiciousness, they tend to overestimate the affective content of stimuli, and they are likely to show emotional overreaction or enhanced sensitivity in other situations (Arts, Walvoort, & Kessels, 2017).

Background Information

This patient is a 65-year-old man who was diagnosed with Korsakoff's syndrome and hospitalized several months prior to this Rorschach examination, which was requested to assist in deciding whether he should remain in a secure facility. Consistent with his memory loss, he was a poor historian and could provide only sketchy information about his past life and current circumstances. He did say that he had been a Protestant minister and an airline pilot, but it was uncertain whether he had in fact done so. Also unknown is whether he has ever been married or had a family, but it was established that he is not presently involved in any interpersonal relationships. As graphic evidence of his limited short-term memory, he did not recognize the examiner or recall having seen him previously following a 10-minute break in the testing. Tables 10.1 and 10.2 present the Structural Summary and Sequence of Scores for his Rorschach protocol.

Interpretation of Rorschach Data

Despite this Korsakoff patient's cognitive limitations, he managed to give a valid Rorschach record of 15 responses and show an average degree of openness to experience, with a *Lambda* of 0.50. His Structural Summary is nevertheless marked by indications of limited coping capacities, problematic interpersonal relationships, low self-esteem, and impaired reality testing. In addition, his Sequence of Scores, with its four *PER* and two *DR* responses, reflect an expansive, personalized, and confabulatory manner of expressing himself.

Notable with respect to his limited coping capacities are his elevated *CDI* of 4, his *EA* of just 4, and his unbalanced *EB* of 0:4. This unbalanced *EB* suggests that he is capable of experiencing and expressing affect, but that he has little ability to think purposefully about what he can or should do. With a *D-Score* of –1 but an *AdjD-Score* of 0, he appears to be experiencing some situational distress. This situational distress flows from his three *m* responses, which identify above-average concern about lacking control of his destiny and reflect his current status as a patient whose fate is in the hands of others.

With respect to his retained capacities to experience and express emotions, his *Afr* of 0.67 indicates that he does not avoid emotionally charged situations. On the other hand, his *FC:CF+C* ratio of 1:3, including a *Pure C*, suggests that he is likely to express affect in an immature way that is more likely to be impetuous and dramatic than it is measured and restrained.

As for his object relationships, there are numerous indications in his record that he is uncomfortable with other people and with himself as well. He shows little interest in other people, little inclination to anticipate or reach out for mutually supportive relationships with others, and little likelihood of having other people play an important part in his life. The Rorschach evidence in these respects

Table 10.1 Structural Summary

			Affect	Interpersonal
***R* = 15**	***L* = 0.50**			
***EB* = 0:4**	***EA* = 4***	***EBPer* = 4.0**	***FC:CF+C* = 1:3**	***COP* = 0* *AG* = 0**
***eb* = 6:2**	*es* = 8	***D* = −1**	***Pure C* = 1**	*GHR:PHR* = 0:1
	Adjes = 5	***AdjD* = 0**	***Const.* = 0:4**	***a:p* = 5:1**
			***Afr* = 0.67**	***Fd* = 0**
***FM* = 3**	***SumC'* = 0**	***SumT* = 0**	***S* = 0**	***SumT* = 0**
***m* = 3**	***SumV* = 0**	***SumY* =2**	***Complex.* = 3:15**	***Human Content* = 1***
			CP = 0	***Pure H* = 0***
				PER* = 4
				Isolation Index* = 0.67
	Cognitive Functioning			Self-Perception
Thinking (Ideation)		Perception (Mediation)	Attention (Processing)	
***a:p* = 5:1**	*Sum6* = 2	***XA%* = 0.60***	*Zf* = 11	***Egoc. Index* = 0.07***
***Ma:Mp* = 0:0**	***Lv2* = 1***	***WDA%* = 0.60***	***W:D:Dd* = 14:1:0***	***Fr+rF* = 0**
***INTELL* = 1**	***WSum6* = 9**	***X−%* = 0.33***	*W:M* = 14:0	***Sum V* = 0**
***MOR* = 1**	***M−* = 0**	*S−* = 0	***Zd* = +1.0**	***FD* = 1**
	Mnone = 0	***P* = 3***	*PSV* = 0	*An+Xy* = 0
		X+% = 0.47	*DQ+* = 2	***MOR* = 1**
		***Xu%* = 0.13**	***DQv* = 3***	***H:(H)+Hd+(Hd)* = 0:1***
***PTI* = 2**	***DEPI* = 3**	***CDI* = 4***	***S-CON* = 6**	***HVI* = No** *OBS* = No
***FM+m* = 6**	***Col-Shd* = 0**			
***RFS-P* = 0.00**	***RFS-S* = 2.68**	***EII-2* = 0.27***	***AdjDMD* = 1***	

Note: The format of the two sections of the table is derived from the Rorschach Interpretation Assistance Program (RIAP). The scores in bold (upper section) are those of the basic variables used for distinguishing between healthy and psychopathological personality functioning as presented in Chapter 4. Noted with asterisks (*) are scores that exceed the normative range (see Chapter 5)

includes an *Isolation Index* of 0.67; a zero frequency of *Pure H*, and *COP* responses; and just one human content response, a poor form quality *Hd* on Card III, which he saw as "An outline of a face in a very poor light," with the center red as the nose, the lower black as the mouth, and the outer red as "shadows of the ears." With respect to his being uncomfortable with himself, his *Egocentricity Index* of only 0.07 suggests low self-esteem and a self-denigrating tendency to regard other people more favorably than he regards himself.

Table 10.2 Sequence of Scores

Card	*Resp.*								*RFS-2*
I	1	*Wo*	*FMpo*		*A*	*P*	*ZW*		1
	2	*Wo*	*Fo*		*A*		*ZW*		3
	3	*Wv*	*FD–*		*Cl*			*PER*	2
II	4	*W+*	*ma.CFo*		*Ls*		*ZW*	*PER*	–1
III	5	*W+*	*ma.YF–*		*Hd, Na*		*ZW*	*PHR*	–4
IV	6	*Wo*	*FMa.FYo*		*A*		*ZW*	*DR*	1
V	7	*Wo*	*FMao*		*A*	P	*ZW*	*DR2*	–5
VI	8	*Wo*	*Fu*		*A*		*ZW*		2
VII	9	*Wv/+*	*Mao*		*Cl*		*ZW*	*PER*	1
VIII	10	*Wo*	*F–*		*A*		*ZW*		–3
	11	*Do*	*Fo*	2	*A*	*P*			4
	12	*Wv*	*F–*		*Cl*			*PER*	2
IX	13	*Wo*	*FC–*		*A*		*ZW*	*MOR*	–3
	14	*Wv*	*C*		*Art*				–2
X	15	*Wv/+*	*CFo*		*Bt*		*ZW*		2

Note: The *RFS-2* column refers to the score of each response on the *Reality–Fantasy Scale Version 2.0*

As for his expansive, personalized, and confabulatory manner of expressing himself, his *PER* response on Card I is a representative example:

> Possibly a cloud formation. [Inquiry] The whole thing. The remnant of some clouds. Almost like I'm flying away from it, at 49 thousand feet. Part of it is below me, smaller, and behind me. [I'm not sure I'm seeing it as you are] The shape of them. That shape indicates wind. Pilots are trained to know that. A lot of fluff, less wind.

The other three *PER* responses he gave were "Images of a volcano like I've seen flying over Hawaii to Japan" on Card IV; "Clouds, like I observed at the Grand Canyon, which you would see if you ever went there, which are called strato-cumulus clouds" on Card VII; and "Reminds me of my life, five or six times flying over a thunderstorm" on Card VIII. Taken together, these structural data and response contents suggest that his interactions with other people rarely consist of mutually pleasurable relationships, but instead serve as opportunities to bolster his limited self-esteem by recounting how far he has traveled, how much he knows, and what he has accomplished in his life.

This man's cognitive functioning is notable for an unusual focus of attention and a poor grasp of reality. With respect to his focus of attention, 14 of his 15 responses were given to *W* locations. It was noted in Chapter 4 and confirmed by the normative data in Table 5.1 that senior adults may differ somewhat from younger people in their *W:D:Dd* ratio. In particular, older people tend to show a slightly decreased frequency of *W* responses, which require energy to formulate. In this case, however, most of the unusual emphasis on *W* responses was the product not of creative effort, but rather of vague global impressions and a personalized and confabulatory expressive style. Seven of his 14 *W* responses were either personalized responses, in which he said more about himself than about what the blots look like, or rambling and disconnected *DR* responses. As further examples of his confabulatory style, one of his *DR* responses was "I don't know how friendly this creature would be, and I'd like to see him up more close," given to Card IV, and the other *DR* response, given to Card V, was "A flying creature, which could be a pretty animal, but I've never had a bad experience with bats, which I've seen flying around in church."

As for his impaired reality testing, his low *WDA%* of 0.60 and elevated *X−%* of 0.33 identify a marked inability to perceive people and events accurately, and his *P* of only 3 compounds his inaccurate perception of the world with limited recognition and endorsement of conventional ways of thinking and behaving. Such gross impairment in reality testing is often considered a symptom of psychotic disorder, and it severely compromises a person's ability to exercise sound judgment. However, his *WSum6* of 9 and *PTI* of 2 are within normal limits and do not suggest thought disorder. His *EII-2* is somewhat elevated, at 0.27. As has been noted in Chapters 4 and 9, however, *EII-2* can sometimes be elevated when *PTI* is not, because it also takes account of disturbing contents and indications of interpersonal problems. In the present case, the *GHR:PHR* ratio of 0:1 would have lent weight to the *EII-2*, but not the *WSum6*.

Conclusion

This 65-year-old man has been diagnosed with Korsakoff's syndrome and is currently hospitalized. He was referred for evaluation to help determine whether he should remain in a secure facility. Due to severe short-term and long-term memory loss, he was able to give only a sketchy account of his past history and current circumstances, although he mentioned having been a Protestant minister and a pilot. Despite his poor memory, he was able to give a valid Rorschach that was notable for evidence of limited coping capacities, problematic interpersonal relationships, low self-esteem, impaired reality testing, and a personalized and confabulatory expressive style.

In particular, he appears largely unable to think purposefully about what he can or should do, to perceive people and events realistically, to reach out for and establish mutually supportive interpersonal relationships, and to regard himself in a positive light. As for his expressive style, he gave numerous rambling and loosely connected responses, many of which included mention of what he had seen while flying. These responses lent some credence to his mention of having been a pilot. However, as often occurs in Korsakoff patients, his personalized confabulations may also have been aimed at covering his memory gaps and bolster his self-esteem. Relevant to the referral question, the most notable of his functioning impairments is his inability to perceive people and events realistically. This poor grasp of reality substantially impairs his ability to exercise good judgment and would warrant a recommendation that he remain in a secure facility.

References

Arts, N. J. M., Walvoort, S. J. W., & Kessels, R. P. (2017). Korsakoff's syndrome: A critical review. *Neuropsychiatric Disease and Treatment, 13*, 2875–2890.

Borsutzky, S., Fujiwara, E., Brand, M., & Markowitsch, H. J. (2008). Confabulation in alcoholic Korsakoff patients. *Neuropsychologia, 46*, 3133–3143.

Kopelman, M. D., Thomson, A. D., Guerrini, I., & Marshall, E J. (2009). The Korsakoff syndrome: Clinical aspects, psychology and treatment. *Alcohol and Alcoholism, 44*, 148–154.

Race, E., & Verfaellie, M. (2012). Remote memory function and dysfunction in Korsakoff's syndrome. *Neuropsychology Review, 22*, 105–116.

CHAPTER 11

Therapeutic Assessment of Acute Depressive Reaction "Disgusting Creatures"

Senior adults commonly experience events that may result in their becoming depressed. Such reactive depression can usually be understood as stemming from a sense of loss. The death of spouses and friends is probably the most widespread precipitant of sadness and may cause people to become at least temporarily discontent, pessimistic, and disinterested in pursuits that previously gave them pleasure. During the first year of bereavement, 10%–20% of surviving spouses develop symptoms of depression, which generally persist if left untreated. Elderly individuals are less likely to become depressed than younger adults during the first months of widowhood. However, the prevalence of major depression increases, and by the end of the second year, 14% of bereaved seniors have major depression, compared with 1%–4% of the elderly population in general (Alexopoulos, 2005; Cole & Dendukuri, 2003). Although they may share many symptoms, major depression should be distinguished from persistent complex bereavement disorder (complicated grief). While anhedonia and self-deprecating feelings are common in depression, seeking proximity to the deceased person is common in complicated grief.

The present case illustrates reactive depression in a woman following the death of her husband. In addition, this case serves to demonstrate the utility of the Rorschach as a therapeutic tool. People generally enter psychotherapy in hopes of being recognized, accepted, and understood. When clinicians suggest to their patients using the Rorschach as part of a collaborative evaluation, they offer them an experience of acceptance and understanding that Lerner (1998) has referred to as an *experience-near* process. In this process, the clinician and the patient work together to integrate the structural data and thematic imagery in a test protocol in ways that can expand a person's self-understanding and foster progress in their subsequent therapy.

As previously noted by Tibon-Czopp and Weiner (2016), Rorschach assessment can be therapeutic in its own right, as well as enriching therapeutic assessment with other measures. The therapeutic benefit of being assessed derives in part from some features it shares with psychotherapy. Most people welcome opportunities to be listened to, understood, and accepted as they are, and they appreciate efforts of others to be helpful to them. Like psychotherapy, clinical assessments engage people in a professional relationship that is dedicated solely to their welfare.

In addition to the indirect therapeutic benefit of providing a positive and potentially helpful experience, Rorschach assessment contributes directly to the welfare of examinees through its utility in treatment planning. For people of all ages, the presence and severity of Rorschach markers of psychological disturbance can help to indicate: (1) whether a person is functioning reasonably well or is in need of psychotherapy; (2) whether a person who needs psychotherapy can be treated adequately on an outpatient basis or requires inpatient care; and (3) whether a person's apparent suicidal tendencies, overwhelming distress, or other emerging difficulties call for crisis intervention. For seniors who have decided to seek psychotherapy, Rorschach findings can suggest which types of therapy are most likely to prove beneficial for them in view of their personality characteristics. For seniors who are already in psychotherapy, Rorschach information concerning their personality style and the nature of their underlying concerns can be useful both to them and to their therapist in establishing the goals of their work together.

Therapeutic assessment is an extended feedback process in which the patient and the examiner collaborate in reviewing the test findings and discussing their implications (Handler, 1999). The collaborative interpretation of Rorschach findings serves as a springboard for further exploration of the personal issues and prior experiences that have caused subjective distress; of how the person has been coping with these issues and experiences; of whether certain means of coping have been more or less helpful in diminishing distress; and of what new coping strategies might be beneficial for the individual. Thus, in contrast to the traditional focus of Rorschach assessment on collecting information, therapeutic assessment applies the Rorschach task in clinical settings as part of the assessment process as well as the therapeutic action. With attention to both the structural data and the thematic imagery, the Rorschach provides a rich source of conclusions, hypotheses, and speculations for discussion in the course of a therapeutic assessment.

Background Information

The respondent in this case illustration is a 65-year-old Israeli woman who entered psychotherapy a few months prior to the present examination. She is a well-educated professional person who retired from her position when her husband became ill and she remained home to care for him. Following his death about one year later, she mourned his loss and withdrew from social relationships and other pleasurable activities. She has three children, and her youngest daughter is currently living with her. She has no known history of psychological disorder or mental health treatment. She has been attending her therapy sessions regularly but barely participating in them. She would answer questions, but she seldom volunteered information about events in her life or her thoughts and feelings. The therapist had not been sensing any development of a therapeutic relationship between herself and this depressed woman. She consequently suggested administering the

Rorschach, and noted that reviewing the patient's responses with her would give them a common language of understanding that would enhance her engagement in the treatment process.

The patient cooperated fully with the Rorschach administration, although she repetitively referred to the cards and many of her percepts as "disgusting." On Card V, for example, she described some birds she saw as "disgusting creatures." Tables 11.1 and 11.2 present the Structural Summary and Sequence of Scores for her Rorschach protocol.

Interpretation of Rorschach Data

This woman has given a valid 21-response Rorschach with a normal-range *Lambda* of 0.62, indicating that she tends to demonstrate openness to experiencing herself, other people, and the world around her. On the other hand, many specific features of how she approaches and deals with events are problematic. She has a notably high *EA* of 11, which indicates substantial psychological resources for coping with the everyday demands in her life. However, the components of her *EA* are markedly imbalanced, with an *EB* of 10:1. This imbalance exceeds the criterion for being pervasively *introversive EB* (*EBPer*) and identifies her as a person who strongly prefers reflective contemplation to affective expression and thinking about matters rather than doing anything about them. Her high *EB* combined with an *es* of only 4 gave her a *D-Score* of +2. A positive *D-Score* is usually associated with a person being well insulated against becoming distressed and able to remain calm and untroubled in situations that would cause most people to become anxious or fearful. Additionally informative is her *eb* of 2:2, which indicates that she rarely allows either disturbing thoughts or unpleasant feelings to come into her conscious awareness.

There are nevertheless some potentially negative consequences associated with a *D-Score* > 0. *D* positive people tend to be set in their ways and satisfied with being the way they are, even if being that way is proving maladaptive. They tend to have little interest in altering anything about themselves, they believe that the environment should accommodate them rather than the other way around, and they typically resist efforts to effect changes in their perspectives or behavior. These personality characteristics have obvious implications for engagement and progress in psychotherapy, as was the clinician's impression in this case.

After considering the implications of this woman's *D-Score*, the next score in her Structural Summary that calls for attention is her *Depression Index* (*DEPI*) of 5. This elevation in *DEPI* is usually associated with either the current presence of a depressed state or susceptibility to recurrent depressive episodes. Several other features of the affective data shown in Table 11.1 deviate sharply from the normal expectation and point to her tendency to: (1) avoid feeling and expressing emotions (*WSumC* = 1.0); (2) disengage from affect-arousing situations (*Afr* = 0.24); and (3) prevent emotional considerations from complicating her life (*Complexity Index* = 1:21). In this respect, her single *Blend* in Response

Table 11.1 Structural Summary

			Affect	Interpersonal
***R* = 21**	***L* = 0.62**			
EB* = 10:1	***EA* = 11.0**	***EBPer* = 11.0***	***FC:CF+C* = 0:1**	***COP* = 1 *AG* = 1**
***eb* = 2:2**	*es* = 4	*D* = 2*	***Pure C* = 0**	*GHR:PHR* = 10:2
	Adjes = 4	***AdjD* = 2***	***Const.* = 0:1**	***a:p* = 7:5**
			Afr* = 0.24	***Fd* = 0**
***FM* = 1**	***SumC'* = 0**	***SumT* = 0**	***S* = 1**	***SumT* = 0***
***m* = 1**	***SumV* = 1**	***SumY* = 1**	***Complex.* = 1:21**	***Human Content* = 12**
			CP = 0	***Pure H* = 7**
				***PER* = 0**
				***Isolation Index* = 0.14**
	Cognitive Functioning			Self-Perception
Thinking (Ideation)		Perception (Mediation)	Attention (Processing)	
***a:p* = 7:5**	*Sum6* = 0	***XA%* = 0.86**	*Zf* = 15	***Egoc. Index* = 0.52***
***Ma:Mp* = 6:4**	***Lv2* = 0**	***WDA%* = 0.85**	***W:D:Dd* = 11:9:1**	***Fr+rF* = 0**
***INTELL* = 1**	***WSum6* = 0**	***X–%* = 0.14**	*W:M* = 11:10	***SumV* = 1***
***MOR* = 3**	***M–* = 0**	*S–* = 0	***Zd* = –8.5***	***FD* = 0***
	Mnone = 0	***P* = 7**	*PSV* = 0	*An+Xy* = 0
		X+% = 0.48	*DQ+* = 8	***MOR* = 3***
		Xu%* = 0.38	***DQv* = 0**	***H:(H)+Hd+ (Hd)* = 7:5**
***PTI* = 0**	***DEPI* = 5***	***CDI* = 2**	***S-CON* = 4**	***HVI* = No** *OBS* = No
***FM+m* = 2**	***Col–Shd* = 0**			
***RFS-P* = 0.10**	***RFS-S* = 1.90**	***EII-2* = –1.57**	***AdjDMD* = 0**	

Note: The format of the two sections of the table is derived from the Rorschach Interpretation Assistance Progran (RIAP). The scores in bold (upper section) are those of the basic variables used for distinguishing between healthy and psychopathological personality functioning as presented in Chapter 4. Noted with asterisks (*) are scores that exceed the normative range (see Chapter 5)

3 on Card I did not include color, which is usually associated with affect, and in reporting "A distorted flower" in Response 21 on Card X, she added, "The colors do not make it any better."

Turning to her interpersonal relationships, the data in Table 11.1 show adaptive strengths. As evidence of interpersonal strengths, she shows considerable interest in other people and positive attitudes toward them, with seven *Pure H* responses, a total of 12 *Human* contents, and a *GHR:PHR* ratio of 10:2. She gives no indications of passivity in her relationships with other people or

Table 11.2 Sequence of Scores

Card	*Resp.*								*RFS-2*
I	1	*Wo*	*Fo*		*A*	*P*	*ZW*	*AG*	4
	2	*Wo*	*Fu*		*Bt*		*ZW*		2
	3	*W+*	*Ma.mp.FVo*	2	*H, Cg*		*ZA*	*GHR*	0
	4	*W+*	*Mao*	2	*H, Ay*		*ZA*	*GHR*	0
	5	*Wo*	*F–*		*Hd*		*ZW*	*PHR*	–3
II	6	*D+*	*Mau*	2	*H*		*ZA*	*GHR*	–1
	7	*D+*	*Mau*	2	*H*		*ZA*	*GHR*	–1
	8	*DSo*	*Fu*		*Sc*				2
III	9	*D+*	*Mao*	2	*H, Hh*	*P*	*ZA*	*GHR*	0
	10	*Do*	*Mpu*		*(Hd)*			*GHR*	–1
IV	11	*Wo*	*Mpo*		*(H)*	*P*	*ZW*	*GHR*	–1
	12	*Ddo*	*FYu*	2	*Hd*			*PHR*	1
	13	*W+*	*Mpo*		*H, Sc*	*P*	*ZA*	*GHR*	–1
V	14	*Wo*	*Fu*	2	*A*		*ZW*	*MOR*	2
VI	15	*Wo*	*Fu*		*Sc*		*ZW*	*MOR*	2
VII	16	*W+*	*Mao*	2	*H*	*P*	*ZW*	*GHR*	0
	17	*D+*	*Mpo*	2	*(H)*	*P*	*ZD*	*COP, GHR*	–1
VIII	18	*Do*	*FMao*	2	*A*	*P*			1
IX	19	*Do*	*CF–*	2	*Bt*				–3
X	20	*Do*	*F–*		*A*				–3
	21	*Wo*	*Fo*		*Bt*		*ZW*	*MOR*	3

Note: The *RFS-2* column refers to the score of each response on the *Reality–Fantasy Scale Version 2.0*

of lacking people who play an important part in her life (*a:p* = 7:5; *Isolation Index* = 0.14).

Nevertheless, this woman's attitudes toward herself appear problematic. She shows an unusual combination of an elevated *Egocentricity Index* (0.52) in the absence of any reflections (*Fr+rF* = 0). This combination of variables usually identifies self-focused people who are paying considerable attention to themselves (the elevated *Egocentricity Index*) but not taking much pleasure in doing so (the absence of *Reflection* responses). Her one *Vista* and three *Morbid* responses provide additional indications of negative attitudes toward herself, feelings of worthlessness, and concerns about her body being inadequate, damaged, or dysfunctional in some way.

Turning to her cognitive functioning, her manner of attending to experience is largely within normal limits, with two exceptions. First, she gives more than half of her responses to *W* locations, which signifies an unusual preference for forming global impressions and focusing on the entirety of situations and experiences, with less attention to their component parts. Second, in addition to this apparent tendency to overgeneralize, she has a large negative *Zd* score of –8.5, which indicates an inclination to make decisions and come to conclusions hastily, without adequate consideration of relevant information. Such haste often leads people to be more impulsive than cautious and more careless than careful.

The perception variables in Table 11.1 indicate good reality testing, with an *XA%* of 0.86 and an *X–%* of 0.14. However, there is an interesting contrast between her *P* = 7, which is usually associated with awareness and endorsement of conventional values and modes of conduct, and her elevated *Xu%* of 0.38, which usually reflects dislike for being conventional and a commitment to thinking about and doing things one's own way. This combination of findings suggests that she may vacillate between these two perspectives, being sometimes unsure in her own mind about whether she prefers to be similar to other people or different from them.

As for her thinking, the previously noted multiple *Morbid* responses indicate a pessimistic view of the world and little positive anticipation of what the future may hold. On the other hand, she appears fully capable of thinking logically and coherently, as attested by her *WSum6* of 0. Her clear thinking and good reality testing are further identified by a *PTI* of 0, a negative *EII-2* score, and normal-range values for *RSP-P* and *RFS-S*.

Based on these findings the therapist drew on the structural data and thematic imagery in the record to formulate some hypotheses about the patient's personality functioning, which she then conveyed to her in a feedback session. She began this feedback session with some observations on the patient's personality strengths, particularly her psychological coping resources (*EA* = 11). She then noted the apparent contradiction between these available resources and the emotional restriction indicated by some of the Rorschach findings (*Afr* = 0.24; *FC*:*CF*+*C* = 0:1). Based on this latter finding, the therapist suggested that the outer world must have been "scary" and "threatening" to her, which were words she used in her very first response to describe a bat she saw in Card I. When confronting the outer world, the therapist continued, she might consider herself to be like the woman she saw in Response 3 to Card I who had "two figures hanging on her… like acrobats." Perhaps, the therapist suggested, this response could reflect feeling trapped by people who are needy and dependent and who require her help, literally "hanging on her." Experiencing the environment as scary and needy, the therapist added, perhaps she identifies herself with the "distorted flower" that she saw in Response 19 to Card X.

This feedback and subsequent instances in which the therapist used Rorschach responses to provide shared terminology for describing the patient's life experiences and outlook (i.e., the common language) helped considerably to advance the therapeutic process. The patient became increasingly cooperative and, within the context of the treatment as a safe place, she began to allow herself to recognize her feelings of helplessness and to discuss her inability to function effectively in interpersonal relationships. Also emerging in the therapy were previously unreported feelings of inadequacy, instability, and exposure to external threat.

Conclusion

This 65-year-old Israeli woman reacted to the death of her husband about a year prior to this examination with a depressed condition in which she avoided social relationships and entertainment activities. A few months before the examination she had begun seeing a therapist who suggested using the Rorschach as a tool for promoting progress in her treatment. The patient gave a valid and unguarded Rorschach, with 21 responses and a *Lambda* of 0.62, but she repetitively referred to the cards and her percepts as "disgusting."

Perhaps the most noteworthy feature of her Rorschach is the extent to which she demonstrated good coping resources (*EA* = 11), insulation against disturbing thoughts or feelings (*es* = 4), and a resulting *D-Score* of +2, which indicates a person who has little interest in making changes and is reluctant to even consider doing so. The data also showed that she is a pervasively introversive person who avoids experiencing and expressing feelings (*WSumC* = 1) and withdraws from affect-arousing situations (*Afr* = 0.24). Nevertheless, she seems interested in people and to view them positively (*P* = 7; *GHR*:*PHR* of 10:2).

She also does not appear to be particularly introspective or psychologically minded (*FD* = 0), but she gave evidence of paying considerable attention to herself (*Egocentricity Index* = 0.53). However, she seems not to take much pleasure in her self-examination (*Reflections* = 0) and instead to harbor many negative and self-critical attitudes toward herself (*V* = 1; *MOR* = 3). She showed some tendencies to overgeneralize (*W*:*D*:*Dd* = 11:9:1) and to be overly hasty in making decisions and coming to conclusions without sufficient basis (*Zd* = −8.5). She showed good reality testing (*XA%* = 0.86; *X−%* = 0.14), but with some vacillation in whether she prefers to be like other people or different from them (*P* = 7; *Xu%* = 0.38). Along with her good reality testing, she appears able to think logically and coherently, as shown by her *PTI*, *EII-2*, *RFS-P*, and *RFS-S* all being within normal limits.

It may seem unusual to consider this woman depressed, despite her *DEPI* of 5, when her Rorschach contains no indication of depressive affect and is in fact notable for indicating avoidance of any kind of feelings. In addition to its emotional facets, however, depression is defined in part by cognitive and behavioral characteristics. This woman's depression is manifested cognitively, in her pessimistic outlook and negative self-attitudes, and behaviorally, in her apparent apathy and withdrawal from social relationships and other pleasurable activities.

In light of the Rorschach findings, the therapist's initial difficulties in working with this woman are not surprising. People who become engaged in psychotherapy and who are likely to benefit from it tend to be emotionally upset, motivated to change, introspective, and comfortable in close relationships (Weiner, 2016). This woman, with her *D-Score* of +2, and *FD* of 0 is none of these. Instead, she is the kind of person who tends to be resistive in psychotherapy and guarded against forming a working alliance with the therapist. It is generally the case that involving a well-defended and unmotivated person in psychotherapy requires them to become upset and consequently motivated to seek and welcome change in themselves. Causing people to become upset may seem paradoxical in a therapy intended to help people feel better, but little progress could be expected in this woman's psychotherapy until and unless she can be persuaded to relax her resistance to it. One place to begin this effort might be her negative self-attitudes, such as by telling her that, whatever she may believe to the contrary, there are clear indications that she considers herself a worthless person and that psychotherapy will give her an opportunity to do something about it.

As shown in this case illustration, establishing a secure working alliance during the assessment process can help senior adults cope with the discouragement, interpersonal discomfort, feelings of aloneness, and subjective distress that often characterize them when they enter psychotherapy. With assessment focused on collaborative elaboration of the senior adult's difficulties, both the patient and the therapist gain knowledge about issues that are likely to arise and need attention in the treatment. This case illustrates the process by which collaborative work on a Rorschach protocol can open lines of therapeutic communication.

References

Alexopoulos, G. S. (2005). Depression in the elderly. *The Lancet, 365*(9475), 1961–1970.

Cole, M. G., & Dendukuri, N. (2003). Risk factors for depression among elderly community subjects: A systematic review and meta-analysis. *American Journal of Psychiatry, 160*(6), 1147–1156.

Handler, L. (1999). Assessment of playfulness: Hermann Rorschach meets DW Winnicott. *Journal of Personality Assessment, 72*(2), 208–217.

Lerner, P. M. (1998). *Psychoanalytic perspectives on the Rorschach*. Hillsdale, NJ: Analytic Press.

Tibon-Czopp, S., & Weiner, I. B. (2016). *Rorschach assessment of adolescents*. New York, NY: Springer.

Weiner, I. B. (2016). Individual psychotherapy. In J. C. Norcross, G. R. VandenBos, & D. K. Freedheim (Eds.), *APA handbook of clinical psychology. Vol. 3: Applications and methods* (pp. 269–287). Washington, DC: American Psychological Association.

CHAPTER 12

Traumatic Stress Condition "Two People Helping Each Other, but It's Hopeless"

Epidemiological studies indicate that, in the general population, 70%–90% of adults over 65 have been exposed to at least one potentially traumatic event (Norris, 1992). Furthermore, trauma- and stressor-related disorders in older adults are more complicated than in younger adults and pose some unique challenges for clinicians. There is evidence in this regard that, with aging, there is a shift from overtly manifest to subthreshold instances of disorder. Older adults complain less than younger people and are more likely to focus their complaints on somatic problems. Age-related changes may also lead to a diversification of symptoms that are spread over a broad range of areas of functioning. As a consequence, strict criteria for any single disorder may no longer be met. In particular, older adults who do not meet full criteria for the diagnosis of stress-related disorders may nevertheless display symptoms associated with the "full-blown" syndrome. Such cases have been labeled in the literature as "subthreshold stress-related disorders" (van Zelst, de Beurs, Beekman, Deeg, & van Dyck, 2003).

It is unknown how many senior adults pass through a long and troubled life without receiving any mental health care. Coping as best they can with unfortunate events in their lives, they endure persistent bouts of anxiety or depression without receiving professional help, whether because of limited awareness of its availability or limited resources for seeking it out. Such is the case in the present illustration, a nonpatient who took the Rorschach and told her life story as a voluntary participant in a research study.

Background Information

This is the case of a 71-year-old Iranian widow who, as just noted, was a voluntary participant in a Rorschach research study. Never having been seen by a mental health professional, she has no history of diagnosed psychological disorder, but she has nevertheless had to contend with traumatic and depressing life events. She married at age 16 and was just 24 years old when her husband died. A younger brother of hers died a year after her husband's passing. She has four children, two girls and two boys. Both of her daughters have emigrated to other countries and are not currently playing a part in her life. The younger of the two girls has received medical treatment for what she described as "a serious disease on her brain." Both of her sons remain in Iran, but she lives alone and has only occasional visits from one of her sons. She completed eight grades of education and has supported herself by working as a cleaning lady. She has recently stopped working and now does some volunteering at a nursing home for the elderly. Aside from spending a few days a week with other elderly people in the nursing home, she does not appear to be involved in any other companionship or enjoyable pastimes.

As far as is known, she is in good physical health and is not taking any medication. During the testing she rarely smiled, and she complained to the examiner of being lonely and having difficulty sleeping. She gave the impression of being someone who tries hard to appear as a psychologically strong and independent person, and she in fact stated that she does not like to depend on anyone else or have anyone depend on her. Tables 12.1 and 12.2 present the Structural Summary and Sequence of Scores for her Rorschach protocol.

Interpretation of Rorschach Data

This woman gave a short record of just 16 responses, which is below normative expectation but satisfies the customary validity criterion of $R > 13$. Moreover, her low *Lambda* of 0.33 indicates that she responded in an open and unguarded fashion and was inclined to reveal rather than conceal her thoughts and feelings. Consistent with her nonpatient status, the Structural Summary data in Table 12.1 fall largely within normal limits. She does not show elevation in any of the six primary findings used in the Comprehensive System to identify psychological disorder. Her *PTI* is 0, her *DEPI* is 4, her *D*-Score is 0, her *CDI* is 2, her *Lambda* is 0.33, and she has no *Reflections*, and each of these scores falls within the normal range. However, her Structural Summary also contains some deviations from normative expectations that, together with some dramatic imagery in the content of her responses, suggest features of recurrent depression and of some stress disorder as well.

Most notable among the deviations in the Structural Summary is the contrast between the *PTI* of 0, which indicates unimpaired capacities to think clearly and logically and perceive people and events realistically, and the *EII-2* of 0.73, which is associated with disordered thinking and poor reality testing. As noted in Chapter 4, the *PTI* and *EII-2* are based on many of the same variables and are usually closely correlated. The apparent discrepancy in this instance is explained by the fact—also noted in Chapter 4—that the *EII-2* differs from the *PTI* in part by taking into account the frequency of *PHR* and such ideationally disturbing contents as *Aggression*, *Anatomy*, *Blood*, and *Morbid*. As shown in the Structural Summary, her *PHR* responses outnumber her *GHR* by a ratio of 2:3. As shown in the Sequence of Scores, 7 of her 16 responses have one or more of these disturbing contents, including four *Morbid responses*. The prevalence of these disturbing contents raises the possibility of a traumatic stress condition.

Table 12.1 Structural Summary

			Affect	Interpersonal
R = 16	L = 0.33			
EB = 4:4	EA = 8	EBPer = 1.0	FC:CF+C = 0:4*	COP = 2 AG = 1
eb = 6:1	es = 7	D = 0	Pure C = 0	GHR:PHR = 2:3
	Adjes = 4	AdjD = 1	Const. Index = 1:4	a:p = 8:3
			Afr = 0.45*	Fd = 0
FM = 2	SumC′ = 1	SumT = 0	S = 0	SumT = 0
m = 4	SumV = 0	SumY = 0	Complex. = 2:16	Human Content = 5
			CP = 0	Pure H = 5
				PER = 0
				Isolation Index = 0.44*
	Cognitive Functioning			Self-Perception
Thinking (Ideation)		Perception (Mediation)	Attention (Processing)	
a:p = 8:3	Sum6 = 2	XA% = 0.81	Zf = 10	Egoc. Index = 0.31*
Ma:Mp = 4:1	Lv2 = 1	WDA% = 0.93	W:D:Dd = 4:10:2	Fr+rF = 0
INTELL = 5	WSum6 = 10	X-% = 0.19	W:M = 4:4	SumV = 0
MOR = 4*	M– = 1	S– = 0	Zd = –1.5	FD = 0*
	Mnone = 0	P = 3*	PSV = 0	An+Xy = 3
		X+% = 0.50	DQ+ = 8	MOR = 4*
		Xu% = 0.31*	DQv = 3*	H:(H)+Hd+ (Hd) = 5:0
PTI = 0	DEPI = 4	CDI = 2	S-CON = 4	HVI = No OBS = No
FM+m = 6	Col–Shd = 0			
RFS-P = –0.19	RFS-S = 2.81*	EII-2 = 0.73*	AdjDMD = 1	

Note: The format of the two sections of the table is derived from the Rorschach Interpretation Assistance Program (RIAP). The scores in bold (upper section) are those of the basic variables used for distinguishing between healthy and psychopathological personality functioning as presented in Chapter 4. Noted with asterisks (*) are scores that exceed the normative range (see Chapter 5)

Two other findings often associated with traumatic stress disorder affirm this initial impression of a traumatic stress condition. First, the *RFS-S* of 2.81 identifies tendencies toward dissociation, a common defensive strategy in response to trauma, used for minimizing felt distress by keeping disturbing thoughts and feelings out of conscious awareness. Second, the *FM+m* of 6 is an indication of intrusive ideation, and the four *m* responses identify in particular concerns about being harmed or damaged by inanimate forces or events over which one has no

Table 12.2 Sequence of Scores

Card	*Resp.*								*RFS-2*
I	1	*Wo*	*Fu*		*Ls, Ay*		*ZW*		2
	2	*D+*	*Fo*	2	*H, Sc*		*ZA*		3
	3	*W+*	*Mapo*		*H, Sc, Ay*		*ZA*	*AG*	−1
II	4	*D+*	*Ma.ma.CFo*	2	*H, Hx, An*		*ZA*	*COP, AB, FAB2*	−5
	5	*Do*	*ma–*		*An*			*MOR*	−4
III	6	*D+*	*Mao*	2	*H, Hh*	P	*ZA*	*COP, DR*	0
IV	7	*D+*	*Mpu*		*Ls*		*ZA*		−1
	8	*Dv*	*Mpu*		*Ls*			*MOR*	−1
V	9	*Wo*	*FMao*		*A*	P	*ZW*		1
VI	10	*D+*	*Fu*	2	*A*		*ZA*		2
VII	11	*Wv*	*C'Fo*		*Cl*			*MOR*	5
VIII	12	*D+*	*FMao*	2	*A*	P	*ZA*		1
	13	*Ddo*	*F–*		*An*				−3
IX	14	*Dv*	*CFu*		*Ls*				1
	15	*Do*	*CFo*		*Bt*				2
X	16	*Dd+*	*Ma.CF–*		*Sc, Bl, H, Ay*		*ZA*	*MOR*	−5

Note: The *RFS-2* column refers to the score of each response on the *Reality–Fantasy Scale Version 2.0*

control. Concerns about being harmed also appeared in the imagery of Response 2, in which she said, "It's two people, one on each side, and each one has a gun to defend himself." She could in this response be showing fear of these armed people, who might shoot her, or identifying with these armed people, who would be capable of protecting themselves. Whichever may be the case, the *Diagnostic and Statistical Manual of Mental Disorders, Fifth Edition* (*DSM-5*; American Psychiatric Association, 2013) specifies defensive avoidance and intrusive ideation as core criteria for diagnosing post-traumatic stress disorder, along with having in fact experienced a traumatic event. The death of this woman's husband and her brother when she was quite young and the subsequent serious illness of her daughter have most certainly exposed this woman to personal trauma.

The four *Morbid* contents shown in the Structural Summary are also noteworthy as indications of pessimistic thinking and a negative self-image and as a criterion score on the *DEPI*. Her *DEPI* of 4, as just mentioned, does not by itself warrant an inference of depression. On the other hand, as also noted in Chapter 4, the *DEPI* seldom produces false positives, but can often generate false-negative findings, and a low *DEPI* should accordingly not be considered to rule out depression. Of further significance, the thematic imagery in many of this woman's responses had a distinctly depressive flavor. These included "Two people helping each other, but it's hopeless" in Response 6 and "A road that I can't see the end of" in Response 7. Other responses with an additionally dissociative quality were "Mountains that are breaking up and falling apart" in Response 8 and "Clouds that are separated from each other" in Response 11.

These indications of some depressive and stress-related features aside, she appears to be functioning reasonably well. She gives evidence of adequate coping resources (*EA* = 8) and is generally able to deal with the demands of her everyday life without becoming unduly upset by them (*D* = 0, *AdjD-Score* = 1). She occasionally shows some cognitive slippage, with a Level 2 *FAB* special score and an *M*– response. Overall, however, her *WSum6* of 10 is within normal limits, indicating her ability to think logically and coherently, and her *M*– is balanced by four good-form *M* responses. With further respect to her cognitive functioning, the findings related to her thinking are notable for her *INTELL* of 5, consisting of one *Abstract* (weighted twice) and three *Anthropology*. This level of *INTELL* usually indicates reliance on intellectualization as a defensive strategy for minimizing felt distress by taking distance from thinking about real objects and present-day events.

With further respect to her cognitive functioning, her *XA%* of 0.81 and *WDA%* of 0.93 indicate that she is capable of perceiving people and events accurately. Accompanying her adequate reality testing, however, is a distinct preference for seeing things in her own way and being a unique rather than a conventional person, as shown by only three *Popular* responses. The structural variables reflecting how people pay attention to their surroundings are also within normal limits, with two minor exceptions. Her *W*:*D*:*Dd* location choices of 4:10:2 suggest that she would have difficulty considering how events relate to each other and functioning effectively in situations that call for concept formation. Also of note are her three *DQv* responses. Like *INTELL*, vague responses often serve a defensive purpose, in this instance minimizing the possible significance of what a person is seeing in the blots by giving objects with indefinite form.

Turning next to her affective functioning, Table 12.1 includes three noteworthy clues to how she experiences and expresses her emotions. Most prominent among these is her *FC*:*CF*+*C* ratio of 0:4. As noted in Chapter 4, *FC* responses are associated with relatively well-modulated and reserved processing of emotion in which feelings emerge and dissipate slowly and are deeply felt but mild to moderate in their intensity. *CF* and *C* responses, by contrast, are associated with relatively unmodulated and spontaneous processing of emotion in which feelings come and go quickly and tend to be superficial, but often quite intense while they last. More numerous *CF*+*C* than *FC* responses is common in children but unusual in adults, especially to the extent of her 0:4 ratio. This finding makes it likely that the depression of which she complains is keenly felt when present, is seldom sustained for any length of time, and is likely to soon recur.

The second point of note in the affective cluster is her low *Complexity Index*, consisting of just two *Blends* among her 16 responses. As with her emphasis on *D* locations, this limited complexity indicates a preference for simplicity in her daily life and limited concern with how events may interrelate.

Third, her *Afr* of 0.45 is slightly below average, which suggests that she is more likely than most people to avoid emotionally arousing situations and keep her feelings to herself. Because close relationships between people usually involve sharing feelings, low *Afr* individuals tend to be socially as well as emotionally withdrawn, and there are indications in the interpersonal variables that such is probably the case for this woman.

The interpersonal cluster of variables indicates that this woman is interested in people and that she views interpersonal relationships as potentially positive and cooperative (*COP* = 2; *Pure H* = 5). The imagery in her two *COP* responses is particularly compelling in this regard. Response 4 was "Two friends hearing some good news, and they are celebrating," and Response 6 was "Two people helping each other to carry a bowl." However, there are also indications that reaching out for and establishing rewarding relationships has been difficult for her. Her ratio of *GHR* to *PHR* of 2:3, with *PHR* greater than *GHR*, is usually associated with ineffective and maladaptive interpersonal behavior. The final point of note is her elevated *Isolation Index* of 0.44, which points to limited involvement in interpersonal and social interactions and the likely absence of people playing an important part in her life.

This implication of an elevated *Isolation Index* is consistent with her actual life circumstances and her complaint of being lonely, in which case her positively toned *COP* could be more representative of wishful thinking than of reality. As probable evidence in this regard, she appended her response of "Two people helping each other carry a bowl" with "But I think they should not help each other." This mixed message about whether people should or should not help each other resonates with the impression she gave during the examination of wanting to be seen as an independent person.

With respect to how she sees herself, the self-perception variables shown in Table 12.1 include two additional deviations from normative expectation. Her *Egocentricity Index* of just 0.31 indicates low self-esteem and suggests that she may have been chronically disposed to regarding other people as more appealing and capable than she is. Her four *Morbid* responses are likely to identify negative views of her body, as in perceiving it as unattractive, damaged, or dysfunctional in some way. Both an *Egocentricity Index* of less than 0.33 and more than two *Morbid* responses receive points on the *DEPI* and lend weight to the previous inference of some depressive features, even though the *DEPI* was not elevated.

One of her images warrants some further speculation about depressive features of her self-image. Her first response on Card I was "It looks like rocks in the

Persepolis." Persepolis was the capital of the first Persian Empire, dating back to 500 BCE, and its ruins remain today as a UNESCO-recognized World Heritage Site. To the extent that she may be projecting herself into this image and identifying with it, as often happens in Rorschach responses, it is as if she were saying to herself, "I'm an ancient ruin, that's what I am." This possibility speaks for itself as a manifestation of depression.

Conclusion

This 71-year-old Iranian woman took the Rorschach as a voluntary participant in a research study. She was in good physical health and had no history of psychological disorder. However, she did appear to be dealing with some of the depressing concerns that often trouble aging people, particularly loneliness, and she showed some signs of residual stress, probably related to some unfortunate past events. With an eighth-grade education, she had supported herself during much of her adult life by working as a cleaning lady. She had recently stopped working, which left her with little to do and largely out of contact with other people, except for spending a few hours a week as a volunteer in a home for the elderly. As for stressful experiences, she was widowed at age 24, her brother died a year later, and her daughter became seriously ill soon after that. She has four children, but has been out of touch with them for many years, except for occasional visits from one of her sons. She lives alone, as she has for many years, and she complained to the examiner of being lonely and having trouble sleeping.

Consistent with her nonpatient status, this woman's Rorschach does not show elevations on the major indices that usually indicate psychological disorder. Her *PTI*, *DEPI*, *D-Score*, and *CDI* are within normal limits. However, her Rorschach did identify aspects of a traumatic stress condition, depression, and interpersonal difficulties that are consistent with her past and current circumstances. With regard to stress, she showed intrusive ideation with a large *FM+m*, including four *m* responses, indicative of concerns about being at the mercy of inanimate forces, as well as a high prevalence of ideationally disturbing contents of *Aggression*, *Anatomy*, *Blood*, and *Morbid*. She invested effort in avoiding emotional distress, as evidenced by a heightened *RFS-S* suggesting dissociative tendencies. She also used numerous *INTELL* contents as a defensive strategy for minimizing felt distress by taking distance from thinking about real objects and present-day events.

As for her depressive features, her Rorschach is notable for indications of low self-esteem, with a low *Egocentricity Index* and the implications of four *Morbid* responses for pessimistic thinking and negative attitudes toward her body. These impressions of depression are heightened by the thematic imagery in some of her responses, such as seeing objects as "falling apart" and efforts as being "hopeless."

With respect to interpersonal difficulties, her Rorschach suggests that she is a socially withdrawn person with limited capacity to form and sustain close relationships with other people and without having many people play an important part in her life, as evidenced by a low *Afr*, more *PHR* than *GHR*, and a markedly elevated *Isolation Index*.

As with her generally normal Rorschach protocol being consistent with her nonpatient status, these indications of a traumatic stress condition, depression, and interpersonal difficulties are consistent with her life history and current circumstances. Noteworthy in this regard are: the history of death and illness in her family; her having stopped working and now having few interests or activities that can help her ward off boredom; her living alone, not being in touch with her children, and having little in the way of other companionship; and her stated complaints of being lonely and having difficulty sleeping. The Rorschach in this case has thus done a good job of indicating generally normal functioning in an elderly nonpatient with no history of psychological disorder, while at the same time identifying underlying troubling concerns and feelings.

References

American Psychiatric Association (2013). *Diagnostic and statistical manual of mental disorders* (5th ed.). Arlington, VA: Author.

Norris, F. H. (1992). Epidemiology of trauma: Frequency and impact of different potentially traumatic events on different demographic groups. *Journal of Consulting and Clinical Psychology*, *60*(3), 409–418.

van Zelst, W. H., de Beurs, E., Beekman, A. T., Deeg, D. J., & van Dyck, R. (2003). Prevalence and risk factors of posttraumatic stress disorder in older adults. *Psychotherapy and Psychosomatics*, *72*(6), 333–342.

CHAPTER 13

Manic Defenses "Could Be a Conflict but It's Nice to Me"

On occasion, senior adults who are functioning reasonably well in their daily lives and do not have a diagnosable affective disorder nevertheless pass through brief episodes of depression and mania. When depressed, they feel sad, listless, pessimistic, and dissatisfied with themselves, their thought processes slow down, and they become behaviorally apathetic and withdrawn. When manic, they feel happy, energetic, optimistic, and pleased with themselves, their thought processes accelerate, and they become behaviorally active and expansive (Del Corno & Plotkin, 2017).

From a psychodynamic perspective, manic episodes can be understood at least in part as defenses against underlying depressive thoughts and feelings. Abundant good spirits can help ward off depressing emotions; self-glorification can provide protection against feelings of worthlessness; and enthusiastic participation in numerous activities can help overcome a loss of interest in the world. The present case illustrates the use of such manic defenses to gain or regain a sense and picture of psychological well-being together with persistent signs of susceptibility to depressive episodes.

Background Information

This respondent is a bright and well-educated 75-year-old British man born in London into a financially well-off family. He recalls his father as having been quite strict and his mother as having been "a beautiful angel" who always attended to her appearance. His parents lived into very old age, approaching 100, and died only several years ago. He said that he feels as if it was only yesterday when they passed. In his early 20s he started a successful business, in which he is still engaged in working. Less successful than his business has been his personal history, which has been marked by problematic marriages and serious illnesses in two of his four children.

During his adult life, he has had three long-term relationships with women, but with each of them he eventually became dissatisfied with their relationship and broke it off. As for his children, his oldest and youngest daughters both were diagnosed with mental disorders in their adolescence. The oldest daughter died in her early 20s and the youngest never fully recovered. He feels somewhat responsible for the illnesses of his daughters, which he attributes in part to his becoming divorced when they were little girls. Following the death of his oldest daughter, he sought psychotherapy, but dropped out after two sessions because he felt "there was no point to it." Nevertheless, he reported having occasional periods of depressed mood.

Despite his psychological misfortunes, he has been able to remain in excellent physical health. He looks younger than his age, has no somatic complaints, watches his diet, goes regularly to the gym, and is not taking any medication. He is a self-reliant man who lives alone and is fully able to take care of his daily needs. He was administered the Rorschach as a voluntary participant in a study concerning personality and attitudes. During a preliminary interview, he appeared to be making an effort to be cheerful, but nevertheless gave some indications of being sad and lonely. Some of his Rorschach responses appeared to make him uncomfortable, but he generally seemed to take pleasure in exercising his imagination. Tables 13.1 and 13.2 present the Structural Summary and Sequence of Scores for his Rorschach protocol.

Interpretation of Rorschach Data

This man gave a valid 28-response Rorschach with an average-range *Lambda* of 0.56, indicating an adaptive openness to experience and willingness to be forthcoming in reporting his thoughts and feelings. However, there is little else in his Structural Summary that would be considered average, with score elevations in almost every cluster of variables. If there is one word that would describe this man and his Rorschach protocol, it would be *complex*. The primary indication of this complexity is his *Complexity Index* of 14:28, signifying that 50% of his responses were *Blends*, compared to an average expectancy of 20%–25% *Blends*. Moreover, four of his *Blends* have more than two determinants. Further attesting his complexity is a sharp contrast between numerous structural scores indicative of underlying concerns and an extensive, flowing, and seemingly pleasurable elaboration of his thematic imagery.

To begin with the structural data, he gives evidence of being at times markedly troubled by both intrusive ideation and unwelcome affects (*es* = 7:12). Fortunately, however, he also has a substantial reservoir of psychological coping resources (*EA* = 19) and thus has a *D-Score* of 0. When his *es* is adjusted for indications of situational anxiety, perhaps related to being examined, he has an *AdjD-Score* of +3 and a corresponding *AdjDMD* of 3. These +3 *AdjD-Scores* indicate that he is basically a stable and well-defended person who can conquer his concerns and meet the demands of his daily life with aplomb. Prominent among his psychological defenses against experiencing distress is a considerable capacity for using intellectualization as a way of taking distance from real-life concrete concerns (*INTELL* = 9).

Turning more specifically to his affective functioning, he has a *DEPI* of 5, which is usually associated with susceptibility to depressive episodes and is accordingly consistent with his self-report of such episodes. Unlike most people who

Table 13.1 Structural Summary

			Affect	Interpersonal
R = 28	**L = 0.56**			
EB = 12:7	**EA = 19**	**EBPer = 1.7**	**FC:CF+C = 0:6***	**COP = 2 AG = 4***
eb = 7:12*	*es* = 19	**D = 0**	**Pure C = 2***	*GHR:PHR* = 1:13
	Adjes = 9	**AdjD = +3***	**Const. Index = 3:7**	**a:p = 12:7**
			Afr = 0.40	**Fd = 1***
FM = 4	**SumC′ = 3**	**SumT = 0**	**S = 1**	**SumT = 0***
m = 3	**SumV = 0**	**SumY =9***	**Complex. = 14:28**	**Human Content = 8**
			CP = 0	**Pure H = 1**
				PER = 3*
				Isolation Index = 0.04
	Cognitive Functioning			Self-Perception
Thinking (Ideation)		Perception (Mediation)	Attention (Processing)	
a:p = 12:7	*Sum6* = 5	**XA% = 0.75**	*Zf* = 12	**Egoc. Index = 0.32***
Ma:Mp = 7:5	**Lv2 = 0**	**WDA% = 0.77**	**W:D:Dd = 6:20:2**	**Fr+rF = 0**
INTELL = 9*	**WSum6 = 15***	**X−% = 0.21**	*W:M* = 6:12	**SumV = 0**
MOR = 8*	**M− = 3***	*S−* = 1	**Zd = −1.0**	**FD = 0***
	Mnone = 1	**P = 5**	*PSV* = 0	*An+Xy* = 1
		X+% = 0.46	*DQ+* = 7	**MOR = 8***
		Xu% = 0.29	**DQv = 0**	**H:(H)+Hd+ (Hd) = 1:7***
PTI = 1	**DEPI = 5***	**CDI = 3**	**S-CON = 5**	**HVI = No** *OBS* = No
FM+m = 7*	**Col-Shd = 3***			
RFS-P = −0.68*	**RFS-S = 2.99***	**EII-2 = 3.00***	**AdjDMD = 3***	

Note: The format of the two sections of the table is derived from the Rorschach Interpretation Assistance Program (RIAP). The scores in bold (upper section) are those of the basic variables used for distinguishing between healthy and psychopathological personality functioning as presented in Chapter 4. Noted with asterisks (*) are scores that exceed the normative range (see Chapter 5)

are depressed, however, and in contrast to his just-mentioned stability, he gives evidence of being an emotionally labile person who exerts little control over his feelings (*FC:CF+C* = 0:6). This loosely controlled emotionality also stands in contrast to indications that he is basically an introversive person who prefers reflective contemplation to affective expression (*EB* = 12:7).

Further suggestive of underlying and possibly depressing concerns are this man's apparently negative interpersonal attitudes and devalued perception of

Table 13.2 Sequence of Scores

Card	*Resp.*								*RFS-2*
I	1	*Wo*	*Fo*		*A*	*P*	*ZW*		4
	2	*Do*	*Mao*		*Hd*			*AG, PHR*	0
	3	*Ddo*	*Fu*		*Hd, Sx*				2
II	4	*W+*	*Ma.ma.CFo*	(2)	*H, Ay, Hx, Ex*		*ZW*	*COP, AG, MOR, AB, PHR*	–1
	5	*D+*	*Ma.CFo*	(2)	*A, Hx*		*ZA*	*FAB, COP, AG, AB, PHR*	–5
III	6	*Ddo*	*F–*	(2)	*A*			*MOR*	–3
	7	*D+*	*Mp.ma.C.C'o*	(2)	*A, Cg, Hx*		*ZD*	*FAB, MOR, AB, PHR*	–5
IV	8	*D+*	*Ma.FYo*		*(H), Cg*	*P*	*ZA*	*DR, GHR*	–1
	9	*Do*	*FMa.FYu*		*Ad*			*INC, MOR*	–1
	10	*Do*	*Fu*		*Hd, Sx*			*PER*	2
V	11	*Wo*	*Fo*		*A*	*P*	*ZW*	*PER*	4
	12	*Wo*	*Mp.FMp.FC'o*		*(A)*		*ZW*	*MOR, PHR*	–1
VI	13	*D+*	*mp.FYo*		*A, Hh*	*P*	*ZA*		1
	14	*Do*	*Fu*		*A*				2
	15	*Do*	*Mau*		*Hd, Sx*			*PHR*	–1
	16	*Wo*	*FMau*		*A*		*ZW*		–1
	17	*Do*	*Fu*		*Fd*			*PER*	2
VII	18	*Do*	*Ma.FY–*	(2)	*A, Hx*			*AG, INC, PHR*	–5
	19	*Do*	*FYo*		*A*				2
	20	*Do*	*Ma.FY–*	(2)	*A, Hx*			*PHR*	–5
VIII	21	*Do*	*Fo*	(2)	*A*	*P*			4
	22	*D+*	*Mp.FYu*		*(H), An*		*ZA*	*MOR, PHR*	–1
	23	*Do*	*CF.FY–*		*Ad*				–3
IX	24	*DS+*	*Mp.FY.CF–*		*Hd, Hx, Id*		*ZS*	*MOR, PHR*	–5
	25	*Do*	*F–*		*Ge*				–3

Table 13.2 (Cont.)

Card	*Resp.*								*RFS-2*
X	26	*Wv/+*	*C.Mp*		*Hx*		*ZW*	*AB, MOR, PHR*	-5
	27	*Do*	*Fo*	*(2)*	*A*				3
	28	*Do*	*FMa.FC'o*	*(2)*	*A*				1

Note: The *RFS-2* column refers to the score of each response on the *Reality–Fantasy Scale Version 2.0*

himself. He is inclined to regard other people as damaged or dysfunctional in some way and as more likely to be competitive than collaborative (*GHR:PHR* = 1:13; *AG* = 4). On the other hand, he did appear to be reaching out for a relationship with the examiner by way of three *Personal* responses that were more of the personally informative than the self-glorifying variety: "I've seen some strange women in my time" in Response 10 on Card IV; "I've seen bats" in Response 11 on Card V; and "A kind of fish I once ate in a Chinese restaurant" in Response 17 on Card VI. This last *Food* response might identify some underlying need to depend on other people, but just one such response in a record should be interpreted tentatively.

As for how he perceives himself, this man gives evidence of low self-esteem and a tendency to compare himself unfavorably to other people (*Egocentricity Index* = 0.32). He seems particularly likely to view his body as damaged or dysfunctional in some way (*Morbid* = 8). Two other interpretive findings among the self-perception variables are his *FD* = 0, which suggests that he is not by nature an introspective person given to inspecting himself, and his *H:(H)+Hd+(Hd)* of 1:7, which suggests that he has had some difficulty forming a clear and stable sense of his identity—that is, what he is like as a person and what he values and believes in.

The Rorschach data concerning of this man's cognitive functioning are mostly within normal limits. He appears to be a well-organized person who is slightly more likely to focus on the details of situations than on their global significance, but who is nevertheless adaptively attentive and precise in viewing his environment (*W:D:Dd* = 6:20:2; *Zd* = –1.0; *DQv* = 0). He is also capable of perceiving events realistically and recognizing conventional values and patterns of behavior (*XA%* = 0.75; *P* = 5). On the other hand, however, three of the seven *DQ–* scores shown in the Sequence of Scores occur in conjunction with *M* responses. A total of three *M–* responses identifies some potentially maladaptive tendencies to misperceive the nature, needs, and intentions of other people. Such misperceptions could play a role in the previously mentioned interpersonal difficulties suggested by his numerous *AG* and *PHR* responses. His thinking processes are also characterized by the previously mentioned *INTELL* of 9, which is an index of broad interests as well as a defensive style, and by his previously mentioned *MOR* of 8, which is an index of pessimistic thinking as well as negative self-attitudes.

Finally, with respect to his cognitive functioning, the overall summary scores in his record differ in two respects. First, he has a normal-range *PTI* of 1, but an elevated *EII-2* of 3.00. Both of these indices are measures of disordered thinking and impaired reality testing, and they are usually closely correlated. However, they differ in that the *EII-2* also takes into account the presence of such disturbing contents as *Morbid*, *Aggression*, and *Sex*. The combination of an unremarkable *PTI* and an elevated *EII-2* usually identifies the presence of disturbing contents, which is the case in the present protocol with its eight *MOR*, four *AG*, and three *Sx* responses. Second, he has a low *RFS-P* of –0.68, which usually indicates preoccupation with inner thoughts and fantasies at the expense of attention to the external world, and a high RFS-S of 3.00, which usually indicates a tendency to fluctuate between imaginal and reality-bound ways of thinking and forming impressions.

Also standing out in the Structural Summary is his *WSum6* of 15, which is somewhat above the normal range and suggests some engagement in incoherent and illogical thinking. However, this slightly elevated *WSum6* appears to be due more to his highly imaginative and free-flowing response style than to disordered thinking. In this regard, the manner in which he related his responses and the imagery in them was as informative, if not more so, as their structural features. He approached the Rorschach task with considerable energy and enthusiasm and appeared to take pleasure in elaborating his responses and exercising his imagination. In so doing, he often delivered rambling and sometimes loosely connected responses and comments that suggested mixed emotions, use of denial as a mechanism of defense, an uncertain self-image, and concerns about hostile feelings being directed his way.

The following Response 9 on Card IV exemplifies his tangential associations and commentaries:

> In this object I can see a pair of eyes on the tail, looking at me. The head is in the middle. It's not a very good-looking thing. You wouldn't like putting it on a child's wall. The eyes are here, with tentacles. I don't get a warm feeling from it. If he would walk in my direction, I would run and cry for help.

A loosely connected stream of thought was similarly evident when he added comments to his responses such as "I wouldn't like to see that on my wall"; "The man who painted this was very weird"; or "Rorschach was a disturbed man." With respect to projecting mixed emotions, he said about his impression of two people dancing in Response 4 on Card II that "It's both comforting and distressing"; he described the figures seen in Response 7 on Card III as being "either happy or sad or both"; and in Response 26 on Card X he saw "A mixture of colors showing a little bit of happiness, sadness, and optimism." In two instances, he used explicit denial to counteract negative emotions. In Response 5 on Card II, he said about an interaction between two bears that "It could be a conflict, but it's nice to me," and in Response 24 on Card IX, he saw "A depressed face with sad eyes, maybe trying to look down at something optimistic."

As for his uncertain self-image, he reported two contrasting images that would seem to have different implications for how he views himself. In Response 12 on Card V, he said, "It's like a butterfly that's not a good-looking butterfly, the ugly duckling, if you know the story." In Response 16 on Card VI, he said, "A peacock," and continued with "Did you know that the males are more decorated than the females, just the opposite of humans?" It may well be that he basically identifies himself with the ugly and relatively helpless duckling, but defends himself against this inferior image by seeking instead to identify with the superior image of a beautiful, strutting peacock.

Concern about hostile feelings being directed his way is suggested by the frequency of aggressive content and eyes in his responses. Response 2 on Card I was "Hands that are about to strangle something"; the human figures in Response 4 on Card II "may be kicking each other to death"; Response 8 on Card IV was "I can see eyes looking at me"; the previously quoted Response 9 on Card IV included "a pair of eyes on the tail, looking at me"; Response 18 on Card VIII was "Two angry fish, with these little spots in the middle being the eyes"; Response 20 on Card VII was "A couple of angry-looking eyes"; and Response 28 on Card X was "Two angry-looking beasts." These responses suggest a recurrent experience of feeling observed by other people who might judge him unfavorably and perhaps act in ways that would be harmful to him. Such concerns are likely to play a role in his previously mentioned discomfort in social situations and his apparent avoidance of close interpersonal attachments.

Conclusion

This 75-year-old British man was examined as a voluntary participant in a study concerning personality and attitudes. He is functioning well as a self-reliant person who lives alone, is in good physical condition, and is still working in a business he started as a young man. However, his personal life has been clouded by problematic marriages and mental illnesses of his daughters, one of whom died and the other never fully recovered. He himself has never been diagnosed with a psychological disorder, but he did report having occasional episodes of depressed mood.

His background and Rorschach responses identify a complex man with three sides. One side is his just-mentioned good daily adjustment, together with Rorschach evidence of substantial psychological coping resources and a good ability to defend himself against disturbing thoughts and feelings (*EA* = 12; *D-Score* = 0; *AdjD-Score* = +3). On his second side, he gives evidence of numerous underlying and potentially depressing concerns. These include indications of pessimistic thinking (*MOR* = 8), low self-esteem (*Egocentricity Index* = 0.32), and social discomfort, with tendencies to avoid close attachments and misperceive the nature and intentions of other people (*GHR:PHR* = 1:13; *M–* = 3). On his third side, he appears remarkably successful in warding off such concerns by adopting an energetic, expansive, and exuberant approach to life and by denying any threats to his equanimity.

The Rorschach evidence of his successful coping style comes mainly from the thematic imagery in his responses and his manner of relating them. In his thematic imagery, he frequently followed negative with positive affect, as in seeing figures as being "sad" then "happy," situations as being "distressing" then "comforting," and possible representations of his self-image as being an "ugly duckling" or a "peacock." As for his response style, he typically delivered long and creative responses, giving free rein to his imagination and taking pleasure in doing so.

This man's reliance on denial as a way of maintaining good spirits, sustaining creative energy and enthusiasm, and warding off underlying depression is a good illustration of manic defenses at work. In his case, these defenses have served him well and contributed to his functioning psychologically within the normal range. There will nevertheless be times when his defenses do not fully quiet his concerns about his personal adequacy and his relationships with other people, which will make him susceptible to the types of depressive episodes that he has reported experiencing.

Reference

Del Corno, F., & Plotkin, D. (2017). Symptom patterns in the elderly. Part V in V. Lingiardi & N. McWilliams (Eds.), *Psychodynamic diagnostic manual* (2nd ed., pp. 751–888). New York, NY: Guilford Press.

CHAPTER 14

Medical Condition and Somatization "A Slight Indication of a Butterfly"

The *Diagnostic and Statistical Manual of Mental Disorders, Fifth Edition* (*DSM-5*; American Psychiatric Association, 2013) has a new diagnostic category defined as Somatic Symptom and Related Disorders. This new category includes several diagnoses with common characteristics, particularly distressing somatic symptoms sometimes associated with abnormal thoughts about and preoccupation with the symptoms. The symptoms may or may not have a medical explanation. Somatic symptoms are observed quite frequently in senior adults. When the symptoms become prolonged or impair personality functioning, they constitute a diagnosable disorder. However, senior adults with somatic complaints are usually brought or referred to nonpsychiatric medical settings, and clinicians in these settings should be alert to possible mental health problems that have not been recognized or are being denied. Since older people generally have various chronic medical conditions that cause physical symptoms, it is quite challenging to distinguish between normal concerns about these symptoms and abnormal preoccupation with somatic difficulties, which usually characterizes individuals with somatizing personality. However, because many medical conditions are associated with psychological symptoms, providing a *DSM-5* diagnosis is even more compelling (Mailis-Gagnon, Nicholson, Yegneswaran, & Zurowski, 2008).

A major aspect to consider for a differential diagnosis is the exclusion of a depressive syndrome with somatic aspects, which has been defined as *masked depression* and is most frequently seen in older people. In these cases, somatization may overlap with ongoing depression and/or generalized anxiety that find somatic rather than verbal expressive channels. Senior adults who overuse the somatic channel are usually not aware of their emotions and are unable to articulate them. Bodily concerns become repetitive, spiral out of control, and invade the person's daily activities, beyond the limitations imposed by their physical state. Senior adults with chronic somatic symptoms are usually preoccupied with the details of external events while being detached from their own subjective experience (Lingiardi & McWilliams, 2017).

The particular type of individuals whose affects are channeled through bodily sensations have been described as *normotic*, meaning that they are well-adapted individuals who function *abnormally normal* (Bollas, 1989). These normotic individuals seem to be disaffected (McDougall, 1984; Ogden, 1989), in that they are removed from subjective experience to the point of being inordinately stable, secure, comfortable, and socially extroverted. They are inclined to reflect mainly on material matters and objects and information that relate to material phenomena, and they have little interest in feelings, fantasy, speculation, or aspects of their inner life. This firm commitment to external reality often becomes a problem, not the solution to any problem (Winnicott, 1971).

Clinical experience and empirical evidence suggest that habitual tendencies to express dysphoric affect by somatic symptoms is quite common among senior adults, and progressive use of the symptoms as a defense for avoiding unpleasant affect may evolve. Most often, however, these individuals present a confusing personality picture in which generally adaptive functioning is interrupted by apparently justified physical symptoms. As would be expected from their normative functioning, these senior adults may provide a normative Rorschach protocol with no prominent deviations. A masked depressive disorder might go unnoticed and the presence of psychopathology might be difficult to determine because the medical condition becomes the dominant issue. Clinicians who use the Rorschach in evaluating senior adults with somatic complaints should accordingly look for any discrepancies between indices pointing to adaptive functioning and indices showing difficulties associated with subjective experience. In line with this conception, the present case illustration explores the Rorschach data of a well-adjusted 65-year-old man. The analysis of his Rorschach protocol focuses on the question of whether his somatic symptoms hide a diagnosable depressive disorder.

Background Information

This is a 65-year-old married and retired man, born in England and living in the east of England. He has been vocationally successful and reports having been an A-Level student during his educational years. Physically, he reports a disability diagnosed as spondylitis in the spine, which most frequently causes lower back pain and other somatic symptoms that exacerbate with aging. These symptoms have become a major concern for him, and he reports recurring and disturbing thoughts regarding their impact on his life. Mentally, he has no psychiatric history and is not currently taking any psychotropic medication. Tables 14.1 and 14.2 present the Structural Summary and Sequence of Scores for his Rorschach protocol.

Interpretation of Rorschach Data

The most prominent finding in the Rorschach protocol of this 65-year-old man is his negative score on the *EII-2* of –1.07, which signifies well-adapted normative functioning. As noted in Chapter 4, the *EII-2* was developed as a measure of psychological impairment and thought disorder. The index comprises five

Table 14.1 Structural Summary

			Affect	Interpersonal
R = 17	**L = 0.89**			
EB = 4:2	**EA = 6**	**EBPer = 2.0**	**FC:CF+C = 2:1**	**COP = 0* AG = 1**
eb = 5:0	es = 5	**D = 0**	**Pure C = 0**	GHR:PHR = 4:1
	Adjes = 4	**AdjD = 0**	**Const. Index = 0:2**	**a:p = 6:3**
			Afr = 0.42	**Fd = 0**
FM = 3	**SumC′ = 0**	**SumT = 0**	**S = 0**	**SumT = 0**
m = 2	**SumV = 0**	**SumY = 0**	**Complex. = 3:17**	**Human Content = 4**
			CP = 0	**Pure H = 3**
				PER = 1*
				Isolation Index = 0.18
	Cognitive Functioning			Self-Perception
Thinking (Ideation)		Perception (Mediation)	Attention (Processing)	
a:p = 6:3	Sum6 = 0	**XA% = 0.88**	Zf = 15	**Egoc. Index = 0.35**
Ma:Mp = 1:3	**Lv2 = 0**	**WDA% = 0.88**	**W:D:Dd = 11:6:0***	**Fr+rF = 0**
INTELL = 2	**WSum6 = 0**	**X–% = 0.12**	W:M = 11:4	**SumV = 0**
MOR = 0	**M– = 0**	S– = 0	**Zd = –8***	**FD = 0***
	Mnone = 0	**P = 7**	PSV = 2	An+Xy = 0
		X+% = 0.71	DQ+ = 8	**MOR = 0**
		Xu% = 0.18	**DQv = 0**	**H:(H)+Hd+ (Hd) = 3:1**
PTI = 0	**DEPI = 2**	**CDI = 2**	**S-CON = 1**	**HVI = No** OBS = No
FM+m = 5	**Col–Shd = 0**			
RFS-P = 1.00*	**RFS-S = 2.45**	**EII-2 = –1.07**	**AdjDMD = 0**	

Note: The format of the two sections of the table is derived from the Rorschach Interpretation Assistance Program (RIAP). The scores in bold (upper section) are those of basic variables used for distinguishing between healthy and psychopathological personality functioning as presented in Chapter 4. Noted with asterisks (*) are scores that exceed the normative range (see Chapter 5)

component variables that are derived from the CS and entered with different weights to form an equation. This index reflects the Ego Psychology model, and its variables are assumed to indicate deficits in ego functions that impair adaptation to external reality. With respect to its statistical distribution, individuals who are well adapted are expected to have an *EII-2* score of less than 0, which indicates high functioning, even in people who show substantial difficulties related to their

Table 14.2 Sequence of Scores

Card	*Resp.*								*RFS-2*
I	1	*Wo*	*Fo*		*A*	*P*	*ZW*		4
	2	*Wo*	*Fo*		*A*	*P*	*ZW*	*PSV*	4
	3	*Wo*	*Fu*		*A*		*ZW*		2
II	4	*Wo*	*FCo*		*A*		*ZW*		2
	5	*Wo*	*F–*		*A*		*ZW*		–3
III	6	*D+*	*Ma.FMao*	2	*H, A*	*P*	*ZD*		0
IV	7	*W+*	*Mpo*		*H, Hh*	*P*	*ZA*		–1
V	8	*Wo*	*Fo*		*A*	*P*	*ZW*		4
	9	*Wo*	*Fo*		*A*	*P*	*ZW*	*PSV*	4
	10	*W+*	*Mp*	2	*H*		*ZA*		–1
VI	11	*W+*	*Mapo*		*Sc, Fi*		*ZW*		1
VII	12	*D+*	*Mp.mapo*	2	*Hd, Cg, Ay*	*P*	*ZD*		–1
VIII	13	*Do*	*Fu*		*Sc*				2
	14	*D+*	*FMau*	2	*A, Bt*		*ZA*		–1
IX	15	*D+*	*FMa.CF–*	2	*A, Bt*		*ZA*	*AG*	–4
X	16	*Do*	*Fo*		*Ay, Sc*				3
	17	*W+*	*FCo*	2	*A, Ls*		*ZW*	*PER*	2

Note: The *RFS-2* column refers to the score of each response on the *Reality–Fantasy Scale Version 2.0*

subjective experience. Consequently, clinical conditions in which the disturbance is masked by areas of apparently normal functioning, such as those characterized by somatic symptoms, might not be captured when measured solely by this index.

To explore these conditions, Tibon, Porcelli, and Weinberger (2003) have suggested using the *RFS* jointly with the *EII-2*. As has been noted (see Chapter 4), the two derivations of the *RFS* (*RFS-P* and *RFS*-S) are aimed at describing psychopathological states in terms of collapse of potential or transitional space between reality and fantasy (Winnicott, 1971). In keeping with the application of Ogden's (1989) model to Rorschach work, a deviant score on the *RFS-P* pointing toward the reality pole (*RFS-P* > +0.65 in adults) speaks to conditions in which reality robs fantasy of its vitality and the capacity to imagine is impaired.

In Rorschach terms, individuals experiencing this form of collapse of potential space toward the reality pole may have difficulty generating responses. They may begin their response to a card by insisting that it is just an inkblot and claiming that they are unable to see it as anything else. When they give codable responses, perhaps only after being prompted, their explanations in the inquiry are often limited to a cataloguing of the parts of the percept and are based on form only. Some of these respondents are nevertheless keen observers and, as an example, will note what details are missing from Card V that would make it look like a real bat (Smith, 1990). Given that the Rorschach stimuli do bear some concrete resemblance to real objects, which they can be assumed to represent, these respondents do not adapt to the basic task of the test, which is to "misperceive" the stimulus as being something more than an inkblot (Exner, 2003). Instead, they are unable to cross the threshold where perception as recognition becomes perception as interpretation (Leichtman, 1996).

With respect to the present case illustration, indications of well-adapted personality are additionally evident in Rorschach Comprehensive System (CS) variables indicating accurate and conventional—or even overly conventional—perception (*XA%* = 0.88; *WDA%* = 0.88; *X–%* = 0.12; and *P* = 7) and capacity for coherent and logical thinking (*WSum6* = 0; *Lv2* = 0). His appropriate adjustment to external demands is further supported by his adequate, although quite restricted and simplistic, affective functioning (*FC:CF+C* = 2:1; *Complexity Index* = 3:17) and his ability to identify with other people (*Human Content* = 4; *Pure H* =3), despite lacking anticipation of engaging in collaborative activities with them (*COP* = 0). The lowered score on the *EII-2* and the other indications of adaptation in the Rorschach protocol give no evidence of impaired functioning or psychopathology. However, the apparent ability of this senior adult to adjust himself successfully to external demands is sustained by the coupling of his relatively low adaptive resources (*EA* = 6) with an *es* of 5, resulting in his *D-Score* of 0.

This man's successful adjustment is also maintained by a coping strategy that adheres closely to reality and limits his ability to relate to internal experience (*RFS-P* = +1.00). His elevated *RFS-P*, which substantially exceeds the normative range, points to a reality-bound and conventional approach. This strategy, which is reflected as well in other deviant CS scores that point to avoidance of self-inspection (*FD* = 0) and little attention to himself (*Egocentricity Index* = 0.32), reveals a markedly narrow and reserved pattern of functioning and experiencing, which may serve him well, as shown by the insignificant constellations (*PTI* = 0; *DEPI* = 2; *CDI* = 2; *HVI* = ns; *AdjDMD* = 0).

In agreement with his excessively reality-bound approach is the frequency of his mostly common and unelaborated contents ("a bat"; "a butterfly"; "insects"), with 11 percepts referring to animals, as well as his comments during the test: "A slight indication of a butterfly" (Card I, Response 2); "Definitely a butterfly-type thing. Can't think of anything else" (Card II, Response 4).

Worth noting, however, is Response 15, which is his only response to Card IX ("Can't see a lot in this one, not to start off…could be two animals or insects confronting each other") and stands out by virtue of its scoring with *FM.CF–* and *AG*. It is reasonable to consider that this ambiguously colored card may have provoked associations of aggressive drives. Such associations may have threatened his internal sense of control and capacity for obtaining stabilized self-cohesion, either because of unresolved neurotic conflicts or because of substantial deficits in his capacity to process emotions. This threatening association might have activated a strategy of coping with the outer stimulus (the blot) that differed from his customary narrow frame of reference as shown in his otherwise unimpaired perception of reality. Interestingly, this style of coping, which is highly unusual for this person and probably quite distressful, is not reflected in Rorschach markers of distress.

Conclusion

This 65-year-old British man, diagnosed with spondylitis, which might impair his otherwise well-adapted functioning, was assessed as part of a normative project. Indeed, he produced a Rorschach protocol that looks normative, with no evidence of impaired ego functioning or psychopathology (*EII-2* < 0). His relatively low availability of psychological resources for coping with situations (*EA* = 6) made assessment of his personality functioning in general and his inner experience in particular quite challenging. The Rorschach protocol in the present case revealed a personality picture of an aging man who is preoccupied with searching for concrete, reality-bound facts and establishing an accurate perception of the external world, while persistently avoiding any internal imagery or affect that might "contaminate" this perception with his subjective experience. Viewed from a psychodynamic perspective, he appears to feature a personality structure in which bodily symptoms are used to express ideas and affects. In line with this conception, the experiential self is deflected from subject to object. External reality and object relationships are thereby drained of their meaning.

The present findings suggest that, in the evaluation of well-adapted seniors with somatic symptom patterns, the *EII-2* should be used jointly with the *RFS* as a complementary index. In general, the *EII-2* might be more sensitive than the *RFS* to problems of adaptation to external reality, whereas the *RFS* is more useful than the *EII-2* for assessing people in whom the very adaptation to external reality is regarded as the problem, not the solution. In these cases, the *RFS* derivations would enable clinicians to detect aspects of personality that would not be captured if the *EII-2* were used alone. In well-adapted senior adults whose major symptom patterns are somatic, abnormality is most often masked by extremely concrete and reality-oriented experience. Using the *EII-2* jointly with the *RFS* can be essential for differential diagnosis and for understanding their subjective experience.

As has been noted, somatization can be an elusive symptom pattern in which underlying psychopathological states may not be reflected in maladaptive functioning. Assessing the quality of personality functioning in apparently well-adapted senior adults with somatic complaints may illuminate implicit psychopathological phenomena, particularly depressive disorders. Exploring their inner experience may provide clues to the effectiveness of their physical symptoms in neutralizing subjective distress and to treatment recommendations.

References

American Psychiatric Association (2013). *Diagnostic and statistical manual of mental disorders* (5th ed.). Arlington, VA: Author.

Bollas, C. (1989). Normotic illness. In M. Fromm & B. Smith (Eds.), *The facilitating environment: Clinical applications of Winnicott's theory* (pp. 317–344). Madison, CT: International Universities Press.

Exner, J. E., Jr. (2003). *The Rorschach: A comprehensive system. Vol. 1: Basic foundations and principles of interpretation* (4th ed.). Hoboken, NJ: Wiley.

Leichtman, M. B. (1996). *The Rorschach: A developmental perspective.* Hillsdale, NJ: Analytic Press.

Lingiardi, V., & McWilliams, N. (2017). *Psychodynamic diagnostic manual* (2nd ed.). New York, NY: Guilford Press.

Mailis-Gagnon, A., Nicholson, K., Yegneswaran, B., & Zurowski, M. (2008). Pain characteristics of adults 65 years of age and older referred to a tertiary care pain clinic. *Pain Research and Management, 13*(5), 389–394.

McDougall, J. (1984). The disaffected patient. *Psychoanalytic Quarterly*, 53, 386–409.

Ogden, T. H. (1989). *The primitive edge of experience.* Latham, MD: Jason Aronson.

Smith, B. L. (1990). Potential space and the Rorschach: Application of object relations theory. *Journal of Personality Assessment, 55*, 756–767.

Tibon, S., Porcelli, P., & Weinberger, Y. (2003). The Ego Impairment Index and the Reality–Fantasy Scale. *Journal of Personality Assessment*, 84, 315–317.

Winnicott, D. W. (1971). *Playing and reality.* New York, NY: Basic Books.

CHAPTER 15

The Après Coup Effect "Like a Butterfly that Is Folded"

Exposure to traumatic experiences in childhood can cause psychological disturbances or dysfunctions that persist into or recur during adulthood. This possibility becomes especially important to consider in older individuals, not only because of the potential harmful impact of trauma on physical and mental health, but also because the stresses of late life may be particularly likely to trigger recall of early-life traumatic events. This persistence or recall of psychological dysfunction in the aftermath of a troubling event is described by Del Corno and Plotkin (2017) as the *après coup effect*, which they define as a "deferred retroactive impact" and has also been referred to as an "aftershock" phenomenon. In keeping with this formulation, senior adults who appear to be functioning well in their daily lives and show good cognitive and affective coping capacities may nevertheless give evidence on the Rorschach of considerable underlying distress or long-term difficulties suggestive of a diagnosable psychological disorder.

The *Diagnostic and Statistical Manual of Mental Disorders, Fifth Edition* (*DSM-5*; American Psychiatric Association, 2013) includes a diagnostic category of Dissociative Disorders and describes a dissociative form of Post-Traumatic Stress Disorder in which the psychological ill effects of traumatizing events can persist, recur, or first emerge long after these events have occurred. This *DSM-5* formulation was based on diverse lines of research conducted mostly with self-report measures of personality functioning. Rorschach indices of psychological distress or dysfunction can also be helpful in identifying a dissociative traumatic disorder and avoiding false-negative conclusions about its presence.

The following case material illustrates such an après coup effect in a 67-year-old British man who was traumatized in childhood and who, despite a psychologically normal life history, gives evidence of emotional scars, particularly with respect to how he views the world, other people, and himself. He was examined as a voluntary nonpatient participant in an Israeli–British research project (Blumberg, Zeligman, Appel, & Tibon-Czopp, 2017).

Background Information

This 67-year-old British man was born and raised in London as the second son in a middle-class family. His father worked as a representative of a small company and his mother was in show business. He studied at the Royal College of Art in London and subsequently taught in various art colleges. He has three children in their 30s from a first marriage and is currently married to his second wife, with whom he has two more children. He has long been involved professionally in various kinds of artwork, including drawing, writing short stories, and composing lyrics and film scripts for radio and TV programs. He is currently volunteering in a community center, where he teaches and instructs non-native English people preparing for an immigration exam. During his childhood and adolescence, he underwent some surgical procedures that he describes as having been extremely traumatic and as eliciting feelings of sadness, anxiety, loneliness, and distress. Tables 15.1 and 15.2 present the Structural Summary and Sequence of Scores for his Rorschach protocol.

Interpretation of Rorschach Data

The Rorschach data presented in the Structural Summary show that this senior adult was invested in the task and inclined to be open and not constricted in his responses (*R* = 31; *L* = 0.55). He gives evidence of substantial cognitive and affective resources for coping with events in his daily life (*EA* = 14.5; *EB* = 8.0:6.5). These resources appear more than sufficient to manage the demands he is facing (*es* = 11; *Adjes* = 9), and he consequently has a *D-Score* of +1 and an *AdjD-Score* of +2. Such positive *D* scores are usually associated with good stress tolerance, behavioral stability, and a likelihood of keeping relatively calm in situations that would alarm most people. However, his stability and stress tolerance also suggest that he is a person who resists change and may be oblivious to matters that should cause him concern.

The data concerning this man's cognitive functioning provide additional evidence of personality strengths. He appears able to perceive people and events accurately (*XA%* = 0.94; *WDA%* = 0.93; *X−%* = 0.00) and to recognize and endorse conventional modes of behavior (*P* = 6). Along with his good reality testing, he shows an unimpaired ability to think logically, coherently, and constructively (*WSum6* = 6; *Lv2* = 0; *Ma:Mp* = 5:3). His adaptive cognitive functioning is summarized by his normal-range *WSum6* = 0, *PTI* = 0, and *EII-2* = −1.11. Also noteworthy in his cognitive functioning is the indication of considerable utilization of intellectualization as a way of taking distance from concrete and here-and-now considerations and thereby minimizing overtly felt anxiety (*INTELL* = 16; *AB* = 7).

Other clusters of variables also include some findings related to good adjustment. In the interpersonal domain he shows substantial interest in other people

Table 15.1 Structural Summary

			Affect	Interpersonal
R = 31	**L = 0.55**			
EB = 8.0:6.5	**EA = 14.5**	**EBPer = 1.2**	**FC:CF+C = 0:6***	**COP = 1 AG = 1**
eb = 7:4	es = 11	**D = +1***	**Pure C = 1**	GHR:PHR = 6:8
	Adjes = 9	**AdjD = +2***	**Const. = 0:6.5**	**a:p = 10:5**
			Afr = 0.41	Fd =1 *
FM = 4	**SumC' = 0**	**SumT = 3***	**S = 1**	**SumT = 3***
m = 3	**SumV = 0**	**SumY = 1**	**Complex. = 9:31**	**Human Content = 11**
			CP = 0	**Pure H = 6**
				PER = 0
				Isolation Index = 0.06
	Cognitive Functioning			Self-Perception
Thinking (Ideation)		Perception (Mediation)	Attention (Processing)	
a:p = 10:5	Sum6 = 2	**XA% = 0.94**	Zf = 24	**Egoc. Index = 0.13***
Ma:Mp = 5:3	**Lv2 = 0**	**WDA% = 0.93**	**W:D:Dd = 20:10:1***	**Fr+rF = 0**
INTELL = 16*	**WSum6 = 6**	**X–% = 0.00**	W:M = 20:8	**SumV = 0**
MOR = 3*	**M– = 0**	S– = 0	**Zd = –6.5***	**FD = 4***
	Mnone = 0	**P = 6**	PSV = 0	An+Xy = 1
		X+% = 0.52	DQ+ = 14	**MOR = 3***
		Xu% = 0.42	**DQv = 1**	**H:(H)+Hd+ (Hd) = 6:5**
PTI = 0	**DEPI = 6***	**CDI = 3**	**S-CON = 6**	**HVI = No** OBS = No
FM+m = 7*	**Col-Shd Blend = 1**			
RFS-P = +0.71*	**RFS-S = 2.00**	**EII-2 = –1.11**	**AdjDMD = +1***	

Note: The format of the two sections of the table is derived from the Rorschach Interpretation Assistance Program (RIAP). The scores in bold (upper section) are those of the basic variables used for distinguishing between healthy and psychopathological personality functioning as presented in Chapter 4. Noted with asterisks (*) are scores that exceed the normative range (see Chapter 5)

Table 15.2 Sequence of Scores

Card	*Resp.*								*RFS-2*
I	1	*Wo*	*FMao*		*A*		*ZW*		1
	2	*Wo*	*Fo*		*Sc*		*ZW*		3
	3	*Do*	*Fo*		*Hd*				3
	4	*Do*	*Fo*	2	*Hd*				3
	5	*Wo*	*FMpo*		*A*	*P*	*ZW*		1
II	6	*W+*	*Ma.CFo*		*H*		*ZW*		0
	7	*W+*	*Ma.FDo*		*Hd*		*ZW*		0
	8	*WS+*	*ma.CFo*		*Hx, Sc, Fi*		*ZW*	*AB*	−1
III	9	*D+*	*Mpo*	2	*H, Ay*	*P*	*ZA*	*AB*	−1
	10	*Wo*	*Mp.Cu*		*H*		*ZW*	*MOR, AB*	−2
IV	11	*Wo*	*FD.TFu*		*A*		*ZW*		1
	12	*Do*	*Fu*		*Fd*				2
	13	*Wo*	*Fu*		*A*		*ZW*		2
V	14	*Wo*	*FMao*		*A*	*P*	*ZW*	*INC*	1
	15	*Do*	*Fo*		*A*				3
	16	*Wo*	*Fo*		*A*	*P*	*ZW*		4
VI	17	*Wv*	*Y*		*Xy*				0
	18	*D+*	*Mau*		*Hd, Ex*		*ZA*	*AB*	−2
	19	*Ddo*	*Fu*		*A*				2
	20	*W+*	*FDu*		*A, Ls*		*ZW*		1
	21	*Wo*	*Fu*		*Ay*		*ZW*		2
VII	22	*W+*	*FMa.FTu*		*A, Hx, Id*		*ZW*	*AB*	−2
VIII	23	*W+*	*CFu*		*Ge*		*ZW*		1
	24	*Do*	*Ma.Cn*	2	*H*				0
	25	*D+*	*Fo*	2	*Sc*		*ZA*		3
	26	*W+*	*mp. CF.FDu*		*Sc*		*ZW*	*AB*	−2

(*continued*)

Table 15.2 (Cont.)

Card	*Resp.*								*RFS-2*
IX	27	*D+*	*Mao*		*H*	*P*	*ZA*	*COP, AG*	0
	28	*D+*	*Mpu*		*H, Hx*		*ZA*	*MOR*	–1
X	29	*Wo*	*Fo*		*Sc*		*ZW*		3
	30	*W+*	*CF.TFu*		*Hd, A*	*P*	*ZW*	*MOR*	2
	31	*W+*	*Mao*		*A*		*ZW*	*FAB, AB*	–5

Note: The *RFS-2* column refers to the score of each response on the *Reality–Fantasy Scale Version 2.0*

(*Pure H* = 6), and in the self-perception domain he gives evidence of psychological-mindedness and openness to introspection (*FD* = 4).

All of this having been said, there is a striking contrast in this man's Rorschach between the indications of good coping resources and mostly effective defenses against becoming upset on the one hand, and evidence of considerable underlying distress on the other. Most notable in this regard is his elevated *DEPI* of 6. This *DEPI* score strongly suggests that he is either currently depressed or highly susceptible to becoming depressed. Illustrative in this regard were his Response 10 on Card III ("A distressing image of a figure with the red in the center suggesting his distress") and his Response 28 on Card IX ("Two figures back to back sulking"). Also of note is the composition of his apparent openness to experiencing and expressing affect (*WSumC* = 6.5), which consists of five *CF*, one *Pure C*, and no FC. For a man who appears committed to keeping tight and precise control over how he perceives and copes with experience (*D-Score* = +2; *X–%* = 0.00; *DQv* = 1), this *CF+C* emphasis represents a marked loosening of affective control that is usually associated more with labile than stable emotionality. What emerges, then, is the picture of a complex man whose overtly positive adaptation and comfort with himself appear to be masking underlying uncertainty and problematic concerns.

With respect to uncertainty, he gives evidence of being both an introspective man, as just noted, and also a person who focuses his attention on the outer world of reality while avoiding fantasy and ignoring his inner thoughts and feelings (*RFS-P* = 0.71). Despite being relatively open to experience (*Lambda* = 0.55), he gives evidence of being prone to examining his experiences less thoroughly than would be desirable in making decisions and coming to conclusions (*Zd* = –6.5), and also of focusing on the entirety of events while overlooking or ignoring their ordinary or commonplace details (*W:D:Dd* = 20:10:1). His hasty decision-making may result in his being more careless than careful, and his global perspective, although possibly reflecting his artistic temperament, can also be serving to shield him from full awareness of events that he would find distressing.

Similarly attesting to this uncertainty is the combination of his previously noted endorsement of conventionality (*P* = 6), which is often associated with wanting to be like other people, with a rejection of conventionality (*Xu%* = 0.42), which is usually associated with wanting to be different from them. In addition, his *Color–Shading Blend* in Response 30 on Card X suggests a tendency to invest situations with both pleasant and unpleasant characteristics and to vacillate between these affective impressions. Similarly uncertain is his expectation about how people are likely to relate to each other, as suggested by his Response 27 on Card IX of "Two figures dancing or fighting."

As for problematic concerns, this man's Rorschach protocol contains evidence of numerous difficulties in establishing and maintaining pleasurable object relationships. His interpersonal cluster of variables includes indications of negative attitudes toward other people and a likely history of discomfort, disappointment, and discord in social interactions (*GHR:PHR* = 6:8). In this regard, he appears capable of forming mutually supportive interpersonal relationships with other people and is interested in doing so (*COP* = 1), but also to be experiencing unmet needs for close personal attachments (*T* = 3). His *Food* response on Card IV was "It looks like an apple core," which raises the possibility that some of his unmet interpersonal needs involve dependency. However, just one such response occurring in a record should be interpreted tentatively, especially when it is not elaborated (such as by commenting on how tasty it looks). This response also has a depressive flavor, as if to fantasize that "someone else ate the apple, and there is nothing left for me except the core."

As for his relationships with himself, the self-perception variables include two indications of a negative self-image. First, he gives compelling evidence of low self-esteem and an inclination to compare himself unfavorably to other people (*Egocentricity Index* = 0.13). Second, he appears to direct his generally pessimistic attitudes in part toward his own body, which he regards as damaged or dysfunctional in some respects and vulnerable to being harmed by external forces (*MOR* = 3).

Conclusion

This 67-year-old British man, who was a voluntary participant in a research study, presents a complex picture of psychological adaptation and underlying problematic concerns. On the positive side, he gives evidence of good psychological coping resources (*EA* = 14.5), solid defenses against becoming upset (*D-Score* = +2; *INTELL* = *16*), and unimpaired ability to think logically and coherently and to perceive people and events accurately (*PTI* = 0; *EII-2* = –1.11). On the negative side, his Rorschach protocol includes numerous signs of depression (*DEPI* = 6) and difficulties in relating comfortably with other people and with himself. These difficulties include a negative view of people and likely social discomfort (*GHR:PHR* = 6:8), unmet needs for close attachments (*T* = 3), low self-esteem (*Egocentricity Index* = 0.13), and concerns about the adequacy of his body and bodily functions (*MOR* = 3).

What we have in this case, then, is a man with no known history of psychological disorder or mental health treatment who has apparently been well adjusted in his family life and in his vocation as an artist and art instructor, but who nevertheless appears to have an underlying depressive disorder. Speculation on the origin of this masked depression, particularly with respect to his negative self-image, brings us back to the title of this chapter, "The Après Coup Effect." In this man's case, we are very likely to be seeing the persistent and long-term effect of traumatic childhood experiences.

References

American Psychiatric Association (2013). *Diagnostic and statistical manual of mental disorders* (5th ed.). Arlington, VA: Author.

Blumberg, H. H., Zeligman, R., Appel, L., & Tibon-Czopp, S. (2017). Personality dimensions and attitudes towards peace and war. *Journal of Aggression, Conflict and Peace Research*, 9, 13–23.

Del Corno, F., & Plotkin, D. (2017). Symptom patters in the elderly. Part V in V. Lingiardi & N. McWilliams (Eds.), *Psychodynamic diagnostic manual* (2nd ed., pp. 751–888). New York, NY: Guilford Press.

CHAPTER 16

Fibromyalgia and Alexithymia "It's Better Not to Think About It than to Suffer"

Fibromyalgia is a chronic pain disorder characterized by widespread muscular and skeletal pain. Among the possible causes of this disorder are recurrent episodes of emotional trauma and psychological distress. When such appear to be the case, this psychosomatic condition is diagnosed in both the *Diagnostic and Statistical Manual of Mental Disorders, Fifth Edition* (*DSM-5*; American Psychiatric Association, 2013) and the *Psychodynamic Diagnostic Manual* (*PDM-2*; Lingiardi & McWilliams, 2017) as Somatic Symptom Disorder. People with this disorder commonly show features of alexithymia.

First identified by Sifneos (1973), alexithymia consists of a limited ability to become aware of one's feelings and express or describe them. This emotional dysfunction often makes it difficult for a person to form mutually pleasurable interpersonal relationships and close attachments to others, and it is typically characterized as well by minimal imaginal capacity and a stimulus-bound cognitive style that leaves little room for fantasy. Taylor and Taylor (2012) and Mohammad and Yaghoubirad (2016) have reviewed empirical research that documents these features of alexithymia and its stability as a personality trait. Numerous other research studies have confirmed the common co-occurrence of fibromyalgia and alexithymia (Di Tella et al., 2017; Huber et al., 2009; Montoro, Reyes del Paso, & Duschek, 2016; van Middendorp, Lumley, Jacobs, van Doornen, Bijlsama, & Geenen, 2008).

Alexithymia may best be conceived of as a disorder of affect regulation reflecting deficits in the cognitive and interpersonal regulation of emotions (Taylor, Bagby, & Parker, 1999). From a developmental psychoanalytic perspective, the capacity for affect regulation emerges from the infant–caregiver interaction. While the parent acts to remedy the child's homeostatic imbalance, as described by Kohut (1977), deficiencies in the early parent–child relationship may restrict the child's development of self-regulatory functions (Grotstein, 1983). This conceptualization is shared by attachment theory, which proposes that disruption of attachment bonds in infancy may lead to a self-regulatory failure and an impaired autonomic homeostasis (Schore & Schore, 2008).

These theoretical notions have recently received empirical support from neurobiological research findings that suggest a developmental structural failure in the cerebral system that is directly involved in homeostatic regulation. This structural failure is seen as leading to a limited capacity to generate affect-regulating symbolic representations. Without access to a more complex capacity for affect regulation, stressful emotions are experienced as primitive, sensorimotor, and undifferentiated bodily sensations, rather than as complex blends of feelings (Score, 2015). Deficits in early object relationships may thus put people at risk of becoming illness-prone and exhibiting developmental arrest, particularly as manifest in a poor quality of self and object representations. The present case illustrates these alexithymic characteristics in a woman abandoned in infancy and currently suffering from fibromyalgia and widespread fearfulness.

Background Information

The patient in this case is a 65-year-old Brazilian woman with diagnosed fibromyalgia who complained to her rheumatologist of episodes of fearfulness on buses and subways and in other crowded places together with a fear of being alone that had emerged following the recent death of her oldest daughter. He referred her for evaluation to a psychiatric outpatient clinic, where she was interviewed and administered the Rorschach.

On interview, she related a lifelong history of stressful life events, beginning with her parents separating and abandoning her while she was still in infancy. She had no further contact with her mother, and her father sent her to live with her maternal grandparents. She has kept some souvenirs from her time with her grandparents, which suggests that these were good years for her, but she was unable to describe any feelings she had for them. When these grandparents died, she was moved to the home of her father, who had since remarried. Her stepmother disliked and mistreated her, she said, and sent her to live with her own parents, who would have been her step-grandparents. She had several stepsiblings from her father's second marriage, including a stepsister who committed suicide and a stepbrother who was struck and killed by a speeding car as she watched him crossing the street. She said she had no feelings about these tragic events, however, because she had never had much contact with either of them.

She remained with her step-grandparents for the next several years, during which she completed an elementary school education, began working as a maid, and became sexually active. She became pregnant with her first steady boyfriend, had an abortion, and broke off her relationship with him. She subsequently became pregnant with another boyfriend, whom she married and with whom she had this child, a girl, and two other daughters. Her marriage did not go well. Her husband drank heavily and was mentally and physically abusive to her. Sexual relations with him were unpleasant, unwanted, and devoid of any affection, she said, and although she feared and hated him, she stayed in the marriage "for the benefit of the children." Her husband had died two years prior the present examination, and she said that she had had no feelings for his loss.

Five months before this examination, her oldest daughter had died at age 37 from lung cancer, for which she had been treated since age 15. The patient said she was close to this daughter and that "I think I suffered with her death" but she cannot describe her feelings at the time. Instead, she said, "It's better not think about it than to suffer." With her limited education, she continued to work as a maid until retiring a few years previously. She is currently living with her youngest daughter and her daughter's son. While presenting this life history, she said, "I have never talked about these things with anyone." Tables 16.1 and 16.2 present the Structural Summary and Sequence of Scores for her Rorschach protocol.

Interpretation of Rorschach Data

Most striking in this valid (R = 17) Rorschach protocol are two indications of extremely limited coping resources: a *CDI* of 5 and an *EA* of just 2. This woman gives evidence of some emotional distress, as shown by both *D* and *AdjD* scores of –1. However, despite her limited capacities for coping effectively with life events, her high *Lambda* of 3.25 makes it likely that she is minimizing her felt distress by maintaining a narrow focus of attention on what is happening around her. She thus appears to have a closed mind to both thoughts and feelings that might be disturbing to her, which is confirmed by her *EB* of just 1:1. Such a generally closed mind means that even slight deviations from normative expectation on Rorschach variables are likely to have considerable interpretive significance.

With further respect to this woman's feelings, she does not appear to avoid emotionally charged or affect-arousing situations (*Afr* = 0.55), but the Rorschach data identify difficulty expressing her feelings as well as her limited awareness of them. She gave just one color response, a *CF*, but two *C′* achromatic responses, and her resulting 2:1 *Constriction Ratio* indicates that her emotions are more likely to be bottled up than expressed. The nature of these unexpressed feelings is difficult to determine, but her *DEPI* of 5 suggests that they may include some underlying sadness.

As for limited awareness of her thoughts, her elevated *RFS-P* of 1.88 indicates that she is a reality-bound person who attends more to the external world than to her inner experience and who seldom indulges in imaginal thinking. Noteworthy in this regard is that a high positive *RFS-P* has been found to be a good indicator of proneness to alexithymia (Tibon, Porcelli, & Weinberger, 2005). In this woman's test behavior, avoidance of fantasy was apparent in a reluctance to give responses or to elaborate on them. On 3 of the 10 cards, she needed encouragement to give her first response, and she began many of her responses with a noncommittal "I don't know, but it could be…" Among her other comments were "It just looked that way, and I can't describe it," "I can't even imagine what this might be," and "I can't put these parts together to make anything."

Table 16.1 Structural Summary

			Affect	Interpersonal
R = 17	**L = 3.25***			
EB = 1:1	**EA = 2***	**EBPer = 1.0**	**FC:CF+C = 0:1***	**COP = 0* AG = 0**
eb = 2:3	*es = 5*	**D = −1**	**Pure C = 0**	*GHR:PHR = 0:2*
	Adjes = 5	**AdjD = −1**	**Const. Index = 2:1***	**a:p = 0:3***
			Afr = 0.55	**Fd = 1***
FM = 2	**SumC′ = 2**	**SumT = 1**	**S = 2**	**SumT = 1**
m = 0	**SumV = 0**	**SumY = 0**	**Complex. = 3:17**	**Human Content = 2**
			CP = 0	**Pure H = 0***
				PER = 0
				Isolation Index = 0.12
	Cognitive Functioning			Self-Perception
Thinking (Ideation)		Perception (Mediation)	Attention (Processing)	
a:p = 0:3*	*Sum6 = 3*	**XA% = 1.00**	*Zf = 6*	**Egoc. Index = 0.35**
Ma:Mp = 0:1*	**Lv2 = 1***	**WDA% = 1.00**	**W:D:Dd = 4:8:5***	**Fr+rF = 0**
INTELL = 1	**WSum6 = 5**	**X−% = 0.00**	*W:M = 4:1*	**SumV = 0**
MOR = 3	**M− = 0**	*S− = 0*	**Zd = −4.0***	**FD = 0***
	Mnone = 0	**P = 3***	*PSV = 0*	*An+Xy = 3*
		X+% = 0.76	*DQ+ = 1*	**MOR = 3***
		Xu% = 0.24	**DQv = 0**	**H:(H)+Hd+ (Hd) = 0:2***
PTI = 0	**DEPI = 5***	**CDI = 5***	**S-CON = 5**	**HVI = No** *OBS = No*
FM+m = 2	**Col–Shd = 1**			
RFS-P = 1.88*	**RFS-S = 2.25**	**EII-2 = −0.18**	**AdjDMD = 0**	

Note: The format of the two sections of the table is derived from the Rorschach Interpretation Assistance Program (RIAP). The scores in bold (upper section) are those of the basic variables used for distinguishing between healthy and psychopathological personality functioning as presented in Chapter 4. Noted with asterisks (*) are scores that exceed the normative range (see Chapter 5)

Turning to her object relationships, this woman seems capable of forming close and mutually supportive relationships with other people (*T* = 1), but she appears unlikely to anticipate that interpersonal relationships will in fact be collaborative (*COP* = 0). The *Pure H* = 0 in her record suggests minimal interest in other people and a limited capacity to identify with them. As shown in Table 16.2, the two human content responses she did give did not occur until the last two responses

Table 16.2 Sequence of Scores

Card	*Resp.*								*RFS-2*
I	1	*Wo*	*Fo*		*A*	*P*	*ZW*		4
II	2	*Do*	*Fo*		*A*			*DV*	3
III	3	*Ddo*	*Fo*	2	*A*				3
	4	*Ddo*	*Fo*	2	*An, Ay*			*MOR, DV2*	-5
	5	*Do*	*Fo*	2	*Bt*			*MOR*	3
IV	6	*Do*	*FT.FMpo*		*A*				1
	7	*Wo*	*Fo*		*Bt*		*ZW*	*MOR*	3
V	8	*Wo*	*Fo*		*A*	*P*	*ZW*		4
VI	9	*Wo*	*Fu*		*Fd, An*		*ZW*		2
VII	10	*Do*	*FMpu*	2	*A*				-1
	11	*Do*	*Fo*	2	*A*				3
VIII	12	*Do*	*Fo*	2	*A*	*P*			4
	13	*Do*	*Fo*		*A*				3
	14	*DdSo*	*CF.FC'o*		*An*		*ZS*	*INC*	2
IX	15	*Ddo*	*Fu*		*Sx*				2
	16	*D+*	*FC'.Mpo*		*Hd*		*ZA*	*PHR*	-1
X	17	*DdSo*	*Fu*		*Hd*			*PHR*	2

Note: The *RFS-2* column refers to the score of each response on the *Reality–Fantasy Scale Version 2.0*

in her record, and both of them are *PHR Hd* responses, which often point to social ineptness and reflect a history of problematic and unrewarding interpersonal relationships.

In addition, the content of these last two responses may identify some underlying sources of concern to her. Response 16 was "Two heads of a baby," which might symbolize helpless beings who are cared for by other people. Response 17 was a human body "from the waist up," which might suggest anxiety about or aversion to sexuality. With further respect to the possible implications of the "baby" response, her *a:p* ratio of 0:3 and the presence of a *Food* response suggest some passive–dependent personality characteristics. She may thus be a person who longs for other people to make decisions for her and tend to her needs, but who unfortunately lacks the initiative as well as the necessary social skills to reach out for and establish such relationships.

The self-perception data in this woman's protocol are notable for indications of negative attitudes toward herself (*MOR* = 3). These negative self-attitudes might involve dissatisfaction with her bodily condition (e.g., her fibromyalgia), and they could extend more broadly to seeing herself as physically or psychologically vulnerable to being hurt or harmed. Also significant among the self-perception variables is the absence of *FD*, which suggests that she is not inclined to be reflective or psychologically minded and which would be consistent with her reality-bound tendency to avoid thoughts and feelings.

The data concerning her cognitive functioning include several deviations from normative expectation in how she attends to, perceives, and thinks about people and events. Her focus of attention is unusual in two respects. First, 5 of her 17 responses (29%) are to *Dd* locations, which indicates excessive attention to unusual features of her environment at the expense of sufficient attention to its ordinary and commonplace elements. Second, her *Zd* of –4.0 indicates that she is an *underincorporator*, which is a person who makes decisions hastily and comes to conclusions quickly without taking into account as much relevant information as they should consider.

Along with her unusual focus of attention, this woman also appears to perceive the world in unusual ways. The Rorschach evidence in this regard is her *P* of only 3, which speaks to a distaste for conventionality and a wish to be her own person and to do things her own way. These indications of individuality rather than conformity are somewhat surprising in view of her apparently passive–dependent orientation, which usually involves attempting to please other people by being like them rather than different from them. It may be that she struggles within herself between wanting to depend on other people and, in view of her life experiences, believing that other people cannot be counted on to be concerned with her welfare and that she must be able to fend for herself.

Finally, with respect to her cognitive functioning, and perhaps consistent with her narrow frame of reference, her *XA%* of 1.00 indicates that she is fully capable of perceiving people and events realistically. Along with her unimpaired reality testing, she appears capable for the most part of thinking logically and coherently (*WSum6* = 5). There is a *Level 2* special score in the record, a *DV2* on Response 4, which the examiner coded for "The head of a skull." Perhaps this response could be considered just a *DV1*, but either way it would not by itself call for any inferences of disordered thinking. It might, however, represent an attempt to defend herself by devaluating a threatening human figure.

Conclusion

This case illustration provides a good example of congruence among a person's manifestations of psychological disorder, life history, and Rorschach responses.

The patient is a 65-year-old Brazilian woman with fibromyalgia who complained to her rheumatologist of fearfulness on buses and subways and in other crowded places. He referred her for evaluation to a psychiatric outpatient clinic, where she was interviewed and administered the Rorschach. Fibromyalgia has several possible causes, one of which is emotional stress, and it often co-occurs with alexithymia, a condition that features a limited ability to become aware of one's feelings and express or describe them to others. This emotional dysfunction often makes it difficult for a person to form mutually pleasurable interpersonal relationships and close attachments to others, and it is often characterized as well by minimal imaginal capacity and a stimulus-bound cognitive style that tends to disallow fantasy. Developmental psychoanalytic theories attribute this dysfunction to deficiencies in the early dyadic infant–caregiver relationship.

Recurrent episodes of severe stress have characterized this woman's life. Abandoned by her mother in infancy and by her father soon after, she was shuttled between her sets of grandparents. Later reunited with her now-remarried father, she encountered a stepmother who disliked and mistreated her and soon sent her to live with her own parents. She remained with these step-grandparents while completing an elementary school education and shortly thereafter beginning what would be her lifelong work as a maid. During this time, a stepsister committed suicide and a stepbrother was killed by a speeding car as she watched him cross the street. Illustrative of her alexithymic avoidance of emotion, she stated in giving her life history that she had no feelings about these tragic events, because she had never had much contact with either of them.

As a teenager, she became pregnant with her first regular boyfriend, had an abortion, and terminated this relationship. She later became pregnant with another boyfriend, married him, and had this child, a girl, and two other daughters. Her husband became an abusive drunkard, and she said that sexual relations with him were unwanted and unpleasant. Her husband had died two years prior to this examination and, once again consistent with her alexithymia, she said that she had no feelings for his loss. Her oldest daughter had developed lung cancer at age 15 and died at age 37, five months prior to this examination. She was unable to describe her feelings at that time and said, "It's better not to think about it than to suffer." In concert with her reticence, she commented to the interviewer that she had never before talked with anyone about these matters.

Her Rorschach responses captured many features of her alexithymic style. A *Lambda* of 3.25, an *EB* of 1:1, and an *RFS-P* of 1.88 indicated a narrow frame of reference and an avoidance of both thoughts and feelings. The *EA* of just 2 combined with the *CDI* of 5 were evidence of limited coping resources, but her closed-mindedness appears to have kept her subjectively felt distress at a minimum (*D-Score* = –1). There was nevertheless some indication in her responses of negative attitudes toward herself and possibly some accompanying sadness (*MOR* = 3; *DEPI* = 5). Also consistent with common consequences of alexithymia, the absence of *COP* and *Pure H* and the *PHR* responses in her record suggested limited involvement with other people and probable difficulties in establishing pleasurable and collaborative interpersonal relationships.

In her cognitive functioning, she demonstrated good reality testing and an ability for the most part to think logically and coherently, with an *XA*–% of 1.00 and a *WSum6* of 5. Interestingly, however, she also showed some preference for being different from other people and doing things her own way, with five *Dd* and only three *P* responses. These indications of individuality rather than conformity contrast with suggestions in her record of a passive–dependent orientation. Her need for the support of other people who will take care of her may be causing her concern about not having or losing such comforting relationships. Relevant in this regard is her previously mentioned report of experiencing fears of being alone since the recent death of her daughter. A final point of note is that her response of "A human body, from the waist up" may reflect her expressed distaste for sexual relationships, perhaps resulting from her unpleasant marital experience.

References

American Psychiatric Association (2013). *Diagnostic and statistical manual of mental disorders* (5th ed.). Arlington, VA: Author.

Di Tella, M., Ghiggia, A., Tesio, V., Romeo, A., Colonna, F., Fusaro, E., Torta, R., & Castelli, L. (2017). Pain experience in fibromyalgia syndrome: The role of alexithymia and psychological distress. *Journal of Affective Disorders, 208*, 87–93.

Grotstein, J. S. (1983). Some perspectives on self psychology. In A. Goldberg (Ed.), *The future of psychoanalysis* (pp. 165–201). New York, NY: International Universities Press.

Huber, A., Suman, A. L., Blasi, G., & Carli, G. (2009). Alexithymia in fibromyalgia syndrome. *Journal of Psychosomatic Research, 66*, 425–433.

Kohut, H. (1977). *The restoration of the self.* New York, NY: University of Chicago Press.

Lingiardi, V., & McWilliams, N. (2017). *Psychodynamic diagnostic manual* (2nd ed.). New York, NY: Guilford Press.

Mohammad, A., & Yaghoubirad, M. (2016). The Big Five personality dimensions and mental health: The mediating role of alexithymia. *Asian Journal of Psychiatry, 24*, 59–64.

Montoro, C., Reyes del Paso, G. A., & Duschek, S. (2016), Alexithymia in fibromyalgia syndrome. *Personality and Individual Differences, 102*, 170–179.

Schore, A. N. (2015). *Affect regulation and the origin of the self: The neurobiology of emotional development.* New York, NY: Routledge.

Schore, J. R., & Schore, A. N. (2008). Modern attachment theory: The central role of affect regulation in development and treatment. *Clinical Social Work Journal, 36*(1), 9–20.

Sifneos, P. E. (1973). The prevalence of "alexithymic" characteristics in psychosomatic patients. *Psychotherapy and Psychosomatics, 22*, 255–262.

Taylor, G. J., & Bagby, R. M. (2012). The alexithymia personality dimension. In T. A. Widiger (Ed.), *Oxford handbook of personality disorders* (pp. 648–673). New York, NY: Oxford University Press.

Taylor, G. J., Bagby, R. M., & Parker, J. D. (1999). *Disorders of affect regulation: Alexithymia in medical and psychiatric illness.* Cambridge, UK: Cambridge University Press.

Tibon, S., Porcelli, P., & Weinberger, Y. (2005). The Ego Impairment Index and the Reality–Fantasy Scale: Comment on Viglione, Perry, and Meyer (2003). *Journal of Personality Assessment*, *84*(3), 315–317.

van Middendorp, H., Lumley, M. A., Jacobs, J. W. G., van Doornen, L. J. P., Bijlsama, J. W., & Geenen, R. (2008). Emotions and emotional approach and avoidance in fibromyalgia. *Journal of Psychosomatic Research*, *64*, 159–167.

CHAPTER 17

Obsessive–Compulsive Personality "I'm Looking for a Symbolic Response"

Aging is itself a potential source of stress, particularly with respect to coping with changing family, social, and work-related circumstances over which the person has little or no control. Del Corno and Plotkin (2017) observe in this regard that aging is commonly experienced as a threat to one's ability to exercise control. This concern is particularly prominent in senior adults with obsessive–compulsive personality characteristics, given the centrality of control issues in obsessive ruminations and compulsive actions. However, the potentially depressing and anxiety-provoking impacts of declining control can be minimized in various ways that constitute enrichment of aging, rather than resignation to it. Among these ways are applying old skills to new ventures, replacing customary interests and pastimes with fresh ones, and reflecting on one's identity and autobiographical narrative. The emergence of a new perspective on one's past and current life circumstances can enable the psychologically healthy elderly person to take on the role of the "wise old man" who enjoys a new personality style, with new habits and new roles that follow urges and dreams of what Winnicott (1965) defined as the *true self*.

In fact, although the elderly lose some roles, skills, and identities in the macro level of their relationships, they may acquire new ones in the micro-level context. This is particularly important among elderly people who show a fixed type of personality traits, even if not a diagnosable personality disorder. Such a fixed type often protects the elderly from experiencing depressive and anxiety symptoms. Emotions and impulses are perceived as dangerous and are possibly avoided. Feelings of fear, shame, and anger become ruminative thoughts, addressed by a variety of defenses or through actions designed to exert control.

Normative senior adults who function adaptively are rarely likely to seek psychotherapy solely for the purpose of obtaining a new perspective on aging. As would be expected from their generally normative functioning, senior adults who do not show any adaptation difficulties may provide a normative Rorschach protocol with no prominent deviations. A masked depressive disorder might go unnoticed and the presence of psychopathology might be difficult to determine if adaptation is used as the main criterion. Clinicians who use the Rorschach in evaluating senior adults should therefore look for any discrepancies between indices pointing to adaptive functioning and indices showing difficulties associated with subjective experience. The following case illustration explores the Rorschach data of a 67-year-old retired educational supervisor with obsessive–compulsive traits who participated in a nonpatient sample of an Israeli–British research project (Blumberg, Zeligman, Appel, & Czopp-Tibon, 2017).

Background Information

This respondent is a 67-year-old British man, born and raised in a city in west England. His parents, both of whom had worked in high-level positions, are faithful Catholics. He is married and has two children. Following his graduation from an MA program in education and music, the couple moved to a city in south-eastern England, where he was employed by the state-funded Catholic educational system. He had advanced to a supervisory position by the time of his retirement about two years ago. As an adolescent, he had decided to abandon religion because of what he said were "some philosophical questions" that he had asked himself. These questions had substantial implications for his views on how he should behave. Accordingly, he reported that his job as a teacher and a supervisor in a Catholic school required some "false patterns of behaviors" during his career.

Since his retirement, he and his wife have spent most of their time caring for their parents, who had been diagnosed with dementia, and helping them find ways of remaining engaged in activities that were within their capacities. He himself is currently serving as a volunteer consultant in crisis intervention within his community. He has no known history of diagnosed psychological disorder or mental health treatment, and as just noted, he was examined as a voluntary participant in a normative data collection research study.

Asked to describe his major personality traits on self-report questionnaires (see Blumberg, Zeligman, Appel, & Czopp-Tibon, 2017), he presented a picture of a senior adult who sees himself as a moralistic, warm, egalitarian, task-oriented, responsible, contented, sympathetic, calm, and emotionally stable person. These personality characteristics were apparent as he applied himself diligently and with enthusiasm to the Rorschach task and appeared intent on seeing as many different things as possible in the blots. In doing so, he politely expressed doubts about the possibility of learning anything about his personality from his responses. He also began some of his Rorschach responses with such comments as "This is just an inkblot" or "I can't see anything." Nevertheless, he persevered in giving 90 distinct responses with more than five responses to each of the 10 cards. In accord with recommended procedures, only the first five responses to each card were coded. Tables 17.1 and 17.2 present the Structural Summary and Sequence of Scores for his resulting 50-response Rorschach protocol.

Interpretation of Rorschach Data

The most striking feature of this senior adult's Rorschach protocol was his obsessive concern with searching the blots and finding as many responses as possible.

Table 17.1 Structural Summary

			Affect	Interpersonal
***R* = 50**	***L* = 0.85**			
***EB* = 4.0:7.5**	***EA* = 11.5**	***EBPer* = 1.9**	***FC:CF+C* = 2:6***	***COP* = 0* *AG* = 2**
eb* = 10:11	*es* = 21	***D* = -3***	***Pure C* = 1***	*GHR:PHR* = 7:5
	Adjes = 10	***AdjD* = 0**	***Const. Index* = 1:7.5**	***a:p* = 9:5**
			***Afr* = 0.43**	***Fd* = 0**
***FM* = 5**	***SumC'* = 1**	***SumT* = 1**	***S* = 1**	***SumT* = 1**
***m* = 5**	***SumV* = 1**	***SumY* = 8**	***Complex.* = 8:50**	***Human Content* = 11**
			CP = 0	***Pure H* = 4**
				***PER* = 1**
				***Isolation Index* = 0.20**
	Cognitive Functioning			
Thinking (Ideation)		Perception (Mediation)	Attention (Processing)	Self-Perception
***a:p* = 9:5**	*Sum6* = 0	***XA%* = 0.86**	*Zf* = 26	***Egoc. Index* = 0.06***
***Ma:Mp* = 2:2**	***Lv2* = 0**	***WDA%* = 0.87**	***W:D:Dd* = 16:30:4**	***Fr+rF* = 0**
INTELL* = 6	***WSum6* = 0**	***X–%* = 0.08**	*W:M* = 16:4	***Sum V* = 1***
***MOR* = 2**	***M–* = 1**	*S–* = 0	***Zd* = –14***	***FD* = 2**
	Mnone = 1	***P* = 4**	*PSV* = 2	*An+Xy* = 3
		X+% = 0.48	*DQ+* = 19	***MOR* = 2**
		Xu%* = 0.38	***DQv* = 0**	***H:(H)+Hd+ (Hd)* = 4:7***
***PTI* = 0**	***DEPI* = 7***	***CDI* = 1**	***S-CON* = 7**	***HVI* = No** *OBS* = No
FM+m* = 10	***Col-Shd* = 3***			
***RFS-P* = 0.82**	***RFS-S* = 2.09**	***EII-2* = –2.24**	***AdjDMD* = 3***	

Note: The format of the two sections of the table is derived from the Rorschach Interpretation Assistance Program (RIAP). The scores in bold (upper section) are those of the basic variables used for distinguishing between healthy and psychopathological personality functioning as presented in Chapter 4. Noted with asterisks (*) are scores that exceed the normative range (see Chapter 5)

As just noted, his resulting 90 responses were reduced for purposes of coding and interpretation to the first five responses to each card, resulting in an *R* of 50. His productivity nevertheless makes obvious his full cooperation and enthusiastic engagement in the Rorschach task, which for him was a novel and unfamiliar activity. The data in Table 17.1 confirm in this regard that his mind is currently open to new interests and perspectives and that he is prepared to act spontaneously and with some creativity (*Lambda* < 0.99; *Xu%* > 0.30).

Table 17.2 Sequence of Scores

Card	*Resp.*								*RFS-2*
I	1	*Wo*	*FMa.FC'u*		*A*		*ZW*	*AB*	–2
	2	*W+*	*Fu*		*Ge*		*ZA*		2
	3	*W+*	*Fu*		*Ge*		*ZA*	*PSV*	2
	4	*Wo*	*FDu*		*Ls*		*ZW*		1
	5	*Do*	*Fo*		*Hd*			*PHR*	3
II	6	*Do*	*C*		*Bl*			*MOR, PER*	–2
	7	*DS+*	*ma.CFo*		*Sc*		*ZA*		1
	8	*W+*	*VF.CFu*		*Sc, Bl*		*ZW*	*MOR*	1
	9	*Do*	*ma.CFo*		*Ex*			*GHR*	0
	10	*Do*	*FCo*		*A*				2
III	11	*Do*	*Fo*		*H*	*P*		*GHR*	4
	12	*Do*	*Fo*	2	*A*				3
	13	*Do*	*Fu*		*Ge*				2
	14	*Do*	*Fu*		*Ge*				2
	15	*Do*	*Fo*		*A*				3
IV	16	*Do*	*Mpo*		*A*				1
	17	*Wo*	*Fu*		*(H)*	*P*	*ZW*	*GHR*	–1
	18	*Do*	*Fo*		*Hd*			*PHR*	3
	19	*Ddo*	*Mp.YF–*		*H*			*AG, PHR*	–5
	20	*Ddo*	*YFu*		*(H)*			*GHR*	–1
V	21	*Wo*	*FMao*		*A*		*ZW*		1
	22	*W+*	*FD.YFu*		*Sc*		*ZA*		1
	23	*D+*	*F–*		*Hd*		*ZA*	*PHR*	–3
	24	*Dd+*	*Fu*		*Ls*		*ZA*		2
	25	*Do*	*Fu*		*Ge*				2
VI	26	*Wo*	*FYu*		*Xy*		*ZW*		1
	27	*W+*	*FY–*		*Ge*		*ZW*		–3
	28	*Do*	*Fu*		*A*				2

(*continued*)

Table 17.2 (Cont.)

Card	*Resp.*								*RFS-2*
	29	*Do*	*Fu*		*A*			*PSV*	2
	30	*Ddo*	*Fu*		*(H)*			*GHR*	–1
VII	31	*Wo*	*Fu*		*An*		*ZW*		2
	32	*Do*	*Fu*		*A*				2
	33	*Wo*	*F–*		*Ge*		*ZW*		–3
	34	*D+*	*Mao*	2	*H*	*P*	*ZA*	*AG, GHR*	0
	35	*D+*	*FMao*	2	*A*		*ZA*		1
VIII	36	*Do*	*Fo*		*A, Sc*				3
	37	*W+*	*CF.YFu*		*H, Art*		*ZW*	*GHR*	1
	38	*D+*	*Mpo*		*Sc*		*ZA*		1
	39	*D+*	*Mao*		*(H)*		*ZA*	*GHR*	–1
	40	*Do*	*FMpo*		*A, Xy*				1
IX	41	*W+*	*CF.Y*		*Art*		*ZW*		–2
	42	*Do*	*Fo*		*A*				3
	43	*+*	*FCo*		*Bt*		*ZA*		2
	44	*D+*	*FYo*		*Sc*		*ZA*		2
	45	*D+*	*Mao*		*Sc*		*ZA*		1
X	46	*W+*	*Mpnone*		*Hx*		*ZW*	*AB, PHR*	–5
	47	*Do*	*Fo*		*A*				3
	48	*Do*	*Fo*		*A*				3
	49	*Do*	*FMao*		*A*	*P*			1
	50	*W+*	*TFo*		*Sc*		*ZW*		2

Note: The *RFS-2* column refers to the score of each response on the *Reality–Fantasy Scale Version 2.0*

The data also indicate that he is functioning cognitively much like his psychologically healthy senior peers who participated in the new international normative sample reported in Chapter 5, with no thinking or perceptual disturbances. In this respect, the absence of any scored item on the *PTI*, the *WSum6*, and the *LV2* indices, as well as the perceptual accuracy shown in his *FQ* scores (*XA%* = 0.86; *WDA%* = 0.87; *X–%* = 0.08), are particularly worth noting. His scores on the

Reality–Fantasy Scale (*RFS-P*; *RFS-S*) are also within the normal range, indicating his ability to move smoothly between attention to the outer world of reality and the inner world of fantasy and imagination.

Nevertheless, although his manner of focusing attention on his environment is normative (*W*:*D*:*Dd* = 16:30:4), he shows a substantially impaired ability to process stimulus input efficiently (*Zd* = −14). This markedly deviant *Zd* score points to an extremely low level of cognitive activity devoted to organizing the stimulus field. In addition to his normative cognitive scores, except for the *Zd*, this highly intelligent senior adult has normal-range scores on the *EII-2* of less than 0 and the *CDI* of less than 4. Taken together, these Rorschach findings identify psychologically healthy cognitive functioning and generally adaptive patterns of coping with experience, with no signs of decreasing mental capacities. The exception in this regard would be his apparently characteristic tendency to pay extraordinary amounts of attention to the components of situations and events, and even to be swallowed up by details (his original 90-response record), while paying minimal attention to the relationships between them (his *Zd* of −14).

With respect to this senior adult's affective functioning, his Rorschach protocol shows that he is currently experiencing considerable subjective distress (*D-Score* = −3) accompanied by loosely controlled and occasionally intense emotions (*FC*:*CF*+*C* = 2:6; *Pure C* = 1). His experienced distress appears to be largely situational in nature (*AdjDMD* = 3), but nevertheless acutely felt, given its contrast with the basic balance between his coping resources and the ordinary demands of his daily life (*AdjD-Score* = 0). His loosely controlled emotionality, combined with apparently minimal capacity to mute his feelings (*Constriction Index* = 1:7.5), may have played a role in an apparent susceptibility to becoming depressed, which is indicated by his highly elevated *DEPI* of 7.

This maximum *DEPI* score of 7 is found in the records of only 2% of nonpatient adults (Meyer, Erdberg, & Shaffer, 2007) and 3% of senior adults (see Chapter 5). Like many other Rorschach indices, *DEPI* can sometimes generate false-negative results, but it rarely produces a false-positive finding. This man's *DEPI* thus provides compelling evidence of a depressed emotional state that includes not only difficulty modulating affects pleasurably (*Color–Shading Blend* = 3), but possibly some self-destructive thoughts or behaviors as well (*S-CON* = 7). It might be thought that an *S-CON* elevation in older people is a normal feature of their concerns about aging, but such is not the case. Normative nonpatient senior adults have a mean *S-CON* of 5.03 (see Chapter 5), which is only slightly higher than the mean *S-CON* of 4.67 found in nonpatient adults (Meyer et al., 2007).

This man's feeling distressed despite having ample coping resources (*EA* = 11.5) is attributable to his *eb* of 10:11, which gives him an *es* of 21 with indications of both disturbing thoughts (*FM*+*m*) and unpleasant emotions (*SumShd*). Although his distress is largely situational, as has been noted, it is nevertheless real, and he appears sometimes unable to avoid situations in which the demands of reality are difficult for him to meet, even with his substantial coping resources. Generally speaking, this combination of a high *EA* with a much higher *eb* typifies people with considerable coping capacities who expose themselves to demands that exceed their capabilities to manage effectively and consequently cause them distress.

From a psychodynamic perspective, experienced distress is an alerting sign of unconscious conflicts between drives and constraints. Life changes associated with aging are related to an increased likelihood of experiencing anxiety and its behavioral manifestations. These negative reactions may be particularly difficult to avoid or control in individuals who, like this British education professional, perceive themselves as responsible, predictable, and controllable. In general, there are two types of control—outer and inner—that a person can exercise over maladaptive impulses and their behavioral manifestations. Outer control consists of externally channeling urges and drives into appropriate forms of expression without needing to repress them. In Rorschach terms, for example, a person can respond to the color parts of a blot while taking full consideration of their form elements. The *FC:CF+C* ratio is relevant in this regard because it identifies a person's capacity for affect modulation and emotional control. In the present case, this man's *FC:CF+C* ratio of 2:6 has been identified earlier as indicating loosely controlled emotionality, and such an unbalanced ratio rarely occurs in nonpatient adults. A score of $CF+C > FC + 2$ has normatively been found in just 15% of adults (Meyer et al., 2007) and 11% of senior adults (see Chapter 5).

As for inner control, *M* responses can indicate the use of creative ideation to guard against troubling affect, especially when they have good form quality and exceed the *WSumC*. The four *M* responses in the present protocol fall short of exceeding the *WSum6* of 7.5, and one of them is an *FQ*–. This insufficient emotional control—internally as well as externally—raises the risk of his on occasion being overwhelmed by emotions. Routine patterns of controlling impulse expression that were effective in the past may well prove less so in the present, when ruminations about health problems and other difficulties become common.

At the same time, however, this man appears to be at least somewhat successful in defending himself against worrisome impulses and emotions by intellectualization. His *INTELL* of six indicates a well-developed capacity to take distance from concrete, here-and-now, and anxiety-provoking concerns by focusing instead on abstractions and on figures and objects that are fictitious, far away, or impersonal. As examples of abstraction, his Response 1 on Card I was "A flying insect, largely black, which makes it sinister"; in giving Response 8 on Card II, he said, "I'm looking for a symbolic response"; and his Response 46 on Card X was "I'm looking at pleasant aspects of nature." With respect to fictitious figures, the four *H* responses shown in the Sequence of Scores are accompanied by an equal number of *(H)* contents. Viewing from afar was the stance he took in Response 4 on Card I of "It's a view of earth from outer space" and in Response 41 on Card IX of "Merging colors, like in an aerial photograph." Indicative of his taking an impersonal stance are the six *Geography* contents shown in his Sequence of Scores.

In his object relationships, this man gives evidence of some adaptive strengths and also some limitations in how he sees other people and himself. As personality strengths, he shows substantial interest in other people (*Human Content* = 11), a generally positive view of what people are like (*GHR*:*PHR* = 7:5), adequate capacity to form close personal attachments (*T* = 1), and unimpaired resources for coping with interpersonal situations (*CDI* = 1). As a potential limitation, on the other hand, he appears to perceive interpersonal interactions as more likely to be competitive than collaborative (*COP* = 0; *AG* = 2). Additionally, despite his interest in people and his adequate coping resources, he may at times experience social discomfort, which is suggested by his seeing more partial or fictitious human figures than real and fully functional ones (*H*:(*H*)+*Hd*+(*Hd*) = 4:7). With respect to his self-perception, he shows a desirable inclination to be introspective and examine his own attitudes (*FD* = 2). However, he also gives evidence of some negative self-attitudes that contribute to his previously noted elevation in *DEPI*. These attitudes include low self-esteem (*Egocentricity Index* = 0.06), self-criticism (*V* = 1), and resulting tendencies to compare himself unfavorably with other people.

In a feedback session with this senior adult, the examiner began by noting both his impressive ego strengths and his extremely high level of subjectively felt distress. Presentation of this picture of his personality functioning led him to question what the major source of this apparent distress might be. The examiner suggested that it might come from fears of losing control as a result of deteriorating cognitive skills. He was quite surprised at this hypothesis having emerged from his Rorschach responses, and he admitted that he is terrified by the prospect of experiencing age-related decline in his cognitive capacities. He was reassured in this regard that his test data did not show any indications of cognitive decline.

Conclusion

This 67-year-old British man with graduate degrees in education and music had retired two years prior to this examination following a successful career in the state-funded Catholic educational system. He is married and has two children, and since his retirement, he and his wife have been devoted to caring for their parents, who have been diagnosed with dementia. He is in addition currently providing volunteer service as a crisis intervention consultant. He has no known history of psychological disorder or mental health treatment and he was examined as a volunteer participant in a research study.

In responding to the Rorschach, he seemed intent on seeing as many things as possible in the blots. This intention led to his giving 90 responses, with more than five responses to each of the 10 cards. Following recommended procedures, only the first five responses to each card were coded, resulting in a 50-response protocol. These Rorschach data identify mostly normal-range cognitive functioning, with unimpaired abilities to perceive people and events accurately and to think logically and coherently, as summarized by a *PTI* of 0, an *EII-2* of less than 0, and *RFS-P* and *RFS-S* scores within normal limits. The one exception in this regard is his apparent tendency to make hasty decisions and to form premature conclusions with insufficient consideration of relevant information (*Zd* = –14).

With respect to his emotional functioning, there are indications in his responses of situational anxiety and depressive concerns. He has ample psychological coping resources (*EA* = 11.5), but also considerable experienced distress (*es* = 21), which gives him a *D-Score* of –3. Much of this distress appears to be situational rather than persistent (*AdjD-Score* = 0). He nevertheless appears susceptible to depressive episodes (*DEPI* = 7) marked by low self-esteem (*Egocentricity Index* = 0.06) and difficulty experiencing pleasure (*Col–Shd Blends* = 3). There is also some possibility that he may at times have harbored self-destructive thoughts, as suggested by an *S-CON* of 7. It might be thought that an *S-CON* elevation in older people is a normal feature of their concerns about aging, but such is not the case.

Interpersonally, he gives evidence of substantial interest in other people (*Human Content* = 11), a generally positive view of what people are like (*GHR*:*PHR* = 7:5), an adequate capacity to form close attachments (*T* = 1), and unimpaired resources for coping with interpersonal situations (*CDI* = 1). On the other hand, there is some indication that he regards interpersonal interactions as more likely to be competitive than collaborative (*COP* = 0; *AG* = 2). With respect to his self-perception, he shows an adaptive inclination to be introspective and to examine his own attitudes and motivations (*FD* = 2). However, he also gives evidence of some negative self-attitudes that contribute to his previously noted elevation in *DEPI*. These attitudes include low self-esteem (*Egocentricity Index* = 0.06), self-criticism (*V* = 1), and resulting tendencies to compare himself unfavorably with other people.

Despite his situational anxiety and susceptibility to depression, this man appears to have been able to sustain a stable psychological adjustment and a productive personal and professional life by successful utilization of intellectualization as a mechanism of defense. In this regard, he shows a well-developed capacity to take distance from concrete, here-and-now, and anxiety-provoking concerns by focusing instead on abstractions and on figures and objects that are fictitious, far away, and impersonal. Such intellectualization is a hallmark of an obsessive–compulsive personality style, which he identified at the beginning of the examination by searching for and finding in the inkblots 90 impressions to report. His personal style might further be described as characterized by a deconstruction of customary formal and conceptual boundaries in favor of creating original compositions with symbolic meanings, in which object and form are defined by experience and personal understanding.

In a feedback session, this intelligent British senior showed a good capacity to use the Rorschach assessment process as a means of enhancing his personal development and openness to experience. It is worth noting in this regard that both the assessment and the feedback sessions were based on the premise that any assessment encounter is essentially therapeutic. From a *relational psychoanalytic* perspective, this premise conceptualizes the assessment process as a person-oriented and experience-near interaction that preserves both asymmetric and mutual relationships between the two persons involved in the encounter (Aron, 1992). The relational vision of the mind also underlies the conceptual implications of this British senior's normative-range scores on the *Reality–Fantasy Scale*. From the perspective of this vision of the mind, meaning in human experience is generated by the mutual, dialectical, and enriching tension between reality and fantasy. Clearly dichotomized phenomena such as reality and fantasy are thus not at odds with each other, but rather constitute an ongoing dialectical tension that fosters healthy personality functioning.

References

Aron, L. (1992). Interpretation as expression of the analyst's subjectivity. *Psychoanalytic Dialogues, 2*, 475–507.

Blumberg, H. H., Zeligman, R., Appel, L., & Tibon-Czopp, S. (2017). Personality dimensions and attitudes towards peace and war. *Journal of Aggression, Conflict and Peace Research, 9*, 13–23.

Del Corno, F., & Plotkin, D. (2017). Symptom patters in the elderly. Part V in V. Lingiardi & N. McWilliams (Eds.), *Psychodynamic diagnostic manual* (2nd ed., pp. 751–888). New York, NY: Guilford Press.

Meyer, G. J., Erdberg, P., & Shaffer, T. W. (2007). Toward international normative reference data for the Comprehensive System. *Journal of Personality Assessment*, 89(Suppl. 1), S201–S216.

Winnicott, D. W. (1965). Ego distortion in terms of true and false self. In D. W. Winnicott. *The maturational processes and the facilitating environment: Studies in the theory of emotional development* (pp. 140–152). London: The International Psychoanalytic Library.

PART V

Conclusion

CHAPTER 18

Concluding Remarks

As stated in its Preface, this book was written to assist mental health professionals in their work with senior adults and to acquaint general readers with psychological information about aging in the twenty-first century. Our text demonstrates in particular the clinical utility of Rorschach assessment in the evaluation and treatment of seniors coping with age-related developmental issues. Toward this aim, Part I of the volume presents two introductory chapters that address current research and perspectives on aging (Chapter 1) and historical developments in the Rorschach assessment of senior adults (Chapter 2). These chapters describe a newly emerging image of aging that runs counter to many traditional beliefs and stereotypes and shows how scholars and clinicians can enrich their understanding of the Rorschach task and its applications in personality assessment and psychotherapeutic work with older people. In Part II of the book, we elaborate the nature of the Rorschach Inkblot Method as a measure of perception, association, and behavior (Chapter 3) and explore the interpretive significance of the structural variables, thematic imagery, and sequence analysis in a Rorschach protocol (Chapter 4).

Part III of the book consists of three chapters in which we present newly collected cross-cultural Rorschach data that have not previously been available. Chapter 5 presents reference norms on 274 nonpatient senior adults from Brazil, Iran, Israel, Italy, Portugal, Spain, and the US and compares these data with those presented by Meyer, Erdberg, and Shaffer (2007) for 4,704 nonpatient adults from 17 countries. These new data prove noteworthy in two respects. First, they show substantial cross-country similarity, which speaks to the applicability of Rorschach assessment irrespective of a person's social and cultural background. Second, they also show substantial similarity between the Rorschach protocols of nonpatient senior adults and those of younger nonpatient adults. None of the variables in the senior sample deviate markedly from the normative standards for adults in general. With particular implications for clinical diagnosis, furthermore, the senior adults were no more likely than the Meyer et al. adults to show elevations on the *PTI*, *DEPI*, or *S-CON* indices. Accordingly, customary Rorschach guidelines for distinguishing between healthy and psychopathological personality functioning are equally applicable in the assessment of younger and older adults.

Chapter 6 compares the cross-cultural Rorschach reference values of two groups of senior adults from several countries around the world. These data show that contemporary reference samples of nonpatient senior adults divided into two age groups of younger-old (60–70) and older-old (71–87) closely resemble each other and the composite adult sample of Meyer et al. (2007) in their Rorschach data. There are nevertheless some differences in the Rorschach structural scores that reflect expected developmental changes in old age. In general, the data represent cognitively healthy senior adults at all ages with the predicted decrease in processing new information carefully and perceiving novel stimuli accurately. The normative age changes in cognitive functioning, affective experience, interpersonal relatedness, and self- perception, as demonstrated by the Rorschach structural scores, are consistent with the theoretical conceptualization of personality development in old age and provide empirical evidence of the lifespan developmental perspective on personality. In particular, our results strengthen the conception that seniors have preserved capacity and are capable of functional plasticity throughout old age. Empirically, our results are equally applicable to the Rorschach Comprehensive System (CS) and the Rorschach Performance Assessment System (R-PAS; Meyer et al., 2011), making it possible for clinicians to compare their Rorschach data with the composite international reference values.

Chapter 7 compares the Rorschach protocols of 203 French and Spanish patients with mild to moderate Alzheimer's dementia with the data from our international nonpatient senior adult sample. Whereas the Rorschach protocols of the nonpatient senior adults are largely indistinguishable from those of adults in general, the Alzheimer's patients show some distinct functioning deficits, consisting in particular of impaired cognitive functioning and a limited ability to muster coping resources. These deviations from the Rorschach performance of psychologically healthy senior adults contribute to understanding the subjective experience of patients with Alzheimer's disease and to providing high-quality clinical care, particularly with respect to the emotional and social aspects of this disease. The comparative data also make it clear that evidence of cognitive impairment and diminished coping resources should not be attributed to normal aging, but are instead likely to identify inroads of psychological disorder or the onset of dementia.

With this background information and normative reference data in hand, Part IV of the book presents 10 case illustrations (Chapters 8–17). These case illustrations include cases of dementia, a broad range of diagnosable psychological disorders, and cases of symptom formation in otherwise adequately functioning seniors. The scope of these cases attests the extensive applicability of Rorschach assessment across a wide spectrum of adjustment difficulties and psychological disorders seen in clinical practice. Moreover, the majority of the case illustrations show the utility of Rorschach assessment in helping well-adjusted seniors cope with age-related subjective distress.

In general, the interpretation of each Rorschach protocol integrates theoretical perspectives and empirical evidence. Following psychoanalytically oriented

Rorschach scholars (e.g., Handler, 1999; Lerner, 1998; Weiner, 2003), we apply four different psychodynamic perspectives: *Ego Psychology*, *Object Relations*, *Self Psychology*, and *Relational Psychology*. In each of the case illustrations, the discussion begins with the structural data and continues with attention to the thematic imagery. The presentation of each case is based on two underlying assumptions: first, the Rorschach is a personality assessment instrument, and the interpretation of a Rorschach protocol should accordingly focus on identifying personality characteristics; and second, personality characteristics can be conceived of as psychodynamic systems in which subjective experience and observable behavior are determined by a complex interaction of cognitive capacities, emotions, defenses, and attitudes. There are numerous ways of translating these assumptions into specific procedures for exploring the meaning and implications of Rorschach responses. Freud (1904/1953) said about different ways of conducting psychotherapy that "All that lead to recovery are good" (p. 259). So let it be for the diverse but equally fruitful approaches to Rorschach interpretation. For our purposes, we have formulated and recommend a specific interpretive strategy that was employed in the 10 case illustrations.

This interpretive strategy can be described with reference to the Structural Summary, which appears as the first table in each of the case illustrations. The interpretation begins with examination of the variables in the upper left quadrant of the Structural Summary. These variables provide information about a respondent's approach to the Rorschach task and openness to experience; about the extent of the person's available coping resources and preferred style of drawing on these resources; and about whether these coping resources are sufficient to meet the demands of the person's daily life, which produces a calm state of mind, or are exceeded by those demands, which typically generates subjectively felt distress.

Following this overview of coping resources and style, the interpretation turns to the four core domains of personality—cognitive functioning, affective experience, interpersonal relatedness, and self-perception—with variables related to each of them clustered in the other three quadrants of the Structural Summary printout. Variables related to cognitive functioning are further subdivided into three clusters of variables that measure aspects of attention, perception, and thinking. The order in which these clusters of variables are interpreted is dictated by the location of the most frequent deviations from normative expectation, and these are indicated by asterisks in the first table of each case illustration. If either the attention, perception, or thinking cluster is notable for deviations from the normative range, the affective experience followed by the interpersonal relatedness and self-perception clusters are interpreted. If either the interpersonal relatedness or self-perception cluster is notable for the deviant scores, they are interpreted jointly as aspects of object relations.

Additionally in this interpretive strategy, the summary indices appearing in the bottom lines of the Structural Summary are considered along with the clusters to which they relate. Thus, the analysis of coping style and capacity takes account of the *CDI*, the *FM+m*, and the *AdjDMD*; interpretation of the cognitive variables considers the *PTI*, *EII-2*, *RFS-P*, *RFS-S*, and *OBS*; evaluation of the affective variables includes the *DEPI*, *S-CON*, and *Col–Shd Blends*; and the *HVI* is considered part of the interpersonal cluster. After the Structural Summary has been addressed, the interpretation continues with a reading of the responses with an eye to thematic imagery that may reveal or suggest aspects of the respondent's view of the world, outlook on life, and attitudes toward themselves and other people.

The personality characteristics that are identified with this interpretive strategy establish the Rorschach as a highly useful diagnostic and therapeutic tool. With respect to differential diagnosis, aspects of an individual's cognitive functioning, affective experience, interpersonal relatedness, and self-perception play a role in many types of psychological disorder. Specific Rorschach deviations in these personality domains can accordingly help to identify and discriminate among these disorders. Cases in point are the implications of Rorschach indications of thought disorder for schizophrenia, of self-criticism for depression, of stress overload for anxiety disorder, of interpersonal withdrawal for schizoid disorder, of hypervigilance for paranoia, and of self-admiration for narcissistic disorder.

As for its being a therapeutic tool, Rorschach assessment can facilitate psychological treatment in three respects. First, Rorschach information can assist in treatment planning by identifying a particular patient's need for change and suggesting ways of engaging this person in a therapeutic process. Treatment recommendations based on Rorschach findings were illustrated in the Chapter 11 case illustration. Second, in preparation for entering psychotherapy, or beneficial in their own right, Rorschach findings lend themselves well to a feedback session in which test evidence of coping strengths and psychological concerns can be profitably shared and discussed with the person who has been examined. Such feedback session was described in the Chapter 17 case illustration. Third, follow-up Rorschach assessment can prove useful in monitoring progress and change in psychotherapy.

The final point of significance is that the large-scale international sampling of nonpatient adults and senior adults reported in Chapters 5–7 shows: (1) that the Rorschach scores of elderly people without neurocognitive impairment closely resemble the scores of younger adults; and (2) that personality characteristics tend to be stable over time and only minimally affected by aging. In the Rorschach assessment of older people, then, no age-based allowances should be made for scores that fall outside of the normal expected range. Rather, test results that deviate from normative expectations should be considered indicative of adjustment difficulties or psychological disorders that call for further evaluation.

References

Freud, S. (1953). On psychotherapy. *Standard edition* (Vol. 7, pp. 257–268). London, UK: Hogarth Press (original work published 1904).

Handler, L. (1999). Assessment of playfulness: Hermann Rorschach meets D. W. Winnicott. *Journal of Personality Assessment*, *72*, 208–217.

Lerner, P. M. (1998). *Psychoanalytic perspectives on the Rorschach*. Hillsdale, NJ: Analytic Press.

Meyer, G. J., Erdberg, P., & Shaffer, T. W. (2007). Toward international normative reference data for the Comprehensive System. *Journal of Personality Assessment*, 89(Suppl.), S210–S216.

Meyer, G. J., Viglione, D. J., Mihura, J. L., Erard, R. E., & Erdberg. P. (2011). *Rorschach Performance Assessment System*. Toledo, OH: Rorschach Performance Assessment System, LLC.

Weiner, I. B. (2003). *Principles of Rorschach interpretation* (2nd ed.). Mahwah, NJ: Lawrence Erlbaum Associates.

Index

For Product Safety Concerns and Information please contact our EU representative GPSR@taylorandfrancis.com
Taylor & Francis Verlag GmbH, Kaufingerstraße 24, 80331 München, Germany

www.ingramcontent.com/pod-product-compliance
Ingram Content Group UK Ltd.
Pitfield, Milton Keynes, MK11 3LW, UK
UKHW022313250926
475702UK00046B/743
9780367243814